Great Experiments

in

Behavior Modification

Great Experiments
in
Behavior
Modification

abstracted by
JERRY WILLIS and DONNA GILES
under the general editorship of
B. R. Bugelski

HACKETT PUBLISHING CO., INC.
P.O. BOX 55573
Indianapolis, Indiana 46205

Copyright ©1976 by
Hackett Publishing Company, Inc.
Printed in the United States of America
Cover Design: Melissa M. Goldsmith
First Printing

**Library of Congress Cataloging
in Publication Data**

Willis, Jerry W
    Great experiments in behavior modification.

    (Great experiments in psychology series)
    Consists of abstracts of 116 articles.
    Includes indexes.
    1. Behavior modification — Abstracts.   I. Giles,
Donna, 1949-   II. Title. III. Series.
BF637.B4W54   361'.06   76-7365
ISBN 0-915144-20-4
ISBN 0-915144-19-0 pbk.

To Edna and Curley,
whose encouragement and support
are so appreciated, and to Lavice,
a warm, genuine, caring mother.

Preface

In several courses on behavior modification for students in psychology and in education, we have often found it useful to assign original articles in the field. The articles generally give the student more information about a particular procedure or the research methodology employed than is available in general introductory texts. In addition, reading the articles beforehand allows class time to be spent discussing the more interesting aspects of the research rather than lecturing on the study itself.

Assigning journal articles is not without its problems, however. Putting an article on a reading list is often equivalent to the kiss of death. Students who attempt to read it in the library often find it neatly removed from the journal by an operation so skillful it would be a tribute to the field of surgery. In libraries in which security is lax, entire journals often disappear mysteriously. Even when articles are readily available, students often complain about the amount of technical material contained in the average article, which they find unpalatable in an introductory course.

A solution to the above problems is the use of précis or abstracts of important articles which are provided for the students. Properly written, these précis can give the student the necessary detail to understand and interpret the research, while eliminating the drudgery of wading through all the ancillary information in the original article, which was written primarily as a means of communicating with other researchers and experienced practitioners. We found this approach a practical one, avoiding some of the problems of other alternatives while retaining their advantages. This book is the product of work in several courses in the past four years.

The articles selected for abstracting are, in our opinion, some of the most original and/or well-executed studies available. They do not exhaust the population of such articles in the field, however. In addition, please note that only *empirical* studies are included. Thus, influential position papers and review articles are not included, nor are research articles that could not be summarized appropriately in one or two pages. In addition, although the work of most of the important figures in the field is represented in the articles, there are some notable exceptions, such as Andrew Salter, Hans Eysenck, Arthur Staats and Knight Dunlap. Omission in no way implies that these and many other leaders have not made substantial contributions to the field. But regrettably, in selecting the final set of articles, it was necessary to consider a number of variables such as the topics to be covered, the space available, and the clarity with which articles could be abstracted. We recognize the frailty of our judgment and would welcome suggestions and comments about material to be included in future editions.

We greatly appreciate the willingness of those living psychologists who gave us leave to abstract their works. Some of the authors suggested clarifying changes, and to these colleagues we are especially grateful. We take full responsibility for whatever errors and distortions we were unable to perceive. We are also grateful to the American Psychological Association and to the publishers of the original studies who gave their approval to this effort. Besides the American Psychological Association, we owe our thanks to *Crime and Delinquency*, abstracted with permission of the National Council on Crime and Delinquency; *Psychology Today* and its publisher, Zif Davis Publishing Company; *Exceptional Children*, abstracted with permission of the Council for Exceptional Children; the figures from *Criminal Justice and Behavior* reproduced by permission of the publisher, Sage Publication, Inc.; *Perceptual and Motor Skills; Journal of Applied Behavior Analysis; Behavior Therapy; Behaviour Research and Therapy; Journal of Behavior Therapy and Experimental Psychiatry; Journal of Experimental Child Psychiatry;* Prentice-Hall, Inc.; *British Medical Journal; Journal of Speech Disorder; American Journal of Mental Deficiency; Journal of General Psychology; Behavior Modification in Children; The Psychological Record;* and *Psychonomic Science*.

We would like to thank several people who provided support, suggestions, and guidance. Dick Bugelski, as editor of this series, was very instrumental in helping to shape our efforts into a useful text. Brad Bucher, Anthony Graziano, and Dave Evans made valuable suggestions about the manuscript; and Bill McClelland, as Chairman of the Department of Psychology, University of Western Ontario, provided administrative support for the project and saw to it that we had the resources necessary to complete the book on time. Sandy Leboldus gave us much needed secretarial support and guidance. We are grateful, also, to Alan Noon who so meticulously reproduced many of the figures, and to Jeane Crowder who gave expert help in preparation of the indexes. A special thanks is expressed to Joan Willis, whose patient tolerance and enthusiastic support lasted through what may have seemed an infinity of working weekends and midnight work sessions.

Introduction to the Text

The purpose of this book is to present the best available research in three general fields that have been subsumed under the term behavior modification. In selecting the papers to be abstracted, the editors took into consideration two major factors. One was the quality of the research and the other was the need to provide the reader with a broadly representative view of the work of behavior modifiers, not only in terms of the variety of techniques used but the settings in which the work is carried out, the type of client served, and the target behaviors selected for modification.

In searching for appropriate papers, we considered about 2,000 articles. Our review of the literature pointed up several problems, some of which were not readily apparent to us previously. A major one is that only a few techniques and a few subject populations have received most of the attention of researchers. Literally hundreds of articles exist describing work with the mentally retarded and preschool or elementary school children, for example, while few articles deal with applications of behavioral technology to high school students or disadvantaged adults. Similarly, the literature is filled with studies demonstrating that token reinforcement can change almost any behavior imaginable, but few studies have examined the effects of other procedures, such as behavior rehearsal or "thought stopping."

A second difficulty with the literature is the lack of experimental rigor in many studies. Research in the real world is a difficult undertaking at best, and although the behavioral field has probably made more gains in less time than any of its predecessors, there are still many obvious flaws in the average study. We can hope that the trend of improvement apparent in the last two decades will continue, so that practitioners will be able to place greater and greater confidence in the conclusions of their research. We cannot, of course, endorse the reliability and validity of our sample studies. Readers should be as critical of these abstracts as they would be of the original papers.

The 116 articles abstracted in this text are arranged around nine interest areas. The first, *Pioneer Studies*, contains several early reports that are now classics. The next two sections, *Preschool Studies* and *Educational Applications*, contain a representative sampling of work in those two settings. The section on *Behavioral Counseling* deals primarily with methods used with groups of clients, with the enhancement of desirable behaviors, and with noninstitutionalized clients. Papers in the *Behavior Therapy* section deal with one-to-one treatment procedures or with clients who have severe problems. Other major areas in which behavior modification has been used are *Institutions* (Section 6), in the treatment of law violators (Section 7) and *Communities and Organizations* (Section 8).

The final set of papers deal with research on the training of professional and paraprofessional personnel to carry out behavior modification programs.

The arrangement of the abstracts in these particular sections was based on our experience in teaching courses on behavior modification. Students are generally interested in one or more of these areas and prefer to read sets of abstracts that describe a variety of programs conducted in similar settings. The sections could also have been arranged along other lines, however, such as the type of treatment used, the type of client served, or the research methodology employed. For those who find these alternative arrangements more useful for their purposes, we have provided a set of indexes following the text. These will enable the reader to identify, for example, all the studies that employed a multiple baseline design, or all those that used a particular treatment procedure, such as behavioral contracting. A target behavior index also lists the types of behaviors dealt with in each study.

CONTENTS

CHAPTER III   *Educational Applications*

CHAPTER IV *Behavioral Counseling*

CHAPTER V *Behavior Therapy*

CHAPTER VII *Behavioral Approaches to Juvenile Delinquents and Adult Offenders*

CHAPTER VIII *Community and Organizational Applications*

CHAPTER IX *Training Behavioral Engineers*

Behavior Modification: An Introduction

In 1913 John B. Watson, an American psychologist, published a paper entitled *Psychology As the Behaviorist Views It.* [1] That paper, often referred to as the Behaviorist Manifesto, outlined the major tenets of a behavioral approach to psychology. According to Watson, psychology should be "a purely objective, experimental branch of natural science." Watson's view emphasized observable behavior—what could be seen—rather than concentrating on elements of the "inner man" that could not be directly observed. Watson combined his emphasis on an empirical approach with a theoretical base which assumed that the effects of the environment, rather than heredity, instinct, or divine providence, were the primary determiners of how we behave. His approach, which differed markedly from other popular psychological theories of the day, appealed to a large number of psychologists and to many people outside psychology, as well.

The early behaviorists were heavily influenced by the Russian physiologist, Ivan Pavlov, who first systematically observed the phenomenon he called classical conditioning. While studying the digestive processes of dogs, Pavlov observed that the dogs associated the sounds of the arrival of food (the door opening, the approach of the assistant with the food) with eating. They began to salivate as soon as they heard the door open. Intrigued with this discovery, Pavlov suspended his study of digestion and began his now famous psychological investigations. Some stimuli naturally cause salivation, such as the smell of food or the response of eating itself. Pavlov found that if he rang a bell just before feeding the dogs on several occasions, he could cause the dogs to salivate just by ringing the bell. The stimuli that naturally elicit salivation are called *unconditioned stimuli*. No training is necessary for them to produce the *unconditioned response* (UCR), which for Pavlov's dogs was salivation. If the unconditioned stimulus (UCS) is paired with a neutral stimulus, that is, one that does not naturally elicit the target response, the pairing or association of the UCS and *conditioned stimulus* (CS) will eventually result in the CS alone eliciting the response. In Pavlov's experiments, the sight or smell of food was the UCS, and the ringing of the bell was the CS. Salivation was the UCR. Before

1. John B. Watson, "Psychology as the Behaviorist Views It," *Psychological Review* 20 (1913): 158-177.

pairing the bell with presentation of food, there was no increase in the amount of salivation when the bell rang. After the bell and food were paired several times, simply ringing the bell produced salivation (*conditioned response*), even when food was not presented.

In 1921 John Watson and Rosalie Rayner demonstrated that humans also learn through classical conditioning.[2] If young children hear a sudden, loud noise they will often jump and begin to cry. With the mother's permission Watson and Rayner placed Albert, an eleven-month-old boy, in a room and on various occasions hit a steel bar with a hammer behind him. Along with the loud noise, a UCS that upset Albert, they introduced a furry white rat, which Albert accepted as a plaything. After several joint presentations, the rat was presented alone. Albert looked at it, moved away, and began to cry. Prior to pairing the white rat with the loud, upsetting sound, Albert had shown no fear of the rat, a rabbit, a dog, or a roll of cotton. After the loud noise and the white rat were presented together, however, Albert was very much afraid of the white rat. He was also afraid, although not as much, of the rabbit, the dog, and the cotton. Throughout the study, Albert accepted a set of wooden blocks and happily played with them, even when he was afraid of other stimuli which were like the white rat. The condition describing Albert's fear of stimuli similar to the feared object is called *generalization*.

The basic phenomenon of classical or respondent conditioning has been used to explain a variety of human behaviors, particularly fears and phobias.

A major characteristic of classical or respondent conditioning is that the controlling stimulus comes *before* the response. The child hears a loud clap of thunder and cries; on a different occasion he hears the bell of an ice-cream truck, and runs from his house to the sidewalk. Later the child may also cry when the sky becomes dark because dark skies are associated with loud noise, or be delighted by the sound of a ringing bell.

Watson used the conditioning theory developed by Pavlov and suggested that all human behavior is reflexively conditioned and that all activity can be reduced to muscle movement.

Today, the behaviorism of Watson is considered by most to be a very radical approach which has not been supported by later research. The lengths to which Watson took behaviorism may have been necessary to establish the field as different from other competing theories, but the extremes as well as the dogmatic, overconfident way in which the approach was presented led to its rejection by many in the 1930s. Early behaviorists gave little credit to heredity, but today we know that it plays an important role in setting limits on the potential of any individual. We also know that

2. John B. Watson and Rosalie Rayner, "Conditioned Emotional Responses," *Journal of Experimental Psychology* 3 (1920): 1-14.

the consequences that follow behavior are as important as the stimuli that precede them. A basic behavioral principle is embodied in the statement "We repeat responses that lead to things we like." This type of learning has been named operant conditioning by B. F. Skinner. Skinner worked with rats in his early years and invented the lever-press ("Skinner") box which has become a standard piece of equipment in many psychology laboratories. Later Skinner adapted the box for pigeons. Skinner's pigeons were taught to peck a small disk at one end of a small chamber. When the pigeon pecked the disk, a feeder dropped a piece of grain into the chamber. In the beginning the pigeon received a reward (called a "reinforcer" by Skinner) each time he pecked on the disk. As reinforcements followed, the rate of pecking increased. If the reinforcers were omitted, pecking would decrease in rate (extinction). From this small beginning Skinner and his followers have gone on to show that many of the rules of behavior that they discovered with their pigeons also apply to humans. The relationship of consequences to behavior is outlined in Table 1.

An excellent use of positive reinforcement to modify behavior was reported by Benjamin Franklin. When the minister on a ship complained that the men rarely attended prayers, Franklin suggested that the clergyman take charge of passing out the daily ration of rum each sailor received and

Table 1
Stimulus-Response Relationships

Name of Stimulus	Effects on Environment	Effects of Stimulus on Behavior
Reinforcer	Something positive added	Response occurs more often (reinforcement)
Reinforcer	Something positive taken away	Response occurs less often (punishment)
Punisher	Something negative added	Response occurs less often (punishment)
Punisher	Something negative taken away	Response occurs more often (reinforcement)
Neutral	Adds nothing negative or positive	No effect

Based on Bijou and Baer (1960)[3] and Michael (1975)[4]

3. Sidney Bijou and Donald Baer, *Child Development, Volume One* (New York: Appleton-Century-Crofts, 1961).

4. Jack Michael, "Positive and Negative Reinforcement, a Distinction That Is No Longer Necessary; or a Better Way to Talk About Bad Things," in E. Ramp and G. Semb (eds.), *Behavior Analysis: Areas of Research and Application* (Englewood Cliffs, New Jersey: Prentice-Hall, 1975).

that the ceremony take place just after prayers. The minister followed Franklin's advice and "never were prayers more generally and more punctually attended" (Franklin, 1969).[5] Franklin also commented, "I thought this method preferable to the punishment inflicted by some military laws for nonattendance on divine service."

Franklin's opinion concerning the desirability of reinforcement over punishment is shared by most behaviorists today. Skinner, particularly, has criticized the tendency in many segments of society to use punishment when positive reinforcement more effectively produces changes in behavior. One problem with punishment lies in the model it provides for the person punished. Spanking a child for fighting with her brother may teach the child that physical aggression is acceptable as long as you're the biggest person around.

Another major problem with punishment is that the person who administers punishment comes to be associated with it, just as the white rat was associated with the loud noise. In addition, many types of punishment, such as spanking, verbal criticism, or ridicule, may stop behavior temporarily but may also elicit emotional behaviors which interfere with learning more acceptable responses. Punishment may be necessary sometimes, however, and several of the abstracts in this text provide examples of its application. Generally, it is used in conjunction with some form of positive reinforcement or when efforts to use reinforcement have failed.

Skinner and his followers have carefully studied the effects of consequences on the behavior of both animals and humans. This basic research has provided us with a great many principles on which the techniques of behavior modification are based. Some of these are illustrated on the following pages.

TIMING

Suppose Susie has been arriving late to pick up her date, Fred, on a regular basis for some time now. Fred knows that his praise and attention are rewarding for Susie and decides to use these in an attempt to increase the number of times Susie arrives on time. Suppose Susie finally does come on time. When should she be praised? In the wee small hours of the morning as she's leaving to go home? During the course of their evening together? When she arrives? Or only after she has come promptly several times (to demonstrate that she's really sincere)? The correct answer represents an important concept: *In the beginning, reward immediately.* Interested individuals often feel that they should wait until others have "proven" their intentions before rewarding them. Studies indicate, however, that the

---

5. Benjamin Franklin, (Submitted by B. F. Skinner), "Operant Reinforcement of Prayer," *Journal of Applied Behavior Analysis* 2 (1969): 2.

quickest way to change behavior is to reward it as soon as the change occurs.

NUMBER OF REWARDS

In any sort of human observation, subjective or objective, it is common to note wide variations in the amount of compliments, praise and attention, or other rewards given by different people. Many rarely praise, allowing a positive behavior to go by unnoticed instead. For those people, rewards are like water in the desert, commodities to be conserved at almost any expense, doled out only as is absolutely necessary. Take for a moment university professors who guard their "A's" as though they were personal possessions, dispensing them with great reluctance and only to those students who walk on water. The result may well be that students of these professors do not work as hard or consistently as they might, because the probability of being rewarded (the number of reinforcers) is so small that such students become discouraged. Another important concept, then, is as follows: *The more often a response is rewarded, the greater the likelihood that the individual will continue to make that response.*

GENERALIZATION AND DISCRIMINATION

Now suppose your brother and his friends come into the house from their neighborhood football game. They have been outside shouting and roughhousing. You've been sitting at your desk trying to read Homer in the original Greek. Now as they come inside to have a cola and listen to your latest top-of-the-charts album, they continue to shout loudly and begin to wrestle in the livingroom. You would like them to stop the nonsense. If the goal is to change this behavior, it may not be reasonable to completely eliminate shouting and wrestling from the boys' behavior. These are natural and adaptive behaviors in some settings. Instead, a more appropriate goal might be to help the boys *discriminate* where these behaviors are acceptable and where they are not. Let us look at Skinner's pigeons again.

Suppose you have a pigeon who has learned to peck a white disk to receive grain. Now we put the pigeon in a chamber that has two disks—one blue, one green. If the pigeon is hungry, he will probably peck at a disk. In fact, he will probably peck at both disks from time to time. As long as both disks bring reward (food), the pigeon will peck at both disks. But if we turn off the feeder connected to the blue disk, the pigeon quickly learns to peck only the green disk. The fact that the pigeon was willing to peck the green and blue disks when he had learned to get food by pecking at a white disk is called *generalization.* The process of learning that pecking at the blue disk no longer provides food, while the green one does, is called *discrimination.*

Besides turning off the feeder connected to the blue disk, there is another method by which to teach the pigeon to peck only the green disk. Suppose both disks provide food, but pecking on the blue disk also produces a loud noise—a punisher—for the pigeon. Again, the pigeon learns to peck only the green disk; in this manner it can get food and at the same time avoid the unpleasant noise.

In the case of your brother and his friends who are noisily running about the house, you might add a mild punisher, such as, "Cedric, you will have to be a little less noisy if you want to continue to listen to my records." If Cedric and his friends fail to reduce their noise you may then say, "Cedric, you are still too noisy. I am taking my records now. I don't mind your listening to them, but this seems unreasonable. I will let you have them when you can keep it down."

SCHEDULES OF REWARD

The way we go about rewarding people for desired behavior is very important. The manner in which rewards are dispensed can be divided into several different categories. These categories are called *schedules.* Table 2 shows the several types of schedules of reward that are commonly used. Below are some examples which will help you understand the table.

Table 2
Schedules of Reinforcement

Schedule	Definition	Use
A. Continuous Reinforcement (CRF)	Every time the desired response occurs the organism is reinforced.	Used in getting behavior going
B. Intermittent Reinforcement	The organism is reinforced occasionally after a desired response occurs.	Used to maintain behavior
1. Time Based	After reinforcement occurs a certain amount of time must pass before the desired response will be reinforced again.	Used to maintain behavior at low and moderate rates
2. Response Based	A given number of responses must occur before reinforcement occurs.	Used to maintain behavior at high rates

CONTINUOUS REINFORCEMENT

Continuous Reinforcement (CRF)—CRF means just what it says. Every time the desired behavior occurs, it is rewarded. This schedule is used most often in the early phases of an effort to change behavior. Continuous reinforcement has the advantage of producing change in behavior quickly. It has the disadvantage of requiring a good deal of attention and effort on the part of the person who is doing the rewarding. There is also another problem. People rarely get rewarded every time they do something right. Even a consistently hard-working, bright student gets less than "A" sometimes, a journalist who writes accurate and exciting accounts is not praised for every article, and few children are praised every time they handle a neighborhood squabble without resorting to a fight. Continuous reinforcement is so different from the usual manner in which people are rewarded that changes brought about using CRF often do not last. CRF is thus best used in the early stages of efforts to get behavior going.

INTERMITTENT REINFORCEMENT

When behavior has been well-established, the next concern is that it continue beyond the continuous reinforcement phase. In some instances, the behavior will continue even if rewards are stopped, because the individual discovers other reinforcers. Susie discovers that she actually enjoys spending the extra time with Fred made possible by her arriving on time.

In other cases, it is necessary to continue formal reinforcement on an intermittent basis. Instead of being rewarded for every response, Susie may be rewarded every other response, then every fifth to tenth response, and finally, only rarely. The emphasis is on a *gradual* shift from CRF to intermittent reinforcement.

Intermittent reinforcement can be of two types—*time-based* and *response-based*. One of the editors worked with a young mother of two boys, ages eight and nine. The boys seemed to be in a continual state of warfare. Fights occurred on an average of five a day. Rarely did an hour pass without some form of altercation over toys, game rules, or which TV program to watch. A training program was initiated involving "tokens" as reinforcers. Initially, this mother gave the boys a token for each twenty minutes of "good behavior." At the end of the week, the boys could spend their tokens on inexpensive toys which she previously had given them, regardless of how they behaved. As the boys began to behave well for longer periods, the time between awarding points was gradually increased. For example, instead of earning one token each twenty minutes, the boys might receive ten tokens at the end of a good morning or twenty at the end of a good day. Eventually, the boys could receive their reward for "a good week."

7

Not all behaviors are best rewarded on a time-based system, however. For example, you probably would not want to reward a salesperson for "number-of-minutes selling." The salesperson could probably make a five-minute job last two hours. Instead, it would be more appropriate to provide rewards for the amount of goods sold. Similarly, if homework is the behavior in question, it would be preferable to reward "amount of homework done" rather than "time spent on homework." Reinforcement here is based on the number of appropriate responses, regardless of time.

DEPRIVATION AND SATIATION

You are working late at school one night and, because it is several hours past your dinner, you stop by the cafeteria for one of its super-special hamburgers before going home. But when you get home, you discover your roommate has finally decided to cook a meal and is so pleased with his efforts, he saved it for you. And what a feast it is: veal paprikash, roast potatoes, and green beans amandine, with Cherries Jubilee for dessert. You know that the most effective way to maintain your roommate's behavior is through positive reinforcement (eating and enjoying), but is the dinner a positive reinforcement for *you*? Not really. The value of any reward varies from time to time. After eating a full meal at the cafeteria, the prospect of eating yet another large meal, no matter how good, is an uninviting event. Your condition is called *satiation*. If you had missed lunch, you would have been in a state of *deprivation* for food. The value placed on a particular stimulus is in part determined by how long it has been since that stimulus occurred (deprivation) and how many times you have been rewarded with that particular stimulus recently (satiation). These are really two sides of the same coin. If it has been eight hours since your last meal, this often occasions the behaviors that produce food. But if you have just eaten a large meal and still have three more hampers of dirty clothes to clean, this sets the stage for clothes-washing behavior.It is easy to see how this phenomenon applies to stimuli such as food; but it is also true of other sorts of rewards as well. In counseling, we often find ourselves helping our clients to produce more positive comments in their contacts with other people. Some people then fall into the trap of settling on one comment, such as "That's nice" for everything they want to reward. "That's nice" may be a reward the first five times, but by the twentieth time in three days (satiation), it may have little impact. For this reason it is better to provide a variety of social rewards for the behavior to be improved. Personalize the social praise: "Fred, I really appreciate how quiet you were this morning when you got up. I was just beat and really needed the rest."

In summary, principles discovered and developed in the operant and classical conditioning laboratories have been adapted by behavior

8

modifiers and behavior therapists to form the basis of treatment techniques. The procedures used focus on when the stimulus or reinforcement is presented (timing), rate of reinforcement (number of rewards), appropriateness of the response to the environment (generalization and discrimination), dispensing of reinforcement (schedules: CRF and intermittent) and history of the individual (deprivation and satiation).

THE FIELD TODAY

Although there were occasional individual pioneers in the decades from 1920-1950 who advocated the use of treatment techniques based on the principles discussed above, a strong movement toward the application of these principles to practical problems did not occur until the early 1960s. During the sixties behavioral approaches to human problems emerged as major alternatives to the then-prevailing psychodynamic and client-centered methods of practice.

These two traditional frameworks for the practice and application of psychology shared several common elements. Both treated the behavior observed as simply an indication or a symptom of the real focus of psychology—the intrapsychic life of the individual. Both assume that the focus of change thus must be internal. Arnold must work through his oedipal complex, Susie must improve her self-concept, Fred must become aware of his inner conflict concerning whether to become a carpenter or a surgeon. Therapy within traditional frameworks has generally meant *talking* with another person, who, it is hoped, understands the way the psyche is wired so that it is possible for clients to better understand their internal workings.

The new behavioral therapies differed on several counts. For the behavior therapist, the behavior observed was important in and of itself. A child who refused to interact with other children and who avoided social interaction was a child who simply did not emit those behaviors, not a child with a poor self-concept or one suffering from lack of ego strength. Instead of assuming that behavior is caused by intrapsychic events, behaviorists assumed that there is a relationship between the behavior and the environment. They assumed that the child refuses to interact with other children because of his learning history and current environment.

Looking outward toward the environment in which a person lives, rather than looking inward, led to major differences in the way behaviorists practice. Simply talking about problems is unlikely to change them if behavior is maintained by what occurs in the environment. Talking is only one small part of an individual's world. Thus, instead of seeing children with behavior problems in play therapy on a weekly basis, many behavior modifiers see the parents of these children once a week in child-management groups. Similarly, if a college student is experiencing feelings of anxiety every time he attempts to ask a woman for a date, behaviorists are not likely to spend weeks talking to the student about his feelings of inadequacy in the situation. Instead, they may institute procedures designed to eliminate the anxious behavior and, if the student lacks the necessary behavioral skills needed to appropriately ask a woman for a date, training may be provided. The behavioral assumption that the environment in which we live controls our behavior led naturally to the assumption that changing behavior means changing the environment. Today psychological treatment is off the couch and out of the psychotherapists' offices. It is in classrooms, on hospital wards, in livingrooms, in factories, and in prisons.

Added to the assumptions that the behavior is important in its own right and that the environment is a major contributor to the development, maintenance, and modification of behavior, there is one more assumption or feature of the behavioral approach: *"Thou shalt evaluate what thou dost."* More than any other attempt to apply psychological knowledge, the behavioral approach has emphasized empiricism, the necessity of gathering objective data on the effects of treatment.

VARIANTS OF BEHAVIORAL PSYCHOLOGY

The three assumptions described above are applicable to the general field of applied behavioral psychology. That field can be subdivided into three overlapping areas. The terms, *behavior therapy, behavior modification,* and *applied behavior analysis* are sometimes used to differentiate the three areas, although they are also used indiscriminately by some. They do, however, represent slightly different emphases within the total field. Behavior therapy is usually associated with practice in hospitals and clinics and particularly, though not exclusively, with techniques based on classical conditioning models. The term behavior modification is often used to identify work in educational and community settings and with the use of operant techniques such as positive reinforcement and shaping. It is frequently used also as a general term to denote the entire area. The third term, applied behavior analysis, denotes a group of practitioners who emphasize the empirical evaluation of technology, usually through the use of within-subjects designs.

Behavior Therapy. As mentioned previously, behavior therapy is loosely associated with treatment techniques based on classical conditioning. In this section, several of the most popular techniques will be discussed. A more detailed description of these as well as many others is available in Rimm and Masters (1974).[6]

6. David C. Rimm and John C. Masters, *Behavior Therapy: Techniques and Empirical Findings* (New York: Academic Press, 1974).

Systematic Desensitization. The most popular form of behavior therapy is systematic desensitization and its variants. If a situation in the environment has become a conditioned stimulus for anxiety, approaching that conditioned stimulus will elicit the undesirable response, anxiety. For example, people who are afraid of being at the top of tall buildings will experience greater and greater anxiety as they move to successively higher floors. In a case reported by Brady (1974),[7] a woman who had such a phobia tried to overcome her fear by systematically placing herself nearer the feared environment, the top floor of a department store. As she rode the escalator from floor to floor, however, she experienced more and more anxiety, until about halfway up she could no longer tolerate her fear and took the down escalator. As she descended she felt less and less anxiety. Being able to do something to reduce anxiety that has been classically conditioned is an example of avoidance learning. The person learns a response, in this case staying away from the top floors of the building, which enables the person to avoid an aversive situation. It also does something else. It prevents the person from ever experiencing the feared situation long enough to extinguish the phobia. Systematic desensitization (SD) is one way of dealing with such problems. In essence, the feared goal or object is approached in a series of small steps while the person is relaxed, a condition that is assumed to be incompatible with being anxious. In the words of Joseph Wolpe, (1958),[8] who developed the procedure, "If a response inhibitory to anxiety can be made to occur in the presence of anxiety-evoking stimuli, it will weaken the connection between these stimuli and the anxiety responses." This principle is sometimes called reciprocal inhibition or counterconditioning. SD involves three steps. The client is first trained in progressive relaxation (see Abstract 28), a procedure originally developed by Jacobson (1938).[9] The person learns to relax one muscle group at a time by first tensing the muscles and then relaxing the tension. The procedure is generally carried out with the client in a comfortable reclining chair or on a couch.

The second component of SD is constructing a hierarchy of anxiety-provoking stimuli or situations. The therapist and the client identify the stimulus situations that produce undesirable anxiety and organize them into meaningful groups. In some instances, there will be only one group, as in the case of the lady who was afraid of being in tall buildings. In other cases, there may be several types of situations that produce anxiety. The situations in the hierarchy are then ordered in terms of the intensity of

7. John P. Brady, "Systematic Desensitization," in W. Stewart Agras (ed.), *Behavior Modification: Principles and Clinical Applications* (Boston: Little, Brown and Company, 1972).

8. John Wolpe, *Psychotherapy by Reciprocal Inhibition* (Stanford: Stanford University Press, 1958).

9. Edmund Jacobson, *Progressive Relaxation* (Chicago: The University of Chicago Press, 1938, revised edition, 1974).

anxiety that they evoke. An example of a hierarchy appears in Abstract 60.

Once the client has learned to relax and the hierarchy has been developed, desensitization itself begins. While relaxed, the client is asked to imagine the scene from the hierarchy that is least anxiety-provoking. If imagining it produces no anxiety or a minimum of anxiety, the therapist instructs the client to begin imagining the next more disturbing scene. Additional instructions about relaxing are generally given when moving from one scene to another. If anxiety is experienced, the client usually signals so by raising his index finger; he is then instructed to stop imagining the scene. The therapist may then drop back to a less potent scene or give additional relaxation instructions.

During the course of therapy, the client proceeds through the hierarchy until it is possible to imagine the most feared scene without experiencing anxiety. As systematic desensitization continues, the client is encouraged to actually practice items that no longer produce anxiety in imagination. For example, if the woman described above is able to imagine being on the fourth floor of a building, an assignment for the week might be to actually go to the third floor of a familiar building. In this way, the scenes that are imagined in the therapy session are related to situations in real life. The client gradually approaches the feared situation "in vivo" as improvement is made (i.e., less anxiety) in therapy.

Implosion Therapy. Whereas systematic desensitization helps the client to gradually approach the feared situation while relaxed, implosion therapy does just the opposite. Treatment by implosion involves having the client imagine very intense levels of the feared situation while experiencing anxiety. The higher the level of anxiety experienced, the better it is. A basic assumption of the treatment is that prolonged exposure to the feared situation will produce extinction of the anxiety. Simply put, the client imagines the feared situation in great detail, often with the help of the therapist, who verbally describes all the gruesome things that could happen. The client feels anxious because of imagining the feared situation, but since the scene goes on and on and nothing happens, the anxiety begins to extinguish. Some writers feel the procedure works by habituating the client not only to the specific fearful experience, but to the experience of unpleasant feelings in general. That is, the person may still feel fearful in the situation but be willing to tolerate it.

There are several terms related to implosion that involve similar procedures. The term *flooding* is used when the client actually confronts the feared situation in reality. *Massed practice* and *negative practice* are used to describe procedures in which clients repeat over and over again behavior that they wish to eliminate. The assumption underlying the treatment is that repeated practice produces aversive side effects such as fatigue and boredom. Since they occur concurrently with the behavior practiced, the aversive side effects become conditioned to the behavior. When that occurs it is reinforcing to stop performance of the behavior and aversive to begin it again.

Aversion Therapy. Because of the important role environment is assumed to play in controlling behavior, a large number of treatment techniques used in behavior modification centers around changing the environment. This is particularly true of operant procedures. For example, if a child finds it reinforcing to misbehave in class and thus gain attention from both teacher and classmates, a common procedure involves instructing the teacher to ignore the misbehavior and praise or otherwise reward the other children when they also ignore it. Once the reinforcement that maintains the behavior is terminated, the behavior itself should extinguish.

There are, however, many behaviors that cannot practically be separated from their reinforcers. This is particularly true of addictive behaviors and sexual deviations. In such cases, aversive therapies have sometimes been tried. Essentially, all these techniques attempt to associate the behavior to be decreased with aversive stimuli. In one common procedure an alcoholic may look at or smell alcohol and at the same time be administered an electric shock, or a person who is attracted sexually to children may view a slide of a child and be administered an electric shock at the same time. By pairing the presence of the alcohol with a noxious stimulus, the therapist hopes to associate some of the anxiety and fear connected to the shock with alcohol. Drinking thus becomes less rewarding because of the aversive emotional responses now associated with it. The mother of one of the editors used this technique unknowingly but quite effectively when she administered doses of castor oil to her children in freshly-squeezed orange juice. Although the "treatment" occurred only a few times during early childhood, the "client" was unable to drink fresh orange juice for more than twenty years.

Variations of the aversive procedure involve application of a punishing stimulus after performance of undesired behavior. For example, the alcoholic may actually pour a drink, pick up the glass, and lift it to his lips before being shocked. This procedure probably combines operant and classical conditioning in that the whole situation is associated with being shocked and the *consequence* of lifting the glass to drink is aversive. A third variation, avoidance or escape learning, requires the client to do something to avoid being shocked. A drink might be placed in front of the alcoholic, for example. If the drink is pushed away, nothing happens, but if it is not, shock follows.

In addition to these procedural variations, aversive techniques use a variety of aversive stimuli, such as drugs that make the client ill, electrical shock, and verbal descriptions of painful or repulsive scenes. When the behavior to be eliminated is imagined rather than performed, and the aversive consequence is also imagined rather than actually administered, the procedure is called *covert sensitization*.

Behavior Modification. Applied operant psychologists emphasize the role of consequences in behavioral change or maintenance. These consequences can be manipulated to produce three major goals: (1) increased desirable behavior, (2) decreased undesirable behavior, and, (3) new desirable behaviors.

Increasing Desirable Behavior. Reinforcement has been discussed at some length earlier. Briefly, it involves the presentation of a consequence that increases the probability of a behavior recurring in the future. Consequences take many forms. For example, there are a variety of social consequences that can be reinforcing, e.g., smiles, praise, recognition, compliments, attention, hand holding, hugs, handshakes, eye contact, and touching are all potentially rewarding. *Contingency management* and *behavioral contracting* are two techniques set up somewhat more formally, so that functional relationships are arranged between particular behaviors and specified outcomes. For instance, one of the editors developed a contract with a Jewish Ph.D. candidate who was experiencing some difficulty completing his thesis proposal. The candidate established eleven stages for proposal completion and deposited $1,100 with the therapist. If the candidate accomplished a particular task by the deadline, $100 was returned to him. If he did not, the $100 was forwarded to the Palestinian Liberation Organization. In this example, both positive reinforcement ($100 returned to him) and punishment ($100 sent to the P.L.O.) were used to maintain the student on target. Contracting is actually a more formalized version of contingency management in which the contingencies, the relationships of reward to behavior, are written out.

Another method of increasing behavior is through the introduction of a *token economy* system using *backup reinforcers*. This technique is modeled after the familiar, larger economy. Briefly, tokens such as points, poker chips, or check marks are earned when subjects emit target behavior and are used to "purchase" various backup reinforcers such as privileges, toys or time-off from tasks. Token economies have been used extensively in behavioral-change programs. Examples can be found in Abstracts 30 and 67.

A fourth important method for increasing desirable behavior is through *modeling* or observational learning. With this technique, there is generally a predetermined role that an individual acts out, either in real life or on video- or audiotape for the subject of the treatment. This technique is based on both theory and data that suggest we learn from the nonverbal as well as verbal behavior of others, regardless of whether those others are actually reinforced for their behavior. Some of the studies which have used modeling as a treatment can be seen in Abstracts 11 and 22.

Decreasing Undesirable Behavior. Some undesirable behaviors are so persistent, or are sufficiently dangerous to the individual and to others, that they require a program to eliminate or decrease them. One of the easiest yet least-used methods of behavior management is *ignoring*. Frequently, just those behaviors that we wish to eliminate are in fact maintained by the attention (approving or disapproving) that they generate. Generally, ignoring must continue over a fairly long period, for example a week, depending on the original rate of behavior. Typically, the behavior at first increases in rate or intensity. This pattern is a common function of any *extinction* or nonreinforcement phase; ignoring is a form of extinction. As ignoring continues, however, the behavior generally decreases. Abstract 21 is an application of this procedure.

Sometimes a more powerful procedure is necessary to decrease behavior, however. *Time out*, a very effective and relatively simple technique to implement, is often used. In time out, the individual is removed from the situation immediately after the occurrence of an undesirable behavior to an environment that is unappealing. Hence, reinforcement that was perhaps available in the form of social contact, pleasant activities, or a comfortable surrounding, is temporarily removed. In time out, it is important to inform the person why time out is occurring and what behaviors are necessary to remain in the more pleasant environment. Time out must be applied carefully, as it can result in a variety of undesirable behaviors. Example of time out is contained in Abstract 65.

A time-honored and much-debated technique for decreasing undesirable behavior is *punishment*. Although research indicates that it generates unfortunate side-effects, such as aggression, it may be effective. Because there are more positive and appropriate techniques for behavior change, it is often not the method of choice. There are times, however, when it is important that a behavior be reduced dramatically and immediately. Children who mutilate themselves and adults who are physically abusive to other people or to objects are two instances of behavior that may require punishment. Punishment is the application of a stimulus or event that decreases the probability of a behavior recurring in the future. Common punishers are electric shock and verbal disapproval. Time out also could be considered a form of punishment. Applications of punishment to suppress deviant behavior can be seen in Abstracts 39 and 84.

Building a New Response. Most of the examples referred to in this chapter involve behaviors that can already be performed, those that are already in the individual's response repertoire. But how are new behaviors trained? Suppose the goal is to teach Arnold appropriate skills for asking Hazel to go out with him. To move from his present behavior to the desired behavior, a procedure called *shaping* is used. Shaping is a training technique whereby *successive approximations* of the desired behavior are rewarded. At first Arnold may be reinforced for very crude approximations, such as simply relaxing as he thinks about talking to Hazel. Next he may be rewarded for remaining relaxed and for saying "Hi, Hazel" in a well-modulated tone. As reinforced behaviors are learned and performed adequately, the therapist calls for behaviors that more closely approximate the desired goal.

Applied Behavior Analysis. The last group of behavioral practitioners is not characterized by use of a particular set of treatment techniques. They tend to use anything that shows promise of being effective, although there is a definite emphasis on operant as opposed to respondent procedures. What differentiates the applied behavior analysts from other subgroups within the field is their dedication, some would call it fanaticism, to applied research. The applied behavior analysts have a particular affinity for within-subjects designs (those that investigate the effects of treatment on individual subjects) and have developed several that are particularly applicable to "real life" settings as opposed to the psychological laboratory. The *Journal of Applied Behavior Analysis,* which began publishing in 1968, is the semi-official organ of this group and has set the standard of research in the field.

Most of the published articles on psychotherapy and other applications of psychological knowledge have been of two types. By far the largest category is that of case studies and anecdotal reports describing the application of a particular treatment in uncontrolled clinical settings. Although the purpose of these studies is, of course, to demonstrate treatment effectiveness, lack of appropriate experimental control and common use of clinical impressions as data considerably limit the usefulness of this type of research.

The most common alternative to the case study is the traditional between-groups design in which one or more groups receive a treatment while a "control" group does not. Although there are a variety of between-group designs which under ideal circumstances can provide researchers with reliable and valid data, a number of writers have pointed out major problems in the use of such designs in applied research (Leitenberg, 1973;[10] Shapiro, 1969.[11])The difficulty of composing matched groups, the ethical questions involved in withholding treatment from clients who need it, and the problem of keeping groups equivalent on every variable except the treatment under consideration, are three commonly mentioned difficulties.

A viable alternative to the weak case study and the problem-laden control-group approach is use of a within-subjects design (Hall, 1975;[12] Baer, Wolf, and Risley, 1968[13]). These designs, developed or adapted by applied behavior analysts, have enabled researchers to study problems that previously had appeared too complex or difficult to evaluate or had

10. Harold Leitenberg, "The Use of Single Case Methodology in Psychotherapy Research," *Journal of American Psychology* 82 (1973): 87-101.

11. M. B. Shapiro, "The Experimental Method Applied to the Individual Psychiatric Patient," in P. O. Davidson and C. A. Costello (eds.), *N = 1: Experimental Studies of Single Cases* (Toronto: Van Nostrand, 1969).

12. R. Vance Hall, *Managing Behavior, Volume One* (Lawrence, Kansas: H & H Enterprises, Inc., 1975).

13. Donald M. Baer, Montrose M. Wolf, and Todd R. Risley, "Some Current Dimensions of Applied Behavior Analysis," *Journal of Applied Behavior Analysis* 1 (1968): 91-97.

generally been the subject of only uncontrolled case studies. Two of the most common within-subject designs are described below:

Reversal Design. A fundamental characteristic of all within-subject designs is use of the subject as his own control. That is, instead of comparing the performance of one group with the performance of another group that was treated differently, the behavior of a single subject or single group at one point in time is compared to the behavior of that same subject or group at another point in time. When a reversal design is used, the study generally has four major phases. First, the "Baseline" or operant level of the target behavior is measured without any attempt to institute treatment. After a clear picture of the level of behavior is obtained, the second phase, treatment, begins. The target behavior is measured continuously, as in Baseline, while treatment is applied. If it changes in the desired direction, there is some indication that the treatment has worked. For example, if the goal is the reduction of smoking and during Baseline the client smoked an average of 45 cigarettes a day, a treatment that reduced the number smoked per day to six would appear very promising. Some researchers, in fact, do stop here. The resulting design is often called *Baseline-Treatment* or *AB*, since only two conditions are involved. Abstract 10 is an example of an AB design. A problem with such research, however, is the fact that treatment is confounded with time. It is possible that something else, unrelated to the treatment instituted but occurring at the same time as treatment, was the actual cause of the changes in behavior. To deal with this problem, a reversal design adds a third phase. After the treatment has had an effect on the target behavior, it is removed for a short period. This phase is sometimes called a reversal because the treatment is removed and replaced with the original Baseline conditions. Reversal can also mean that the treatment is not removed but is applied to a behavior that is the opposite of the target behavior. For example, if parents have been attending to their child only when she is playing cooperatively with her brother, the reversal phase might involve attending to her only when she is not playing cooperatively. The purpose of the reversal phase is to demonstrate that when the treatment condition is no longer applied, the desired changes in behavior are no longer maintained. That is, when treatment is instituted in the second phase, the behavior improves; when it is removed in the third phase, the improvement stops or the behavior worsens. The last phase of a reversal design is a reintroduction of the treatment condition to show that when treatment is applied again behavior improves. Abstract 74 uses a reversal design. They are sometimes also called ABAB designs.

Multiple Baseline Designs. The fundamental characteristic of a multiple baseline design is application of a treatment at several different points in time. This can be accomplished in three ways. The most common multiple Baseline design uses three subjects or groups of subjects. A Baseline is taken on the target behavior. Then, usually after about one week of Baseline, the first subject is placed under the treatment condition, while the other two subjects continue in the Baseline phase. After the effects of treatment have stabilized for the first subject, treatment is instituted for the second subject, and, following the same procedure, for the third. In effect, the design is a series of Baseline-treatment studies, each with a different Baseline length. Varying the point in time at which treatment is instituted shows that the factor that produced the change in behavior is actually the treatment rather than some other variable which happened to occur at the same time as treatment. For example of this type of multiple Baseline see Abstract 75.

A second type of multiple Baseline uses only one subject or one group and measures treatment effects across three different behaviors. A third type also uses a single subject or group and measures the same behavior across three different time periods or stimulus conditions.

Behavioral Observation. A final characteristic of the behavioral field in general and of applied behavior analysis in particular is its emphasis on the use of actual observations of behavior as data. Nonbehavioral research often relies on other forms of data. For example, a study evaluating the effects of group counseling on aggressive behavior in the classroom might involve a paper-and-pencil test which supposedly measures "aggressive tendencies" before and after counseling. The success of treatment is judged by changes in test scores. Frequently, such studies use tests without demonstrating any relationship between changes in scores on the test and actual changes in aggressive classroom behavior. It may be much easier to modify the manner in which students answer the test rather than the manner in which they behave in the classroom.

A similar problem exists when researchers use global ratings of improvement. Some studies, for example, ask parents, teachers, or ward staff to rate the general improvement of individuals based on their contact with them. Behavior analysts have criticized this type of data because of its lack of precision. It represents the *impression* of the observer rather than the actual behavior observed and thus can be influenced by a variety of factors other than improvement in behavior. Parents, for example, may report improvement in their child when objective data indicate there has been no change, perhaps because they expect treatment to have a beneficial effect or because they like the therapists and do not want to disappoint them. (See Abstract 110)

For the applied behavior analyst, the solution to the problems described above is the direct observation of behavior. Instead of relying on personality tests or rating scales, emphasis is placed on measuring change in the target behavior itself. Two major types of behavior observations have been used.

Frequency Data. Sometimes researchers simply count the number of occurrences or frequency of the target behavior. The question answered is "How many times did it happen?" Abstract 85 is a study in which this type of data is used. If the periods of observation vary in length, the *rate* of the behavior rather than its frequency is often graphed. Rate is simply the number of behaviors per minute or hour. If a parent counting the number of disagreements between two siblings counts eight on a day when they were together for four hours and six on a day when they spent three hours together, the rate is the same, two per hour.

Duration Data. Not all behaviors are easily counted. It is hard to tell when some behaviors begin and when they stop. Others may vary considerably in length from one occurrence to another. Johnny may have only one tantrum on Monday while he has seven on Tuesday, but the one on Monday may have lasted all day while the seven on Tuesday may each have lasted less than five minutes. With such behavior it may be desirable to measure *how long* the behavior lasts instead of how many times it occurs. Collection of duration data can involve no more than measuring the amount of time the behavior occurred (see Abstract 10).

Some researchers use a more complicated procedure called *time sampling* in which an observer divides the observation period into several short intervals. The intervals are often ten seconds each, with a five-second period after the interval for recording the behaviors observed. When using time sampling, observers watch for the target behavior during the ten-second interval. If it occurs, they may place a plus sign in a box on the recording sheet. A minus is recorded if the behavior did not occur. Some researchers have used this method to observe a large number of behaviors at one time. The data obtained are in the form of percentages of intervals in which the behavior occurred. An example of time sampling data is presented in Abstract 31.

CHAPTER I

Pioneer Studies

Abstract 1

A Laboratory Study of Fear:
The Case of Peter

MARY COVER JONES (Teachers College, Columbia University), *Pedagogical Seminary*, 1924, *31*, 308-315.

The classic study on treating children's fears.

The work of Watson and Rayner (see Introduction) demonstrated that fears could be conditioned. This study is a sequel to that research and is one of the first studies to demonstrate the effects of a psychological treatment of fear.

Method

SUBJECT AND SETTING: Peter was a relatively normal three-year-old, who had a strong fear of white rats as well as similar objects such as a rabbit, and a fur coat. This fact was discovered during a study of children's fears, and it was decided to attempt to modify the fear. By placing objects in his crib in a playroom, the experimenter discovered Peter was even more afraid of the rabbit than the rat. The rabbit was therefore the feared stimulus to which treatment was applied, while other nontreated stimuli were used to test for generalization of effects.

PROCEDURE: Each day during the initial phase of a three-month treatment, Peter and three other children who did not fear rabbits were brought to the laboratory for a play period. A rabbit was present during the sessions, and Peter was occasionally brought in alone to observe his reactions. The children served as models for nonfearful interaction with the rabbit. After a few days, a more specific treatment was applied. It consisted of bringing the rabbit closer and closer to Peter each day, starting with an initial distance of 12 feet.   The gradual introduction of new situations requiring closer and closer contact with the rabbit were an important part of treatment. Extensive notes were made during the study which indicated whether Peter avoided, tolerated, or welcomed each new situation.

Results

Peter demonstrated progressive tolerance of closer and closer contact with the rabbit, beginning with its presence 12 feet from Peter and finally ending with Peter fondling the rabbit and allowing it to nibble his fingers.

Two setbacks were noted in the progress of treatment. One occurred when a large dog jumped at Peter and frightened him as he was leaving the hospital after an illness. The other occurred when Peter received a slight scratch while helping carry the rabbit to his cage.

By the end of the study (three months), Peter had developed a "genuine fondness" for the rabbit. In addition his fears of other similar objects had either disappeared or been greatly reduced.

Abstract 2

The Elimination of Children's Fears

MARY COVER JONES (Teachers College, Columbia University), *Journal of Experimental Psychology*, 1924, 7, 382-390.

A survey of methods to eliminate children's fears.

Watson has shown how fears might be acquired through conditioning. The next step is to discover how such fears can be eliminated. Seven methods have been described in the literature, and these methods are the subject of inquiry.

Method

SUBJECTS: Seventy children, three months to seven years of age, in a temporary care institution served as subjects. Children were normal in IQ, social status, etc. (Temporary residence due to illness at home, mother working, etc.)

PROCEDURE: All children were screened for possible fears (of the dark, being alone, animals, loud sounds). Those with readily elicitable fears were subjected to one of seven different treatments (sometimes combinations, because the intent was to eliminate fears, not only to study techniques.) The techniques used will be described, along with results.

Materials: White rats and rabbits, frogs, false faces, etc.

Results

One, two, or three cases are described briefly in connection with each technique. The techniques used varied in numbers of attempts or hours, depending on progress.

1. Method of Disuse: Shield child from fear stimuli or situation for a time on the grounds "he'll grow out of it." In three cases, waiting for weeks or months did not result in disappearance of fear. *Conclusion:* An unsafe method.

2. Method of Verbal Appeal: Talk the child out of it: pleasant stories in connection with feared object. Can be used only with older children. *Result:* Hours of talking proved ineffective.

3. Method of Negative Adaptation: Repeat stimulus monotonously; S should get used to it. *Result:* May be indifferent to formerly feared stimulus, but not a positive, pleasant reaction, which was the objective.

4. Method of Repression: Ridicule, social teasing, scolding by play-mates. *Result:* The emotion seems to be resuggested and entrenched.

5. Method of Distraction: Offer a substitute activity; e.g., candy to a crying child. *Result:* Requires someone around to provide substitutes or distractions, which lead only to temporary forgetting.

6. Method of Direct Conditioning: Associate fear stimulus with a positive stimulus; e.g., food in presence of feared object. This method requires care and sensitivity in controlling the situation—e.g., keep a feared animal at a distance that will be tolerated. *Result:* There is a danger of reversed results but this is the only method, except for the next, which worked effectively.

7. Method of Social Imitation: Have a nonfearing S who shows positive behavior present along with the fearful one. *Result:* This method (with no. 6 above) was found to be productive in developing positive behavior.

Conclusion: Only the methods of direct conditioning and social imitation were unqualified successes. The others had some virtues, but they either did not lead to positive adjustments or had undesirable aspects.

Abstract 3

Negative Practice versus Positive Practice in The Elimination of Typing Errors

ROBERT RUHL (University of California), *Journal of General Psychology*, 1935, *13*, 203-211.

An early evaluation of Dunlap's negative practice procedure.

This study compared two methods of eliminating unwanted behavior. The more common procedure, positive practice, involves practicing the correct behavior. The other method, negative practice, was developed by Knight Dunlap and involves practicing again and again the errors or mistakes made, on the assumption that overpractice will eliminate them.

Method

SUBJECTS AND SETTING: The study was conducted in two typing classes in a high school. One was a beginning class, whose members had about two months of experience, and the other was an advanced class with eight semesters of experience. Each of the classes was divided into two groups, one designated *positive practice* and the other *negative practice*.

PROCEDURE: Before treatment the students were given a timed typing test. The errors made on the test were identified, with a list made for each student. For students who received positive practice instructions, the list consisted of the words for which an error occurred, with each word spelled correctly. Students who were in the negative practice section received a list that spelled the words exactly as the student had spelled them. Following the test, the students were given 20 minutes to practice the lists, either the corrected list (positive practice) or the list with errors (negative practice). On the following day, students took the test again and were given another list based on the errors made that day. This procedure continued for eight days.

Results

Analysis of speed and accuracy data across successive days indicated that both the positive and the negative practice sections of the beginning group improved in those areas. The advanced group made little improvement in accuracy, regardless of condition, perhaps because they began at a relatively high level of performance. The advanced group did increase its speed, however, regardless of treatment condition.

Abstract 4

A Study of the Efficacy of Negative
Practice As a Corrective For Stammering

HAROLD FISHMAN (University of California at Los Angeles),
Journal of Speech Disorder, 1937, 2, 67-72.

Successful use of negative practice in speech therapy.

The principles that are assumed to underly negative practice are discussed in Abstract 3. In essence, negative practice simply means performing an unwanted behavior again and again, on purpose. This purposeful practice was used in this study to eliminate stammering.

Method

SUBJECTS AND SETTING: Five cases are described, four males ages 13, 17, 19, and 20, and one female, 12. All had severe speech problems. Treatment was conducted in a small room, with the client and the instructor seated across a table.

PROCEDURE: Each client was asked to read from several types of material for 10 to 20 minutes. Speech errors were recorded, and practice material was made up of short sentences with words to be purposely stammered underlined. The words were those stammered during the reading phase. Clients were told that practicing the stammering would help to eliminate it, but only if the practiced stammer was like the involuntary stammer. Each client was given instructions on exactly how to repeat the involuntary stammer. Then they were asked to: 1) read each sentence on a list three times, while stammering at the underlined words, 2) say each sentence correctly with the instructor three times, and 3) say the sentence correctly once. When the client mastered the material, the sentences were replaced with new ones.

Two clients were seen once a week and were instructed to practice at home, as well, for the duration of the session. Schedules of the other clients are not given.

Results

Three of the cases showed marked improvement after negative practice. One, for example, stammered on 15% of the words read on the pretest and after a month stammered on only 6% of the words on a posttest.

Two cases were worse after treatment. One, for example, stammered on 5% of the words read before treatment and 20% after treatment.

Abstract 5

Enuresis—A Method for Its Study and Treatment

O. H. MOWRER and W. M. MOWRER (New Haven Children's Center), *Journal of Orthopsychiatry*, 1938, *8*, 436-459.

The classic paper on treatment of enuresis.

Enuresis has been the target of a wide variety of somewhat bizarre but unsuccessful treatments. Writers have often considered enuresis as merely an indication of some other problem such as repressed sexuality, deep-seated anxieties, or hostility. While these may be the primary cause of the problem in a few cases, and may be contributing factors in others, the treatment described in this paper is based on the assumption that a great many cases of enuresis are due to the lack of appropriate training.

Method

SUBJECTS: Thirty children (ages 3-13) who wet the bed at night, but who were expected by their parents to have full control, were studied. Children labeled "highly neurotic" or psychotic were not considered suitable candidates for the treatment. In addition, it was emphasized that success would be more likely if there was already a good relationship between the parents and the child.

PROCEDURE: Treatment was based on Pavlovian or classical conditioning principles. The goal was to associate waking up with a full bladder. To accomplish this association, a special mattress pad was developed which basically consisted of two pieces of bronze screening separated by a piece of absorbent cloth. When dry, the pad did not conduct electricity. When wet, however, the pad became a good conductor and closed a circuit that included a battery and an electric doorbell.

The bell served as an unconditioned stimulus for awakening. When the pad was placed on the child's bed, the ringing of the bell coincided with the beginning of bed wetting and with a relatively full bladder.

The child was instructed to get up when the bell rang and go to the bathroom. In theory, a full bladder, which occurs at the same time as the ringing bell, should become a conditioned stimulus for awakening.

The apparatus was used nightly until seven successive dry nights occurred. Then the child was given one or more cups of water more than normal just before going to bed. When seven more consecutive dry nights occurred, use of the apparatus was discontinued, although it was reinstated if a relapse occurred.

Results

All 30 cases were successfully treated. None required more than two months. No evidence of the emergence of other "symptoms" was observed when the children were no longer enuretic.

Abstract **6**

The Treatment of Alcoholism by Establishing Conditioned Reflex

WALTER VOEGTLIN (Shadel Sanitorium), *British Journal of Medical Sciences*, 1940, *199*, 802-810.

Pavlovian methods of treating alcoholism.

Pavlov's basic research on conditioned responses is applied in this early paper to the treatment of alcoholism.

Method

SUBJECTS AND SETTING: The treatment was given to 685 alcoholics who were hospitalized, usually for about five days. Average age was 41. Five to seven sessions of treatment were administered to most patients. Treatment was conducted in a comfortable soundproofed room with subdued light.

PROCEDURE: The patient was brought into the room and given an injection of a drug that produced violent nausea in two to eight minutes. Just before onset of nausea, the patient was given a drink of alcohol and asked to smell the liquor frequently.

Treatment consisted of requiring the patient to drink and smell a wide variety of liquor while experiencing severe nausea produced by the injection. Most of those who experienced the treatment vomited, but those who did not had their stomach emptied via a tube. This prevented the absorption of any of the alcohol consumed. At the end of each session, the stomach of each patient was emptied and washed with warm water, using a tube.

Results

Of 685 patients who were treated over a four-year period, the status of 538 was known. The number of patients who were abstinent comprised the primary data. Reported abstinence level was 97% for the first six months after treatment. For the next 3½ years, the level ranged around a mean of 64%. There was some suggestion that older alcoholics were more likely to remain abstinent, while women and wine and beer drinkers were more likely to return to drinking.

Abstract **7**

The Conditioning of the Human Fetus *in utero*

DAVID SPELT (Muhlenberg College), *Journal of Experimental Psychology*, 1948, *38*, 338-346.

Is there learning before birth?

Can conditioning techniques be applied to the unborn fetus to learn about the impact of environmental factors without resort to surgery? The fetus is known to respond to a loud sound. Can the sound be used as an Unconditioned Stimulus (US) and, when paired with a suitable CS, can learning before birth be demonstrated?

Method

SUBJECTS: Thirteen pregnant and three nonpregnant women. The pregnant women were at or beyond the seventh month of gestation. The responses recorded came from these Ss, but the Ss were, of course, the fetuses.

A large hollow pine box, about 30 inches square × 10 inches deep, served as a sound chamber when struck with an 8-pound force by an oak clapper. The sound (which did not evoke startle responses in the mothers) served as the US and was effective stimulus for a movement of the fetus. A gongless doorbell was strapped to the abdomen. The striker from the doorbell served as the CS, producing a vertical vibration on the surface of the mother's abdomen. Tambours were attached to the abdomen at points where X-rays indicated the head, arms, and leg positions of the fetus. The mothers could detect fetal movements almost perfectly. All fetal movements were recorded by tambours connected to pens writing on a kymograph drum.

PROCEDURE: It was necessary to provide controls for movements of the abdomen that were not made by the fetuses. This was done by testing nonpregnant women (N = 3). Controls were also necessary for pseudo-conditioning and the possible effects of CS alone because of advanced pregnancy (N = 6). Two more Ss before the eighth month of gestation were tested to see if the fetus would react to the sound before the last two months. The controls were effective in that none of the Ss reacted inappropriately. The conditioning procedure consisted of presenting the CS (vibrator) for

29

five seconds, followed by the US (loud noise). Trials were spaced at least four minutes apart, and two experimental sessions were held daily for 30-75 minutes for varying numbers of days with different Ss (because of their entering labor or other reasons).

Results

For the five Ss who were used in the conditioning study (conditioning) proper, these were the findings:

S 10—Sixteen US, followed by 10 CS—no response to CS (control for pseudo-conditioning). After eight sessions of paired stimulation, three successive CRs.

S 17—Three successive CRs after eight sessions.

S 16—After 21 pairings, first CR. After 59 pairings, seven successive CRs. The following day, four CRs; then scattered CRs in extinction.

S 15—First CR after 16 pairings. After two-week rest, 6 CRs after 31 pairings.

S 12—First two CRs after 21 pairings in the seventh session. After extinction following three CRs, S showed spontaneous recovery. The next day, six CRs in 11 tests with CS alone. After 18 days' rest, S gave seven CRs to the first nine test CSs.

Conclusion: Some 15-20 paired stimulations were required to establish conditioning to the level of three or four successive CRs. Experimental extinction, spontaneous recovery, and retention of the CR for about three weeks were demonstrated.

Abstract 8

The Reinforcing Effect of Two Spoken Sounds on the Frequency of Two Responses

JOEL GREENSPOON (Indiana University), *American Journal of Psychology*, 1955, 50, 409-416.

Reinforcement effects in conversation.

"A reinforcing stimulus is a stimulus introduced following a response that increases the probability of occurrence of that response." Not much systematic work has been done in assessing reinforcing stimuli in human behavior. "The purpose of this research was to investigate the effect of the introduction and omission of two spoken sounds following a predetermined response on the frequency of occurrence of that response."

Method

SUBJECTS: Seventy-five undergraduate students in five groups. Apparatus included a tape recorder and microphone.

PROCEDURE: Ss were seated in front of the E where they could not see him. They were instructed to say as many words as they could think of in 50 minutes. Only individual words (no phrases) were called for. For the first 25 minutes, E would say for Ss in Groups I and III "Mmm-hmm" and for groups II and IV "Huh-uh" depending on the words S emitted. For the control groups, nothing was said at any time following the words. For the last 25 minutes (an extinction period) E said nothing to any S. The four experimental groups were arranged as follows:

Group I:	"Mmm-hmm" for "plural" words.
Group II:	"Huh-uh" for "plural" words.
Group III:	"Mmm-hmm" for nonplural words.
Group IV:	"Huh-uh" for nonplural words.

Results

The data were analyzed by the ten five-minute periods in each 50-minute session. The Ss spoke in the range of 700-800 words.

The effects of the spoken reinforcers followed expectations; saying "Mmm-hmm" increased the number of plural words emitted by the Ss and "Huh-uh" decreased this number for Groups I and II. When E reinforced nonplural words, the results followed the same pattern but not so strikingly (no statistically significant group differences). When the reinforcements were omitted (last 25 minutes), the responses showed a decline (not significant in Groups III and IV). The findings for the control groups and Groups I and II are shown in the Table.

It needs to be noted that nonplural words form a proportionally larger class of words than do plurals. When reinforcements were introduced for nonplural words, the class size became a determiner because both kinds of reinforcers increased emission of nonplural words. "Mmm-hmm" thus reinforced both plural and nonplural words, but "huh-uh" decreased only plural words. "The nature of the response is a determinant of the reinforcing character of the stimulus."

Mean Number of Plural Responses for Successive Five-Minute Periods for Control Group and for Experimental Groups in which Contingent Stimulus Was Introduced Following Each Plural Response. (Stimulus omitted last five periods of experimental groups.)

5-minute period	Control Group (No stimulus)	Group I ("Mmm-hmm")	Group II ("Huh-uh")
	Mean	Mean	Mean
1	15.47	25.50	11.33
2	11.20	22.07	7.17
3	11.00	22.43	2.83
4	10.53	19.07	4.83
5	8.40	20.86	3.83
6	8.13	16.21	7.33
7	8.27	11.64	4.83
8	10.87	10.50	3.00
9	6.67	11.43	7.33
10	8.33	9.50	4.83

Abstract 9

Case of Fetishism Treated by Aversion Therapy

M. J. RAYMOND (St. George's Hospital, London), *British Medical Journal*, 1956, 2, 854-857.

Treatment of an unusual sexual problem.

"Exotic fetishism" is a tendency to be sexually aroused or attracted by a particular aspect of the body or by an inanimate object. This study reports an attempt to apply aversive conditioning to a fetish.

Method

SUBJECT AND SETTING: The client was a 33-year-old male, referred by an out-patient department of a mental hospital after he attacked a baby carriage. A check of his record indicated he had committed 12 previous attacks on baby carriages which were known to the police. While in the Royal Air Force (1948), he had attacked empty carriages in a train station and set them on fire. Later, after a stay in a mental hospital, he scratched and cut a carriage (1950) and was returned to the hospital.

He also was known to have attacked a handbag. Upon release, he had several other incidents. He deliberately drove his motorcycle into a carriage containing a baby, squirted oil on another carriage (1952), and splashed a carriage with his motorcycle (1957).

The client reported he had impulses to damage carriages and handbags since age ten, and he estimated he averaged two-three attacks a week. He indicated he masturbated regularly while fantasizing about baby carriages and handbags being damaged by their owners. He was married and had two children, was successful in his work, and was described as a good husband and father by his wife. However, he indicated he could only have intercourse while fantasizing about handbags and carriages. A good deal of his leisure time was devoted to his fetishes and he knew a great deal about them.

A psychiatric examination indicated no psychosis, although the client was depressed because his efforts to deal with his fetishes had all been unsuccessful.

PROCEDURE: With the client's cooperation, an aversive treatment developed. A collection of handbags, carriages, and pictures of these items was obtained and shown to the client just before an injection of a drug producing nausea. The treatment was given twice an hour, day and night, for one week. No food was given and an amphetamine was used to keep him awake at night.

After the first week, the client was allowed home for eight days. When he returned to the hospital, he reported that for the first time he had been able to have intercourse with wife without using his fantasies. After five more days of treatment, he indicated the sight of the objects made him sick. He was then confined to his bed with carriages and handbags about him in the room. Treatment was administered irregularly.

On the ninth day he rang for the nurse and was found sobbing uncontrollably and saying again and again "Take them away." The objects were removed and he was given warm milk and a sedative.

Further treatment included a "booster" session six months later. The client viewed a film of women carrying handbags and pushing carriages. The film was begun just before the onset of nausea produced by injections.

Results

Nineteen months after the initial treatment, the client reported no further difficulties related to the fetish. He had been promoted at work and had experienced no police contacts.

Abstract **10**

The Elimination of Tantrum Behavior
by Extinction Procedures

CARL WILLIAMS (University of Miami), *Journal of Abnormal and Social Psychology*, 1959, 59, 269.

Early research on parental modification of tantrum behavior.

Can extinction procedures be applied to undesirable human behavior?

Method

SUBJECT: A 21-month-old male child who was pronounced medically fit, but who had a history of ill health up to the age of 18 months and who had required special care and attention, was the subject. The child would now demand special attention at bedtime, and the parents could not leave the bedroom till the child was asleep.

PROCEDURE: Child was put to bed in a relaxed manner, and the parent (or aunt) closed the door on leaving the room and did not reenter when the child began to scream with rage. The extinction procedure was repeated in a second series after an original ten-day series.

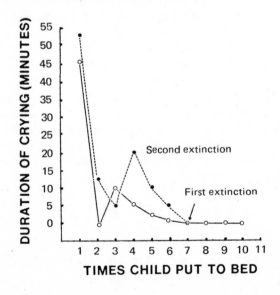

Results

In ten days, the child accepted the putting-to-bed routine without fussing and appeared to welcome the operation. After about a week, the child again had a tantrum episode after his aunt put him to bed, perhaps a spontaneous recovery. A second extinction, requiring only seven days, brought about the quiet acceptance again. At almost four years of age, the child showed no side effects and appeared to be a normal, friendly person.

Abstract 11

Transmission of Aggression through Imitation of Aggressive Models

ALBERT BANDURA, DOROTHEA ROSS, and SHEILA ROSS (Stanford University), *Journal of Abnormal and Social Psychology*, 1961, *63*, 575-582.

The effects of seeing other people behave in an aggressive manner.

Note: This paper includes much interesting material on aggression. The abstract will deal only with the specific imitation aspects of the report.

A test of imitative learning can be considered more crucial if carried out in the absence of the model and in a setting different from the original situation. In this study, Ss were first exposed to a model in one setting and tested elsewhere without the model present. The study, therefore, involves the generalization of imitative patterns.

Method

SUBJECTS: Thirty-six boys and 36 girls in a nursery school, ages 37 to 69 months, with a mean age of 52 months, were the subjects. The children were rated and matched on normal aggressiveness. Male and female adults served as models. Data on sex differences, sex of model, and aggressiveness of *Ss* were collected.

Materials: Assorted nursery-level toys serving as background items for the toy of major concern, an inflated five-foot "Bobo" doll.

Design: Experimental *Ss* were divided into two groups. One group observed an aggressive model; the other group observed a passive or subdued model. A control group did not observe either.

PROCEDURE: An individual child would be invited to play at an attractive task. Seated at a table, the *S* would begin to work with colored pictures. The model would then go to another part of the room where, for ten minutes, he engaged in either: 1) aggressive behavior (lay Bobo on its side, sit on it, punch it on the nose, strike it on the head with a mallet, toss it in the air, and kick it about the room). These were all considered specific behaviors that are unlikely to occur to a child who is likely to punch the clown doll but not much else. 2) The nonaggressive condition. The model assembled a tinker toy and ignored the doll.

After the model left, the experimenter took the child to another building, where the *S* was subjected to a frustrating experience to insure that no inhibiting process would be obscuring aggressive tendencies. The question under study is not aggression itself, but what form it would take. In this room, the *S* was shown some attractive toys and allowed by *E* to start playing with them; *E* then told him the toys were for the other children, and took the child to still another room where he could play with any of the toys there. These included the Bobo doll and mallet, a dart gun, and other aggressive and nonaggressive toys (dolls, trucks, etc.). The *S* spent 20 minutes in this room with the experimenter, who was busy with paperwork. Two observers watched the *S* through a one-way mirror.

Results

All *Ss* were scored for aggressive responses. In the nonaggressive and control groups, 70% of the *Ss* had zero scores. The scores for the various subject breakdowns are shown in the Table.

While some general aggression could be expected due to the frustration imposed on all *Ss*, the precise form of the aggression is the issue. Where the Table refers to imitative aggression, the data represent the number of times the *Ss* distinctly repeated the model's behavior, including the repetition of precise remarks made by the model. The differences between the experimental groups were highly significant in such specific imitativeness. In general, boys showed more aggression than girls following exposure to the male model.

Conclusion: The observation of cues produced by the behavior of others is one effective means of eliciting certain forms of responses, which are of a low probability in themselves, without the necessity of reinforcement.

Mean Aggression Scores for Experimental and Control Subjects
Experimental Groups

Response category	Aggressive		Nonaggressive		Control groups
	F Model	M Model	F Model	M Model	
Imitative physical aggression					
Female subjects	5.5	7.2	2.5	0.0	1.2
Male subjects	12.4	25.8	0.2	1.2	2.0
Imitative verbal aggression					
Female subjects	13.7	2.0	0.3	0.0	0.7
Male subjects	4.3	12.7	1.1	0.0	1.7
Mallet aggression					
Female subjects	17.2	18.7	0.5	0.5	13.1
Male subjects	15.5	25.8	18.7	6.7	13.5
Punches Bobo doll					
Female subjects	6.3	16.5	5.8	4.3	11.7
Male subjects	13.9	11.9	15.6	14.8	15.7
Nonimitative aggression					
Female subjects	21.3	8.4	7.2	1.4	6.1
Male subjects	16.2	36.7	26.1	22.3	24.6
Aggressive gun play					
Female subjects	1.8	4.5	2.6	2.5	3.7
Male subjects	7.3	15.9	8.9	16.7	14.3

Abstract 12

Intensive Treatment of Psychotic Behavior by Stimulus Satiation and Food Reinforcement

TEODORO AYLLON (Anna State Hospital) *Behaviour Research and Therapy*, 1963, *1*, 53-61.

Pioneering research in a mental hospital.

Stimulus satiation is a treatment procedure reflecting the old saying that one can, indeed, have too much of a good thing. In this famous case study, that principle is used to modify a persistent behavior of hoarding.

Method

SUBJECT AND SETTING: The subject was a female psychiatric patient in a mental hospital who had been hoarding towels for nine years. Each day the patient would collect towels from the 40 other patients on the unit and store them in her room. Each day the staff would politely try to get the patient to return the towels because of the problems caused when 40 patients took baths and had very few towels. She refused, and it would be necessary to enter her room and take the towels.

PROCEDURE: First a count of the number of towels the patient had was made. Then the unit staff were instructed to stop both collecting the towels from the patient and telling her not to collect them. They were also told to give the patient an average of seven additional towels a day. Later, the number given her was increased to 60 per day.

Results

At first the patient expressed pleasure in receiving the towels. She made comments such as "Oh, you found my towels, that's wonderful, thank you, nurse, thank you." As the number of towels in her room increased however, she began to make less positive statements such as "It takes me all day to put my things away now, you know . . . I don't think I need so many towels, maybe I have enough now."

Before treatment, the patient had folded the towels and neatly piled them on her bed, bureau, and chair. When her towel count reached about 700, however, she complained she could not stay up all night taking care of the towels. The staff told her to do the best she could, but she became less efficient in caring for her towels and even expressed irritation at their presence. After four weeks of treatment, she threw several at a nurse. When no one picked them up and returned them to her room, she put several more towels outside her room. When they were not returned, she removed hundreds of towels from her room in the following several days, until she had only one.

CHAPTER II

Preschool Studies

Abstract 13

The Organization of Day-Care Environments:
"Zone" versus "Man-to-Man" Staff Assignments

KATHRYN LE LAURIN and TODD RISLEY (University of Kansas), *Journal of Applied Behavior Analysis*, 1972, 5, 225-232.

Staff development in day-care programs.

Like many professional and semi-professional jobs, the operation of a day-care center can be conducted in a variety of ways. Each center director has certain preferred methods of operating, which are usually based on subjective experience and a pet philosophy or theory of day care that appeals to him or her. In reality however, very few of the decisions about the day-to-day operational procedures are based on empirical comparisions of the alternatives. This study attempts to do just that for one frequent task in day-care centers—moving children from one task to the next.

Method

SUBJECTS: Forty-three children, ages three to five, attending a day-care center in an urban poverty area, participated in the study. There were three full-time teachers for the center, as well as one head teacher/administrator.

PROCEDURE: Two ways of allocating staff during trasitions from one area to the next were compared. In the first or "Zone" approach, the staff was assigned to an area and supervised all children in the area (e.g., lunchroom, bathroom, bed area, heads-down, table area). For the other approach, "Man-to-Man," each teacher was given responsibility for a group of six to twelve children and thus moved with the group from place to place.

The study concentrated on the time after lunch when the children moved from lunch to an area where they removed their shoes, and then to a rest area for a nap. Under the Zone procedure, all four teachers supervised lunch until the first child left lunch. One teacher then took her place in the shoe area and helped children get ready for a nap, while another supervised the bathroom area. As more children left lunch, one of the remaining teachers went to the sleep area.

Under the Man-to-Man procedure, each teacher kept all children in the lunchroom until all had finished, then moved them as a group to the succeeding areas.

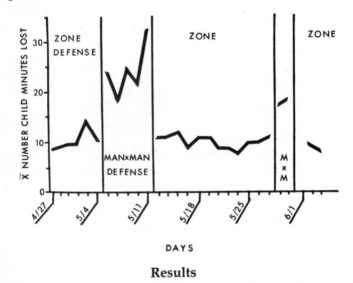

DAYS

Results

Five observers, stationed strategically in the center, recorded the behavior of the children using the play-check method. During the observation period, the observers at the beginning of each 60-second period would count the number of children engaged in activities appropriate to the area.

As shown in the Figure, the Zone procedure was in effect for seven days at the beginning and for two other periods of 12 days and three days. Man-to-Man was used once for five days and again for two days. The Figure indicates that children tended to lose more time or not be engaged in appropriate tasks much more under Man-to-Man procedures than Zone. Transitions took longer for Man-to-Man and produced a lower level of engagement.

Abstract **14**

Collateral Social Development Accompanying Reinforcement of Outdoor Play in a Preschool Child

JOAN BUELL (University of Oregon), PATRICIA STODDARD and FLORENCE HARRIS (University of Washington) and DONALD BAER (University of Kansas), *Journal of Applied Behavior Analysis*, 1968, *1*, 167-175.

Does modifying one behavior affect others?

Behavior modification has a highly successful record of altering a specific target behavior in the desired direction, but what of related behavior? Does modifying one behavior have any effect on related types of responses? Although subjective ratings frequently point to positive side effects, some theorists view behavior change as merely a matter of substituting one inappropriate behavior for another. Rarely are actual objective measurements of target-related behaviors taken, however, in order for this issue to be studied empirically.

Method

SUBJECTS AND SETTING: A three-year old preschool girl was selected as the subject. Although apparently bright, she was well behind the other children at the preschool in use of outdoor play equipment and in the amount and type of verbal behavior she emitted. She rarely spoke to the other children, and when speaking to teachers, she appeared to be imitating her infant brother.

PROCEDURE: Use of outdoor play equipment was designated as the target behavior. Collateral behaviors, that is, behaviors that might be affected by a change in the target behavior, were also measured. They included touching the teacher or another child, speaking to the teacher or another child, using a child's name when addressing him or her, parallel play (playing near other children but not with them), cooperative play, and "baby" behavior.

The behaviors were measured by one or two observers using a 10-second time-sampling technique during all outdoor play, within the preschool day.

Baseline. For the first five days of the study, teacher behavior continued as usual. That is, the child was given random, noncontingent attention.

Reinforcement with Priming. For the next nine days, the child, Polly, was lifted onto the particular piece of play equipment nearest to her, regardless of her protestations (which occurred the first three days), providing she had not been placed on it before. This procedure was referred to as priming. Once she was on the play equipment, the teacher remained near Polly, talking, smiling, approving and generally displaying interest and delight in Polly's performance.

In addition, teachers also continued with random, noncontingent attention to Polly as in Baseline.

Reinforcement without Priming. Priming was discontinued on day 15, buy any self-initiated use of outdoor play equipment by Polly was reinforced as in the previous condition. On day 19, her teachers began to alter their reinforcement schedule from continuous to intermittent. Specifically, they increased the distance between themselves and Polly, in addition to reducing the frequency of their approving comments. This sort of fading was maintained during the remainder of the study; superimposed on it were probe periods of noncontingent reinforceent.

First and Second Probe. Only naturally-occurring, random and noncontingent reinforcement was maintained during the probe conditions. These periods (days 23 to 27 and 37 to 40) were included to show the dependence of behavior on reinforcement. Both probe conditions were essentially the same, except in the second probe Polly was never rewarded for using outdoor equipment and was specifically reinforced within 20 seconds of leaving the play equipment.

Results

Use of outdoor play equipment was clearly affected by the intervention, as the Figure illustrates. Reinforcement appeared to be central in determining the level of Polly's play behavior. When she was not primed, the data indicate her play frequency decreased, but this was transitory, since reinforcement alone increased the frequency to its primed-plus-reinforcement level within five days. Withdrawal of reinforcement in the probe conditions resulted in an immediate and marked decrease in the use of play equipment.

The effects of treatment on collateral behavior were varied. Child-oriented behaviors, that is, touching and speaking to other children, cooperative play with other children, and use of other childrens' names consistently increased over Baseline, but to different degrees.

Teacher-oriented behavior was constant throughout the study, but fluctuated considerably from day to day. It must be noted that teacher-oriented behavior began at a higher frequency than child-oriented behavior and was considered adequate quantitatively for a three-year-old child, although qualitative deficiencies were noted (e.g., a high rate of "baby" talk which decreased across all conditions of the study).

Parallel play, the final behavior measured, was unstable during the entire course of the study.

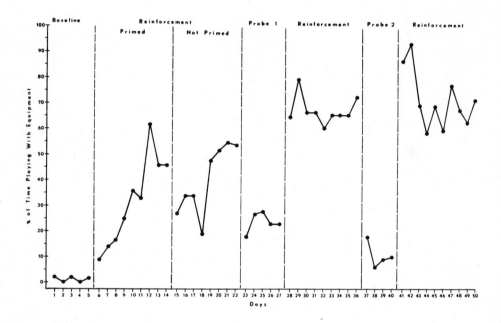

Abstract 15

Reading-related Behavior in an Open Classroom: Effects of Novelty and Modeling on Preschoolers

GARY HASKETT and WILLIAM LENFESTEY (University of North Carolina, Charlotte), *Journal of Applied Behavior Analysis*, 1974, 7, 233-241.

Positive effects of providing models for reading.

The philosophy on which open classrooms are based assumes that there is an innate human tendency to be responsible and to seek personal gratification through growth and learning. Open classrooms thus seek to help the child activate his natural tendencies to explore, learn, and create by providing an environment that is relatively unstructured but rich in learning opportunities. Unfortunately, there is little empirical research on an open system of education to test the effect of these concepts in practice. This study suggests that the addition of some behavior modification techniques into open classrooms may improve the operation of the classes.

Method

SUBJECTS AND SETTING: Eight children, ranging in age from three years, three months to five years, nine months, attending a university preschool, were selected as subjects. All the children scored above the average on intelligence tests, with the lowest IQ being 114.

The preschool class met three days a week for eight weeks, from 9:00 A.M. to 4:30 P.M. Undergraduate students in psychology and education provided care and tutoring for the group.

PROCEDURE: Reading behavior was measured throughout the study by observers who took data each day during two 15-minute free-play sessions at about 1 A.M. and 2 P.M. Reading was defined as a child looking at the pages of an open book.

To record reading behavior, the observer would look at the children for six seconds. Then he or she would take the next six seconds to record on a rating sheet the reading behavior of the children observed. This pattern of observation continued for the entire 15-minute free-play period.

Baseline. During the first seven observation periods (3½ days), there were about one dozen books available to the preschoolers, but no specific attempt was made to encourage the children to read. The books were familiar ones which had been in the preschool since the beginning of the year.

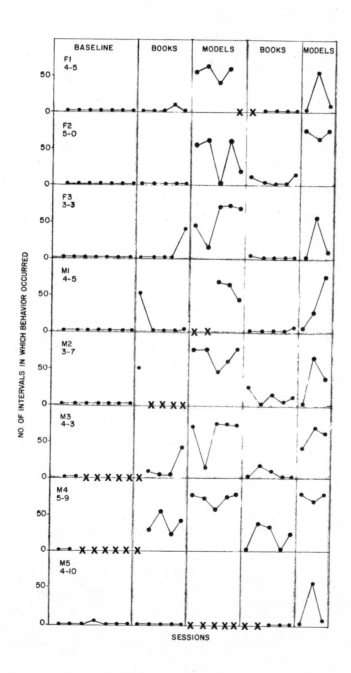

Intervention. For the next five sessions (Books condition) the children were introduced to new reading material every day. Tutors entered the classroom carrying 10 to 15 books, announced their arrival, and placed them with the other books. The tutors did not attempt to encourage the children to read, however. During the next five sessions, the tutors read aloud from the books already present, stopping only to answer questions about the reading material (Models condition). Again, they did not encourage the children to attend or to read from the new books.

For the next eight sessions the Books condition (Baseline, five days) and the Models condition (three days) were replicated.

Results

The Figure shows that although reading was possible as an activity, it did not occur naturally for these preschool children. Even with new books regularly appearing, the amount of time spent in reading related behavior increased only slightly. For most children, it did not increase at all. When modelling was introduced, reading behavior increased across all subjects who were present. When the students no longer saw models reading from the books, the amount of time they spent reading decreased, while reintroducing models produced another increase.

Abstract **16**

Establishing Use of Descriptive Adjectives in the Spontaneous Speech of Disadvantaged Preschool Children

BETTY HART and TODD RISLEY (University of Kansas), *Journal of Applied Behavior Analysis*, 1968, 1, 109-120.

Expanding the child's world through language training.

The richness of the world in which a child lives is in part determined by the child's ability to describe his world. One child may simply see two toys. Another may see a polka-dot talking tiger and an orange-and white-striped elephant. It is especially important for culturally-depriven children to acquire language skills of this sort in order to survive in an educational world oriented toward the middle-class child, in which verbal ability is a major factor influencing success. In this study a program geared specifically toward enhancing the descriptive vocabularies of a group of disadvantaged preschool children is developed.

Method

SUBJECTS AND SETTING: Eight black boys and seven black girls, ages four to five years, were selected from large families with extremely low incomes. Their I.Q. scores, as determined by the Peabody Picture Vocabulary Test, averaged 79. The preschool program was comprised of breakfast (teacher-structured), free-play indoors, group time (teacher-structured), free-play outdoors, and story-time (teacher-structured), and covered a three-hour period, five mornings a week, for the duration of the preschool year.

PROCEDURE:

Baseline. Throughout Baseline, the children were reinforced socially on an intermittent basis for using appropriate descriptive adjectives during the free-play period. In addition, they were corrected intermittently when they used descriptive adjectives inappropriately. If, when requesting a piece of equipment such as a ball, a child used a descriptive adjective ("Could I have the red ball?"), he almost always received it, but there was no particular attention paid to occurrences of nouns and adjectives together during this condition.

Baseline lasted 103 days. The frequency of adjective usage was so low, however, that the authors decided to initiate a second Baseline period. It appeared that many adjectives simply were not within the children's vocabularies. If the frequency was to be increased, the children would first have to learn to say the words.

Baseline: Color-naming at Group Time. The 15 children were divided into two groups, seven in one group and eight in the other. The teacher presented a picture or an object to be identified and described. For example, the teacher might hold up a picture of a duck or a pencil. If the child responded correctly, "The duck is yellow" or, "The pencil is blue," the teacher would say something like, "That's correct. Good answer," or, "That's very good," and give the child a food snack, as well. If the child answered simply "yellow" or "pencil," the teacher approved, asked for a complete sentence, and gave the snack when the child repeated the answer correctly.

This condition followed Baseline and lasted 50 days. When it ended, seven of the children could name the nine colors taught and eight could reliably name six colors. There was still, however, no significant change in their free-play use of adjectives or adjective-noun pairings. The authors noted in the final days of this period, however, that when an item could be obtained only through asking for it with its color, the rate of adjective-use increased considerably. Thus, the third condition was introduced.

Material Contingent on Color Naming. Here, play materials and equipment were not provided unless the child asked for them specifically, using a noun-adjective pair (e.g., blue cow). The children were socially reinforced on every occasion in which they used an adjective-noun pair and, if it occurred spontaneously, were also praised for using an adjective. Five days into this condition, the seven children fluent in color-naming were introduced to a counting contingency in their group time. That is, praise and snacks now depended on the specification of the *number* of objects or items in a picture. Meanwhile, the eight children who could name six colors continued in the color contingency group.

Materials Not Contingent on Color Naming. This condition was included as a check. Materials were dispensed freely, as in Baseline, so that the experimenters could ascertain whether the effects of their training were maintained without specific intervention.

Results

The Figure represents the average rate of descriptive adjectives (size, color, number) per sample hour used by the 15 children across all four experimental conditions. The black bars represent measures of noun-adjective pairs. The white bars are measures of all adjectives, and so include those occurring in a noun-adjective pair.

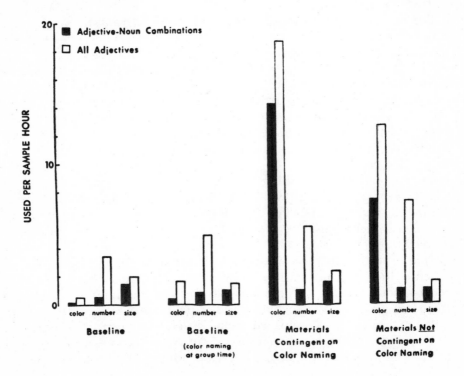

As was indicated by the institution of a second Baseline condition featuring reinforced color-naming at group time, the natural occurrence of descriptors was very low. Average use of color adjectives was 0.5 per hour, while color-noun pairs occurred at only 0.2 per hour. During the second Baseline, the average frequency of color adjectives used by the group of children increased to 1.8 per sample hour. Color-noun pairs increased slightly in frequency, from 0.2 to 0.4. When play materials and snacks were available only through use of noun-adjective pairs, there was a dramatic increase in their usage. Adjective-use jumped from 1.8 to 18.6 per hour, while noun-adjective frequency increased from 0.4 to 14.2.

During the fourth condition, when materials were not contingent on color-naming, the frequency of both adjectives and adjective-noun pairs dropped, but remained well above either Baseline.

The Figure also shows that these results were not simply an artifact of increased verbalizations in general, because use of adjectives relating to size remained almost constant throughout the study.

Abstract **17**

Modification of the Classroom Behavior of a "Disadvantaged" Kindergarten Boy by Social Reinforcement and Isolation

MARTHA ABBOTT, *Journal of Education*, 1969, *151*, 31-44.

Reinforcing the positive; ignoring the negative; and the use of time out in a classroom behavior modification project.

This study is about the type of child who gives teachers gray hair and drives them into the real-estate business. Bobby was a difficult, disruptive, hostile child, who was a continual problem for his teacher. A combination of reinforcement and time-out operations was used by the teacher in an effort to alter the undesired behavior.

Method

SUBJECT: Bobby was one of 12 children enrolled in a kindergarten program in an urban poverty area. Bobby, who had been very disruptive and resistive for some time, was the middle sibling in a family of three children. His mother was described as very lenient, while his father was very strict.

PROCEDURE: During a five-day Baseline period, Bobby's behavior was recorded using the Coping Analysis Schedule for Educational Settings (see Table), in order to determine the operant level of his behavior. When Treatment 1 was initiated, the teacher gave positive social attention for desirable behavior, ignored all inappropriate behavior, and ignored all unacceptable behavior unless it was intolerable, at which time Bobby was given a short negative verbal threat of isolation. If the unacceptable behavior did not stop within five to ten seconds, Bobby was put in isolation for five minutes. Isolation involved taking Bobby to a quiet, bare room near the classroom. After five days under Treatment 1, the use of isolation was extended to include inappropriate behavior that disrupted the class (Treatment 2). This was followed by a brief reversal phase, in which Baseline conditions were again in effect. The teacher disapproved when Bobby was exhibiting inappropriate or unacceptable behavior but gave no verbal warnings and no periods of isolation. He was given attention when he was disruptive, but was not praised when he behaved appropriately.

The fifth and final phase began with a reinstitution of Treatment 2 conditions. Then the amount of social reinforcement for acceptable behavior was gradually reduced from a near-continuous schedule to an intermittent schedule which roughly approximated the amount of adult attention received by other children in the class.

TABLE
Modified Coping Analysis Schedule for Educational Settings (CASES)

DESIRABLE (D)

5a. *Self-Directed Activity*—working independently on an activity or project with interest.
6. *Paying Rapt Attention*—listening and attending with interest to the on-going activity.
7a. *Sharing and Helping*—contributing ideas and interests, volunteering answers, and helping others.
8a. *Social Interaction*—mutual interaction through conversation, games, and joint projects.
9. *Seeking Support, Assistance, and Information*—asking for help, sympathy, and attention from teacher or peers.
10. *Following Instructions Passively*—conforming to expectations without great interest.

INAPPROPRIATE (I)

5b. *Self-Directed Activity*—5a., but at an inappropriate time.
7b. *Sharing and Helping*—7a., but at an inappropriate time.
8b. *Social Interaction*—8a., but at an inappropriate time.
11. *Observing Passively*—being distracted from on-going activity.
12. *Responding to Internal Stimuli*—no observable interaction with environment.

UNACCEPTABLE (U)

1. *Assaultive behavior*—direct verbal or physical attacks or destruction of property.
2. *Negative (Inappropriate) Attention-Seeking Behavior*—loud or annoying disruptive behavior which seems to be directed toward obtaining the attention of others through unacceptable behavior.
3. *Manipulating and Directing Others*—bossing others.
4. *Resisting Authority*—actively or passively refusing to comply with teacher's expectations or requests.
13. *Physical Withdrawal or Avoidance*—flight, moving away, hiding.

Results

The Figure shows the mean level and standard deviation of the three behaviors measured during all five conditions. Bobby's behavior was worst during Baseline and reversal conditions and best during treatment phases. The line across the inappropriate and unacceptable categories shows how Bobby's behavior compared to the average for the class.

(1-Baseline, 2-Treatment I, 3-Treatment II, 4-Reversal, 5-Reintroduction)

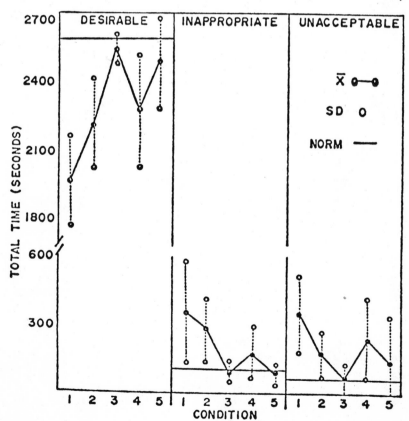

Abstract **18**

Applying "Group" Contingencies
to the Classroom Study Behavior
of Preschool Children

DON BUSHELL, JR. (University of Kansas), PATRICIA WROBEL
and MARY MICHAELES (Webster College), *Journal of Applied
Behavior Analysis*, 1968, *1*, 55-61.

A token reinforcement program for standard classrooms.

A great many early reports of behavior modification in schools involved the
use of special assistants who spent large amounts of time modifying the
behavior of one child. In fact, a frequent criticism of behavior modification
is the time it can take to set up and carry out a program. This study provides
a preschool example of a token economy administered by the regular
teacher of the class, which included all the students as participants.

Method

SUBJECTS: The study was conducted in a preschool classroom with 12
children, three to six years old. There were ten girls and two boys. All were
considered above average in ability, and each had previous experience with
token economies. The children attended school for about 2½ hours per day.
Two teachers handled the class.

PROCEDURE: During the study the children followed a regular pattern each
day. First, the children spent 20 minutes in individual activities, 25 minutes
in a group Spanish lesson, and 30 minutes in "study teams," in which
children who could perform a skill taught less capable children.

While the children worked in the three activities, the two teachers walked
about the room and gave tokens (colored plastic washers) to those who
were "actively working at their various tasks." The teachers did not men-
tion the tokens while administering them and did not award tokens to
children who asked for them. However, social praise such as, "You're doing
fine, keep it up" or "good," was given with the tokens. When the study
teams were operating, the tokens were awarded when the learner accomplished the assigned task.

Both teachers gave out about 120 tokens each day. For about 15 tokens
each day, the children could buy a "special-event ticket," which was re-

quired for entry into the day's special event. The events varied from day to day and included activities such as a movie, trips, art and gym. The exact price of the event was varied from day to day, so that the children never knew when they had earned the exact amount needed.

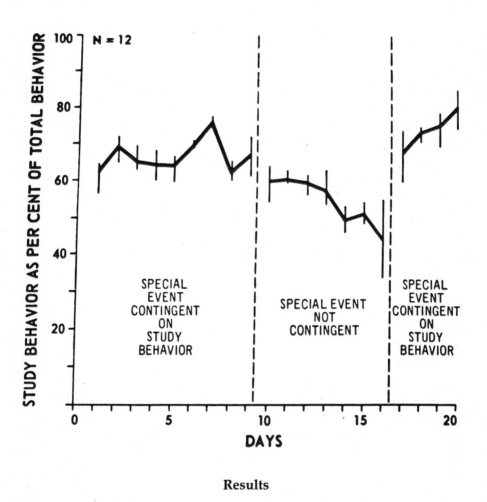

Results

Four observers recorded the behavior of the children from an adjoining observation room.

A time-sampling procedure was used in which each child was looked at in sequence and scored an S—studying—or NS—not studying. The Figure shows the percent of time the group averaged studying during the experiment. In the first and last phases, when the special event was contingent on earning enough tokens, study behavior was high, averaging well above 60%. During the middle phase, when tokens were awarded but were not necessary for the event, study behavior dropped markedly.

Abstract **19**

Effect of Contingent and Noncontingent Social Reinforcement on the Cooperative Play of a Preschool Child

BETTY HART, NANCY REYNOLDS, DONALD BAER (University of Kansas), ELEANOR BRAWLEY and FLORENCE HARRIS (University of Washington), *Journal of Applied Behavior Analysis*, 1968, *1*, 73-76.

Analyzing the effects of the frequency of reinforcement and the contingencies of reinforcement.

There are a number of studies in the literature that suggest adult social-reinforcement has a powerful effect on the behavior of preschoolers. Typically, these studies utilize frequent and contingent reinforcement together. In this study, the roles of frequent reinforcement and contingent reinforcement were assessed separately.

Method

SUBJECT AND SETTING: Martha was a five-year-old pupil at a university preschool which met for 2½ hours each day, five days a week. Martha's behavior at school, although varied and often effective in getting her way, was comprised almost entirely of anti- or nonsocial activities such as independent play, foul language, and taunts ("I can do better than you."). PROCEDURE: A reversal design was used incorporating a Baseline condition and two treatment procedures, noncontingent frequent reinforcement and less frequent but contingent reinforcement of cooperative play.

Baseline. For a ten-day period, intermittent and noncontingent reinforcement typically found in a preschool environment was given to Martha.

Noncontingent Frequent Reinforcement. From days 11 to 17, teachers increased their rate of attention to and approval of Martha. During Baseline, the teachers had attended to or approved of Martha about 20% of the time. During this phase the level increased to 80%. However, the increased level of reinforcement was randomly distributed, so that no specific behaviors were consistently reinforced.

Contingent Reinforcement. For the next 12 days, the teachers positively reinforced only cooperative play behavior. Because Martha's rate of cooperative play was so low, this behavior was shaped into her repertoire. Shaping involved reinforcement first for responsive verbalizations near other children, then for potentially cooperative verbalizations more directly involving another child, and finally reinforcement was given only for actual cooperative play.

The last two phases of the study involved a return to noncontingent frequent reinforcement for four days, and a second phase of contingent reinforcement for eight days.

Results

Because Martha was frequently close to other children but not actually cooperating with them, a measure of the amount of time she spent near her classmates, as well as a measure of the time spent in cooperative play, was taken. The data were taken by an observer who recorded Martha's behavior throughout the day, with the exception of a 20-30 minute group-activity period. The nursery-school day was divided into 10-second intervals, and the observer recorded whether the child was close to other children (proximity) and whether she engaged in cooperative play during each 10-second interval.

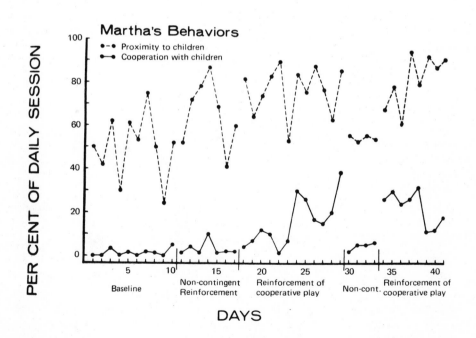

As can be seen in the Figure, proximity to other children was maintained at a high frequency throughout the study, but showed an increased rate after Baseline. Frequent reinforcement, when it was noncontingent, did not increase Martha's cooperative play. However, when reinforcement was contingent on cooperative play, that behavior increased, even though the actual amount of reinforcement was much less than during the non-contingent reinforcement condition (80% versus below 20%) and sometimes even less than the intermittent reinforcement of the Baseline period.

Conclusions. For these data, it would appear that the most salient component of adult social-reinforcement was the contingent relationship between it and the target behavior, rather than the absolute amount of reinforcement provided.

Abstract 20

Effects of Systematic Social and Token Reinforcement on the Modification of Racial and Color Concept Attitudes in Black and in White Preschool Children.

Margaret Spencer and Frances Horowitz (University of Kansas), *Developmental Psychology*, 1973, *9*, 2, 246-254.

Changing responses to racial membership: A step toward an empirical approach to racism.

The fact that members of many minority groups lack pride in the group to which they belong has been recognized for some time, but attempts to empirically study how racial attitudes can be changed are extremely rare. This study represents one of the few attempts to change not only the minority member's view of his race but that of the dominant majority, as well.

Method

SUBJECTS: Twenty-four black and 24 white preschool children, ages three to five years, served as subjects. Social class ranged from lower-class to upper-middle.

PROCEDURE: Two types of stimulus cards were used. On each card an animal was drawn twice—once in white and once in black. The second set of cards contained pictures of children, two per card, who were identical except for their hair and skin color, which identified one as black and one as white.

The experimenters also used the set of one black and one white mechanical puppets. Each puppet could be activated to dispense a marble to the child.

Each child was seen individually for five experimental sessions. Half were seen by a black female experimenter, half by a white female experimenter. In the first session, the child was presented the animal cards and asked to choose one of the animals. For example, the experimenter might say, "Here are two dogs. Everyone says how pretty one dog is. Which is the pretty dog?"

During the second phase of Session one, the children were again asked to choose one of the animals on each card. This time the puppet, who was the same race as the child, reinforced each experimental child (24 Ss) for selecting the black animal when the question was positive (e.g., "Show me the pretty dog."), or the white animal when the question was negative (e.g., "Show me the stupid owl."). The puppet nodded and gave a marble for correct responses. When an incorrect response occurred, the experimenter explained that the puppet felt the other animal was correct. Children who earned marbles contingently could buy a toy at the end of the session. The session ended when the child made no more than one error on the set of six cards, or when all the cards were presented four times. Children in a control group (24 Ss) went through the same sequence of card presentations without receiving marbles and without being corrected for errors. Each child was presented the cards twice.

Two weeks after the first session the children were presented the cards again. Experimental subjects saw each card six times and were reinforced or corrected as in Session one. The control subjects also had six trials per card, but without reinforcement or correction.

The third and fourth experimental sessions were given two weeks apart and were essentially a repetition of the second. However, the cards depicting children were used instead of the animal set. Four weeks after the fourth session the final experimental session was given, which was a repetition of the third.

Between sessions four and five, parents of half of the children in the experimental group participated in the study at home by playing a special

57

game. Each child selected a set of toys they liked and a set they disliked. The parents were given matched pairs of thes toys, a white and a black box, and 20 marbles. The game involved hiding a toy in one of the boxes, showing the child its mate, and asking the child to select which box he thought the matching toy was under. Preferred toys were always under the black box; nonpreferred toys were in the white box. Parents were instructed to play the game daily for four weeks, to give a marble for each correct response, and to correct errors. Marbles were redeemable for prizes.

Results

The data analyzed were percentage of errors per trial. Selecting a white stimulus was always considered an error. Thus, percentages above 50% indicated a white bias. A four-factor analysis of variance (Treatment, Subject's Race, Experimenter's Race, Sessions) indicated treatment had a significant effect, as did sessions. Subject's race and experimenter's race were not significant. Initially, all groups were strongly biased toward white preferences. Error percentages ranged from 70 to 80 per cent. Groups who received the experimental treatments reduced their errors to about 40% (a bias in favor of the black stimulus) , except for the black experimenter-black children group, which only dropped to about 54% error.

The game played at home and age of the subject had no effect on level or changes in error percentages.

Abstract 21

Control of Aggression in a Nursery School Class

Paul Brown and Rogers Elliott (Dartmouth College),
Journal of Experimental Child Psychology, 1965, 2, 103-107.

Catch them being good: A positive approach to dealing with aggression.

The control of aggression in humans has been the concern of a number of psychological theories. Most of these, however, have relied on nonobservable internal events, such as the generation of guilt or anxiety, to explain how aggression can be controlled. Behavioral theorists have focused their attention on external events rather than internal postulates, and have suggested that the consequences of behavior, aggressive or not, have a major influence on whether that behavior will occur again. This study is an early example of the application of behavioral theory to the modification of aggressive behavior.

Method

SUBJECTS: Twenty-seven boys, three to four years old, who were attending a nursery school, served as subjects.

PROCEDURE: Using a rating scale for aggression, an observer counted the number of physically aggressive behaviors (pushing, holding, hitting) and verbally aggressive behaviors (threatening) during the morning free-play hour. Ratings were taken for one week, and after a week of no observation, a two-week treatment period began. Ratings were taken during the second week of treatment. Follow-up observations were taken during the third week after treatment, and in the fifth week treatment was instituted.

Treatment. After explaining to the nursery-school teachers that sometimes the attention given to aggressive behavior contributes to its maintenance, the experimenters told the teachers, "Try to ignore aggression and reward cooperative and peaceful behavior. Of course, if someone is using a hammer on another's head, we would step in, but only to separate the two and leave. It will be difficult at first, because we tend to watch and be quiet when nothing bad is happening, and now, as much as possible, our attention will be directed toward cooperative, or nonaggressive behavior." Examples of appropriate statements of praise were given to the teachers ("That's good, Mike."), as well as instructions to avoid comments such as "Aren't you sorry?" which would constitute giving attention to a child who had behaved inappropriately.

TABLE
Average Number of Responses in the Various Rated Categories of Aggression

Times of observation	Categories of Aggression		
	Physical	Verbal	Total
Pre-treatment	41.2	22.8	64.0
First treatment	26.0	17.4	43.4
Follow-up	37.8	13.8	51.6
Second treatment	21.0	4.6	25.6

Results

Both physical and verbal aggression dropped considerably when the treatment condition was instituted. The results for each of the four rating periods is given in the Table. Verbal aggression decreased when treatment was applied and did not increase once the teachers were told the experiment was over (after two weeks of treatment). Physical aggression did increase, however. Returning to the treatment conditions for a second time produced another decrease in the number of physically aggressive behaviors.

CHAPTER III

Educational Applications

Abstract 22

Modeling Therapy for Test Anxiety: The Role of Model Affect and Consequence

PETER JAFFE and PETER CARLSON (University of Western Ontario), *Behaviour Research and Therapy*, 1972, 10, 329-339.

Novel application of a popular technique.

Modeling is a common treatment technique which has been used to treat a variety of problems. This study represents a somewhat unusual use of it, however, since the focus was test anxiety. In addition to investigating the use of modeling as a therapeutic intervention, this study also compared several ways of conducting the therapy.

Method

SUBJECTS AND PROCEDURE: Twenty female and ten male university students volunteered for the study because they suffered from fear of examinations. The 30 participants scored above the median on the Sarason Test Anxiety Questionnaire. Before treatment, all subjects took several subtests of an individual intelligence test. They also completed two self-report measures of test anxiety. Subjects, in groups of five, then watched one of four videotaped presentations of a male and then a female student taking sections of an individual intelligence test. A control group took only the pre- and posttests.

Calm-Positive. Models in this videotape were very calm and businesslike. Their examiner praised their performance after each section and told them at the end that they had done well above average at the end of the test session.

Anxious-Positive. Models on this tape also performed well and received positive feedback, but behaved anxiously, were restless, and expressed excessive concern regarding their performance.

Calm-Negative. The models were calm and businesslike but did not do well on the test. They were told by the examiner their performance was well below average, and that it was amazing they were ever able to get into college.

Anxious-Negative. In this final condition, the models were very anxious and received the negative feedback described above from the examiner.

Immediately after viewing the videotape assigned to them, each subject took the intelligence test sections previously administered, as well as several subtests which he had not taken previously. The self-report measures were also readministered after treatment.

Results

Subjects viewing the calm-negative, anxious-positive, and anxious-negative videotapes all improved on the portions of the intelligence tests they took, which were also taken by the models they observed on videotape. There was no significant difference between the calm-positive and control group.

On sections of the intelligence test not modelled on the tape, no significant differences between any of the experimental groups and the control group were found. Subjects in groups who viewed an anxious model, however, improved their grades in the introductory psychology class they were taking more than other groups.

The data from the self-report measures of test anxiety suggested that either observing anxious models or observing models receiving negative consequences resulted in some decrease in anxiety.

The data thus suggest that observing calm models who successfully deal with the anxiety-provoking situation may not be as effective as observing an anxious model who does not successfully deal with the problem.

Abstract **23**

Cognitive Modification of Test Anxious College Students

DONALD MEICHENBAUM (University of Waterloo). *Journal of Consulting and Clinical Psychology*, 1972, *39*, 370-380.

Treating anxious thoughts as well as anxious feelings.

Most behavioral approaches to treating test anxiety have used systematic desensitization, on the assumption that reducing the anxiety will alleviate the problem. Some researchers, however, have assumed that test anxiety has two components: emotionality (anxiety) and thinking (worry). The worry component, which may involve behaviors such as ruminating excessively over alternatives, preoccupation with negative feelings such as inadequacy, and concern over performance, is not directly dealt with in systematic desensitization. Another approach, often referred to as cognitive modification, does attend to the worry as well as the anxiety however. Cognitive modification procedures attempt to make the client aware of his thoughts and how they contribute to poor performance. A second component involves a modified systematic desensitization procedure, which requires the client not only to imagine the anxiety-producing scene but to subsequently imagine "coping" successfully with the situation. The client is also taught specific coping behaviors, such as taking slow, deep breaths and self-instructions to pay attention to the task.

This study compared a cognitive treatment procedure to systematic desensitization.

Method

SUBJECTS AND SETTING: Twenty-one volunteers who responded to a university newspaper advertisement for treatment of test-anxiety were the subjects. There were 15 males and six females; with one exception, they were all college students.

PROCEDURE: Before treatment, subjects completed several self-report measures of test anxiety. They were also given two actual tests which were previously shown to be sensitive to the effects of anxiety (a test requiring memorization of series of digits and the Ravens Matrices test). Three groups were then formed randomly with the restriction that each group be balanced for sex and for pretest scores on the anxiety measures.

Treatment.

Group Desensitization. The eight subjects in this group received eight sessions of treatment based on traditional systematic desensitization procedures. They were trained in progressive relaxation, hierarchy construction, imagery, and group desensitization.

Cognitive Modification Therapy Group. The eight subjects in this group were taught to identify anxiety-producing thoughts and self-statements they emitted before and during tests. They were trained also to emit self-statements that facilitated attending to the task and relaxing. The first of these two goals was accomplished through discussions in the group. The second was accomplished through a modified desensitization procedure. The subjects received all the components of traditional desensitization. In addition, they were trained in the use of slow, deep breathing as well as relaxation, because the breathing exercises seem to have a beneficial effect on test anxiety. In addition, during the desensitization procedure itself, subjects were asked to visualize themselves performing specified behaviors such as studying the night before an examination. If they became anxious, they were told to imagine themselves coping with the scene by taking slow, deep breaths and by self-instructions to relax and to pay attention to the task. They were also encouraged to use any self-statements that would help them pay attention to the task and inhibit thoughts irrelevant to the task. In essence, they rehearsed "in their head" behaviors that were likely to help them deal with tests.

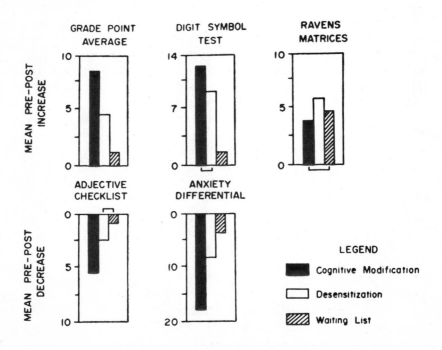

Waiting-list control group. The five subjects in this group were told they could obtain treatment sometime in the future. They took all the pretreatment measures. At the end of treatment, subjects in all three groups took the premeasures as posttests. The tests were administered again after one month.

Results

Analyses of variance indicated there were no significant differences between the groups before treatment. The Figure shows the mean increase or decrease in scores on five of the prepost measures used. Subjects in the cognitive modification treatment generally made greater improvements than those in desensitization, but these differences were not significant, except for grade-point average. Both groups were significantly better than the waiting-list controls. The results for several other measures were similar, with the cognitive group showing most improvement. On one self-report measure, the results indicated that the subjects in the cognitive group treated anxiety more as a beneficial or facilitative factor when taking tests than as a debilitative one.

Abstract 24

Effects of Continuous and Intermittent
Self-Monitoring on Academic Behavior

MICHAEL MAHONEY, BERT MOORE, TERRY WADE and NANCI MOURA (Stanford University). *Journal of Consulting and Clinical Psychology*, 1973, 41, 65-69.

Does keeping track of behavior change it?

Although the simple technique of recording one's own behavior has sometimes resulted in dramatic modification of that behavior, this effect has generally been attributed to covert self-evaluation. The actual paramet-ers of self-monitoring have not been clarified. The authors in this study have chosen to look at the relative results of two self-monitoring schedules against a simple performance feedback technique in order to partial out the role of evaluation.

Method

SUBJECTS AND SETTING: Twenty-seven college students who volunteered for a review program of the verbal and quantitative aptitude portions of the Graduate Record Examination (GRE) were selected. The subjects were each given a three-hour session on a teaching machine programmed with 300 problems, alternating from verbal to quantitative. Subjects were required to choose from four or five solutions and record their answers on a roll which was advanced and on which the questions were prepared in such a manner that students could not change their answers. After responding to the question, the subject advanced the machine to the next problem

PROCEDURE: Subjects were randomly assigned to four conditions: 1) continuous self-monitoring (n = 6); 2) intermittent self-monitoring (n = 7); 3) performance feedback (n = 7); 4) control (n = 7). Subjects were instructed that the project dealt with effective study habits and that amount of review necessary varied from student to student. They therefore had the option of terminating at any time. It was suggested that 90 minutes was adequate, but they need not feel constrained. Subjects were also encouraged to be accurate and told that there were more problems than they could do in the allotted time.

   Continuous Self Monitoring: Immediate feedback for all questions was provided. Students were instructed to depress a counter button each time they answered correctly. A reliability check that denoted which answers the subjects counted as correct was provided, unknown to the subjects.

   Intermittent Self-Monitoring: Instructions were similar in this condi-tion, except subjects were to depress the counter after three correct responses.

   Performance Feedback: Immediate feedback was available, but subjects were not required to tabulate their successes.

   Control: No feedback was given.

   All subjects were informed that results of their overall performances would be available in one week. Any subject who had not informed the experimenter that the review time was sufficient at the end of three hours was told that there was a time limit at the end of that period.

Results

All data were transformed to ranks and analyzed using the nonparametric statistic, Kruskal-Wallis analysis of variance, because of wide inter-group variation. Results showed that self-monitoring groups reviewed significantly longer than the feedback alone and control groups; and that of the self-monitoring groups, the continuous group reviewed significantly longer than the intermittent group. Number of items reviewed, speed, and verbal accuracy were not significantly different for any of the groups. For the quantitative problems, however, both self-monitoring groups were superior and did not significantly differ from each other. The reliability check on continuous self-monitoring showed that the subjects in that group were reliable recorders.

Abstract **25**

Examination Performance in Lecture-Discussion and Personalized Instruction Courses

DAVID BORN, STEPHEN GLEDHILL, and MICHAEL DAVIS (University of Utah) *Journal of Applied Behavior Analysis*, 1972, 5, 33-43.

An alternative to lecturing in the college classroom.

The Personalized System of Instruction developed by Fred Keller has become a popular alternative to traditional or lecture-based methods of teaching university courses. This study is an empirical evaluation of the effectiveness of PSI.

Method

SUBJECTS AND SETTING: Sixty students in a psychology-of-learning course were the subjects. They were assigned to one of four sections of the course, with each section matched on the basis of cumulative grade-point average.

PROCEDURE:

Lecture-Discussion Section. Students attended three, one-hour lectures on the course each week. No part of the grade was dependent on attendance, but the lectures were designed to supplement the reading assignments for the course.

Personalized Instruction Section (Keller). The reading material for the class was divided into 16 units, and a study guide was provided for each unit, which gave study questions the students could use to test themselves. As in the lecture section, there were three hours of class time each week. Proctors (advanced psychology majors who were familiar with the course content) were available to hand out study units, provide tutorial help, and to give unit tests. The unit tests were generally eight to ten sentence-completion, or fill-in, items and two to three short-answer, essay questions. If a student took a unit test and passed it perfectly, he moved on to the next unit and began studying it. If he missed one or more items, he restudied the unit and took a different form of the test until he made a perfect score. Students could decide when they were ready to take the unit tests, but were required to have passed all units to be tested on the mid-term or final before taking either of those examinations.

Modified-Keller Section. Conditions in this section were similar to those in the personalized section. Instead of 16 units, however, the material was divided into 57 small sections, which could be combined or studied individually by students. A student could thus elect to study very small sections of the material and be examined over them, or he could put several sections together and be tested once in the larger amount of content. Students in this section could also earn extra points by doing a project or paper.

Rotating Section. Students in this group worked under lecture-discussion conditions until the first mid-term. Half were then assigned to each of the remaining two conditions until the second mid-term examination. They were then reassigned to the other condition for the remainder of the course.

Results

The major measures of effectiveness were scores on the mid-term and final examinations, which were common to all sections. The examinations that included multiple choice, short answer, and essay items were scored by raters who were unaware of the section from which each examination came. Because the initial matching for assignment to groups was done on the basis of students who preregistered, rather than students who actually attended the first day of class, there were some differences in grade-point average across the groups. Thus, an analysis of covariance was used for comparisons. The data indicated that in terms of overall score the lecture-discussion section was significantly poorer than all other groups. When the scores were broken down into item types, there was no reliable difference between sections on multiple choice items, but the lecture-discussion group was poorer on both fill-in and essay items. The Keller section was better than all groups on essay items.

Data from the rotating section indicated that students with high grade-point averages performed equally well, regardless of the type of instructional format used. Students who had below-average grades, however, tended to do better under the personalized system.

Finally, although the modified Keller provided students with the opportunity to select varying lengths of assignments on which to be tested, almost all chose to be tested in each chapter in the text, which was the same format used in the Keller section. Finally, only three students in the modified section chose to do a project for extra credit.

Abstract **26**

A Note on Some Reinforcing Properties of University Lectures

KENNETH LLOYD, WARREN GARLINGTON, DOUGLAS LOWRY, HELENE BURGESS, HARALD EULER, and WILLIAM KNOWLTON (Washington State University), *Journal of Applied Behavior Analysis,* 1972, *5*, 151-155.

Lecturing: How to keep students out of the classroom.

The lecture is an old and respected (at least by professors) component of university life. Aside from the use of a textbook, it is perhaps the most common form of instruction on college campuses. This study examined the degree to which lectures are reinforcers.

Method

SUBJECTS AND SETTING: Three university courses in psychology were studied. Each used a personalized system of instruction similar to that described in Abstract 25. In addition, a lecture was provided once a week.

PROCEDURE: In each class, attendance at lectures was generally noncontingent, that is, no specific part of the grade was dependent on attending the lectures. In class A, however, students were given 20 points for attending the lecture during the seventh week. In class B, students were told that five questions on the weekly 15-item quiz would be from the lecture during the tenth week, one item from the lecture in week 11, and three from it in week 12.

In class C, during weeks eight-ten, students were required to do a certain amount of work before being allowed to attend the weekly lecture. Thus, lectures were treated as a privilege or reward. Also, class C students who attended the final lecture (14) received 20 points.

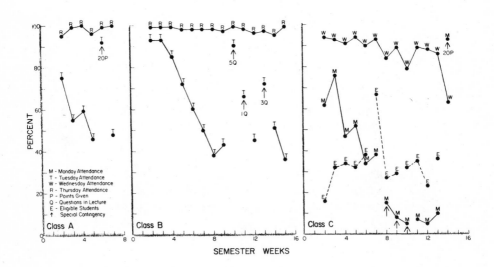

SEMESTER WEEKS

Results

The Figure shows the attendance data from all three classes. The lines at the top of the graph (labeled R or W) indicate attendance rates at quizzes or at sessions in which the quiz was discussed. For class A, attendance at lectures was consistently below attendance at quizzes, except for the week when students earned 20 points by attending the lecture. In class B, attendance gradually declined across the semester, until quiz items were taken from the lecture. When items were no longer based on the lecture, the decline continued. Finally, in class C, attendance to lectures declined across the semester, regardless of the contingency on attendance. The dashed line (E) indicates the percent of students eligible to attend, that is, the number who earned the 35 points during the previous week required for admission. The only day on which lectures were strongly attended in class C was the one in which students earned 20 points for attending.

The results suggest lectures were generally not reinforcing events for students.

Abstract 27

The Application of Operant Conditioning
Techniques in a Secondary School Classroom

LORING W. MCALLISTER, JAMES G. STACHOWIAK, DONALD M. BAER, and LINDA CONDERMAN (University of Kansas and Lawrence High School), *Journal of Applied Behavior Analysis*, 1969, 2, 277-285.

Social reinforcement and social punishment in a high school classroom.

Research related to reducing inappropriate behavior in preschool and in elementary school classrooms has received extensive attention by investigators. Treatment has generally focused on a few particularly disruptive students and has involved a variety of procedures. In this study, techniques for altering inappropriate behavior have been extended to the secondary school level and involve measures to change the behavior of an entire class of students.

Method

SUBJECTS: The experimental group included 12 male and 13 female students with a mean age of 17 years and an I.Q. range of 77 to 114, with a mean of 94.43. These students made up a low-track, junior-senior English class in which 80% of the students were from the lower socio-economic level. There were 13 males and 13 females in the control group. The mean age was 17.04 years, the mean I.Q. was 91.04, and socioeconomic status varied from lower-class (76%) through middle (14%) to upper (4%).

The teacher had one year of experience, which included a low-track class, and taught both experimental and control groups.

PROCEDURE: **Observed Behaviors.** Four behaviors were observed:

1. Inappropriate talking by students (audible vocal behavior engaged in without the teacher's permission.).
2. Inappropriate turning by students (turning around while seated other than when getting work-related material or when attending to a student talking appropriately).
3. Verbal reprimands by the teacher for inappropriate talking or turning around.
4. Praise dispensed by the teacher for appropriate behavior.

Behaviors were recorded as occurring or not occurring for each one-minute interval in a class period. The experimental group had a 70-minute period while the control group had a 60-minute period.

Baseline. This condition lasted 27 days and involved recording the four behaviors without any form of restriction or intervention.

Experimental Condition I. The teacher applied aversive social consequences for inappropriate talking, beginning on the 28th day. Whenever possible, she used the particular student's name and a direct, verbal, stern reproof ("John, be quiet" "Phil, shut up." "You people, be quiet.") No consequences were applied to turning around. In addition, no other punishment was applied to talking (for example, keeping them after school).

When periods of quiet occurred, the teacher socially reinforced the entire class ("Thank you for not talking"). Social reinforcement occurred during the first two minutes of class, after each 15-minute period when a lecture or class discussion was taking place, at the end of silent, seat-work assignments, and at the end of each class, as appropriate.

Experimental Condition II. On the 54th day of the experiment, the teacher began a parallel procedure with students who turned around inappropriately. She continued to socially reinforce or punish talking, as well.

72

Results

Figures 1 and 2 present the data for frequency of talking and of turning around for both experimental and control groups. Intervention in both cases produced a major decrease in the frequencies of both behaviors in the experimental class. For the talking behavior, the Baseline mean of 25.33% of the recorded intervals was reduced to only 5%. The amount of time spent turning around was 15.13% for the experimental group during Baseline, decreasing to a mean of 4.11% when intervention effects had stabilized. The control group means were comparable to Baseline conditions for the experimental group throughout the study.

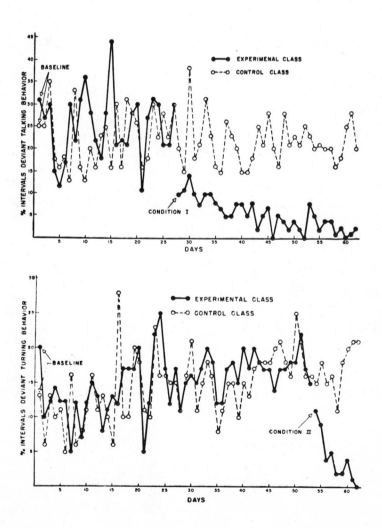

Abstract **28**

Systematic Desensitization and Relaxation of High Test-Anxious Secondary School Students

ROBERT LAXER, JACK QUARTER, ANN KOOMAN, and KEITH
WALKER (Ontario Institute for Studies in Education, University of Toronto), *Journal of Counseling Psychology*, 1969,
16, 446-451.

A critical study of group relaxation training and systematic desensitization.

Severe anxiety about taking tests in school is not an uncommon experience for students. In addition, previous research has indicated that test anxiety reduces the ability of the student to perform on the test. Test anxiety can be considered a sort of specific phobia, which produces fear, or it can be viewed as an indication of a more general or pervasive problem of anxiety which is not specific to one problem. If it is a specific problem, systematic desensitization would appear to be the treatment of choice, while a more general relaxation training program might be more appropriate for anxiety not related to a specific situation. This study evaluated the two alternatives to treatment.

Method

SUBJECTS AND SETTING: Only one of two studies is summarized here. The subjects were 89 students in grades 9-12 in four secondary schools in Toronto who had high scores on two tests of anxiety, who were in some academic difficulty, but could potentially pass the year, and who were recommended by a counselor. The subjects were assigned randomly to one of three groups (control, relaxation, systematic desensitization). Paper-and-pencil tests of test anxiety and general anxiety were administered before and after treatment. Grade-point averages were also computed before and after treatment.

PROCEDURE: One counselor was assigned to each of the schools and was given a seven-day training program in the treatment procedures, which included a theoretical overview and several daily practice sessions.

The counselor met small groups of two to four students for daily 20-minute sessions (in one school there were two, 20-minute sessions per day). Students were also encouraged to practice during other parts of the day. The program of treatment began six weeks prior to final examinations and continued until examinations began. Posttesting occurred during the final examination week.

Treatment Program. For the first two days, students in both the relaxation (R) and systematic desensitization (S.D.) conditions learned to relax while lying on floor mats. Students began with their feet and concentrated on relaxing muscle clusters until they were generally relaxed. Through audio tapes, the students were told to think of the muscle group (e.g., arches of the feet, calf muscles, upper arm, forehead), be aware of the strain when the muscles were tensed, and to concentrate on the feeling of relaxation as tensing was eased. For days three-five relaxation training continued, except the instructions about tensing muscles were dropped. Students in the relaxation group continued to practice relaxation for the remainder of the study.

Desensitization. On the sixth day of training, students in the S.D. condition were given a standard hierarchy of 22 graded aversive stimuli associated with school and evaluation. An item on the mild end of the hierarchy might be "going into a regularly scheduled class," while more anxiety-arousing items included "being called on to answer a question in class by a teacher who scares you," "seeing an exam question and not being sure of the answer," and "having to tell your parents you failed." During the sessions, the first ten minutes were spent relaxing. The remaining time was spent presenting items from the hierarchy. Once the students were relaxed, the counselor verbally described an item and asked the students to close their eyes and imagine the situation. Each description was followed by some comments that encouraged relaxation. If students felt tense as they imagined an item, they were asked to lift their index fingers. The counselor then went back to relaxation training until the students felt relaxed again. Items higher on the hierarchy were not presented until all members of the group were desensitized to lower items. S.D. continued until the 30th day of treatment. During the last ten days, both the R and S.D. groups sat at classroom desks during the treatment sessions to facilitate transfer of the treatment effects to the situation in which examinations would occur.

Results

An analysis of variance indicated that there were no differences between any of the groups, including the no-treatment control group, on any of the academic measures taken. There also was no significant difference on measures of test anxiety. Only on the general test of anxiety was there a significant difference. The relaxation condition had a lower anxiety score than the control group. No other differences were significant.

75

Abstract **29**

Programming Behavior Change and Reintegration into School Milieux of Extreme Adolescent Deviates

MARIAN MARTIN, RACHEL BURKHOLDER, TED ROSENTHAL, ROLAND THARP, and GAYLORD THORNE (Southern Arizona Mental Health Center and University of Arizona), *Behaviour Research and Therapy*, 1968, *6*, 371-383.

Teaching adaptive school behavior to problem students.

Successful therapeutic interventions using behavior modification techniques are becoming increasingly frequent within controlled settings such as hospitals and prisons. An important next step, however, lies in programming those behavioral changes into the natural environment, so that they are maintained by naturally-occurring reinforcers. This study presents an effective method for offering that opportunity to adolescents emitting extremely deviant behavior.

Method

SUBJECTS AND SETTING: The program was carried out in a community mental health center where special educational materials and teachers were provided. Originally, a token economy program was set up to reinforce appropriate behavior of nine adolescents on a fixed ratio and then a variable ratio schedule. All the subjects had been removed from regular classes because of disruptive behavior and attended the experimental classes at the mental health center for half a day (morning). Behaviors targeted were incompatible with disruptive responses such as fighting, sexual promiscuity, stealing, and infractions of school rules. The students ranged in age from 13 to 18 years and had all been involved in homebound programs.

The original token economy program was unsuccessful, as only one adolescent showed signs of making academic progress. It was out of this system, however, that the reported experimental procedure developed.

PROCEDURE: **The Phase System.** Although there were nine students in the token economy, for reasons external to the experiment, there were only five students available when the Phase System began. Table 1 summarizes the Phase System. A counselor saw each student and carefully explained the

Table 1. Phase System Program

Phase I: Preliminary

Required behavior	Reinforcers
1. Attend school 1-4 hr daily.	1. Teacher attention and points.
2. At least 1 hr of good behavior out of the hours attended.	2. Canteen items (20 cents a day; can be saved up) on points.
3. No school work required.	3. Home backup for hourly notes.
4. Know and pass an oral test on the Purpose and Preliminary sections of the Handbook.	

Review: Available every 5 days; three consecutive days of full attendance and all required behavior necessary for promotion. Favorable review after each Phase followed by recognition.

Recognition: A letter to the parents informing them of the child's progress and praising both the child's efforts and that of the home in accomplishing this gain. Child is given praise by teachers and staff.

Phase II: Intermediate

1. Attend school full time.	1. Teacher attention and points.
2. Do some academic work, as set by teachers.	2. Tutoring.
	3. Canteen items and field trips, on points.
3. No behavior which damages property or injuries any person.	4. Increased home backup on a single daily note.
	5. Can see counselor by appointment.
	6. Extracurricular activities.

Review: Available every 20 days. Review board has the option of setting a "condition to be fulfilled" if 20 consecutive days of the required behavior have not been achieved in every category.

Recognition: A letter is sent home inviting the parents to a conference at school at which the child's progress is explained and praise given. The child receives a certificate of progress and an improvement party is held at the school in the child's honor.

Phase III: Advanced

Required behavior	Reinforcers
1. All those listed in I and II	1. Teacher attention and points.
2. No behavior which cannot be tolerated in the classroom.	2. Tutoring.
3. Schoolwork, as individually assigned, at a passing level.	3. Canteen items, as before, no points required.
4. Occupy and discharge satisfactorily one committee job.	4. Trips and objects (ordered from a catalog, maximum value $5.00) on points.
	5. Can see counselor on appointment and for special problems.
	6. Home backup increases, on every other day notes if possible.
	7. Extracurricular activity.
	8. Special course, by staff.

Review: Eligible for review after 10 weeks, or 50 consecutive school days.
Recognition: A letter to the home and parent conference, as above. The child is the guest of teachers and staff at lunch; his certificate of progress is presented at that time.

Phase IV: Honors

---

1. All those listed in I-III.
2. At least some school work at a grade of 3 or above.
3. If possible, attend at least one class in a public school, maintain appropriate behavior and passing work.
4. Become a member of the Student Council.

1. Teacher attention and points.
2. Tutoring, including course(s) carried in public school.
3. Canteen items and trips, no points required.
4. Objects, on points. Can save up for more costly objects.
5. Increased home backups on weekly notes, if possible.
6. Can use separate study room.
7. Counselor, same as Phase III.
8. Extracurricular activities.
9. Special course.

Review: Eligible for graduation at next semester break.
Recognition: A letter and conference, as above. A graduation dinner banquet is given in honor of the child (or children) graduating. The parents are invited and mother is presented with a corsage. The child receives a gift and certificate of graduation.

Phase V: Postgraduate

---

1. Regular attendance at public school.
2. Passing grades.
3. Appropriate behavior in school.

1. Increased home backups, no notes, if possible.
2. Special assistance with school problems, tutoring, and counseling available, as needed.
3. Extracurricular activities.
4. Cash bonus for continued attendance. Grades differentially reinforced with cash, special events, planned with the home.

---

program, outlined reasons for ejection from regular schools, described the required behaviors for progression from one phase to another in this system, as well as the reinforcers that were available.

Phase I. Because the requirements were simple, this phase screened out candidates who were uninterested. Staff could also meet with parents to explain the program, determine the level of cooperation and discuss reinforcers that could be dispensed at home. Parents were given some instruction in reinforcing appropriate behavior and ignoring disruptive responses.

Phase II. A relevant academic program was outlined for the student. Counselors dealt with specific problem behaviors in school and at home.

Phase III. In this phase, academic skills were developed and course credits were earned. Availability of external reinforcers was highlighted through promoting interests and recreation in their own neighborhoods. Activities such as hunting minerals and sewing acquired reward value and could be used to achieve appropriate behavior. In addition, students began participating on committees responsible for recreational activities and for managing the canteen.

Phase IV. During this phase, a gradual reintegration of these students into the regular classroom began through reintroducing them to one course in a public school system. Students were required to comply with rules governing all students while they were within the regular system.

Phase V. Students graduated and were placed in the public school system on a full-time basis.

Throughout the program, demands on students became increasingly complex, with a concurrent decrease in number of tangible reinforcers. These were replaced generally by new reinforcers found in the home and community and were usually social.

Results

The Figure presents partial data for four of the five students during different phases of the program. Initiation of the phase system appears to maintain low levels of disruptive behavior and a high rate of work. A fairly consistent pattern can be detected which indicates that beginning a phase results in slightly increased disruption and slightly decreased work behavior. Anecdotal evidence suggests that this may be due to the increased demands of the phase and attendant difficulty in matching behavior to the new responses required.

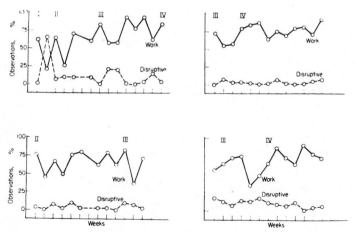

Individual records of work and disruptive behavior, showing effect of phases.

Abstract 30

Contingent Token Reinforcement
in an Educational Program
for Emotionally Disturbed Children

JERRY WILLIS (University of Western Ontario). In Rickard
and Dinoff (eds.), *Behavior Modification in Children*. (Tus-
caloosa: University of Alabama Press, 1974,) 157-170.

Control-group study of token economies.

Much of the research on the effects of reinforcement systems, such as token
economies, have relied on single-subject designs. Although a valuable
means of obtaining research data in the natural environment, the use of
subjects as their own controls can produce problems in interpretation. A
particularly difficult issue is the question of contrast effects. That is, the use
of a Baseline with no reinforcement immediately prior to the institution of a
tangible reward condition may enhance the effectiveness of the reward.
This study evaluated the effects of a token reinforcement system using a
control-group design.

Method

SUBJECTS AND SETTING: Thirty-six children, 5 girls and 31 boys, attending
a summer camp for disturbed children, served as subjects. Their ages
ranged from 8 to 15. During 26 days of camp, they attended class for 1½
hours a day in a specially-designed room. Each student had a small cubical
in which to work. Based on pretreatment educational tests, each child was
assigned to a series of programmed texts in reading, mathematics, science,
or French. Two nights a week, the children came to a "store" where they
could spend points earned at the camp. A variety of merchandise was
available, including candy, soft drinks, toys, clothing, camping items, and
radios.

EXPERIMENTAL GROUPS: The camp population was divided into six cabin
groups, which represented the various age groups at the camp. Two cabin
groups were assigned to each of three treatment conditions.

No Token Reinforcement. Children in this group attended class,
received assignments, and were monitored much as they would be in a
regular classroom. They periodically took tests in the work they were

completing and were required to redo the work if they did not pass the test. No points were awarded to this group for classroom work. They did, however, earn points for other work, such as keeping their cabin clean.

Non-Contingent Token Reinforcement. Children in this group received a "salary" for attending class each day. The salary was actually the median number of points earned by the Contingent Token Group.

Contingent Token Reinforcement. Children in this group were told that the number of points they earned depended upon the amount of work they did and on passing tests on the material. Since all students were working in programmed material that was divided into small sections of work called frames, the points earned were based on frames completed.Most students earned one point per frame completed, although a few who were more or less capable had different ratios. For example, children who were classified as retarded as well as disturbed were paid two points per frame completed, because their rate of work was generally slower than others. Points were earned only when the child passed a test in the work.

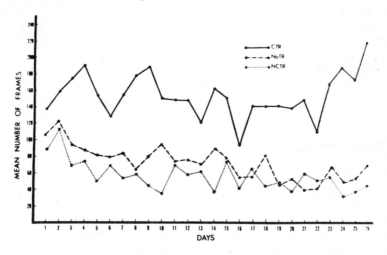

Daily frame rates for the contingent token reinforcement, non-contingent token reinforcement and no token reinforcement groups

Results

Daily rates of frames completed in each group were compared. In a previous year, when all cabin groups worked under similar conditions, the cabins that worked under the contingent token condition were not superior to the other cabins. The Figure shows, however, that the group that received tokens contingently was superior to the other groups throughout the 26 days of the experiment. The contingent group also made significantly greater gains on standardized achievement tests given before and after the study.

Abstract **31**

Behavior Modification of an
Adjustment Class: A Token Reinforcement Program

K. DANIEL O'LEARY and WESLEY BECKER (University of Illinois), *Exceptional Children*, 1967, *33*, 637-642.

An early example of the classroom token-economy.

The use of tokens in classrooom settings is now a common occurrence in many schools. The study described here was one of the early examples of a token system, designed for and applied to a classroom, which could be operated by one teacher.

Method

SUBJECTS AND SETTING: The subjects were 17 emotionally disturbed nine-year-old children attending an adjustment class due to their high rates of undesirable classroom behavior. Observers recorded the behavior of nine of the most disruptive children, using a 20-second observe, 10-second record, format for 22 minutes daily.

PROCEDURE: After a 10-day Baseline period, a token economy was introduced in the classroom. The instructions, "In Seat, Face Front, Raise Hand, Pay Attention, and Desk Clear" were written on the blackboard. The children were told that they would receive tokens for following the instructions. The tokens were actually ratings from one to ten which were written in a small booklet on each child's desk. After instruction and guidance from the experimenter, the teacher would place the ratings in each booklet at the end of lesson periods. At first, ratings were made five times a day, but were gradually decreased to three times a day. Ratings were based on the behavior of the child in class, the child's performance academically, and on the overall behavior of the group. Group ratings were charted on a thermometer chart on the blackboard. High ratings resulted in the reward of popsicles for the entire group.

Points accumulated in the booklets could be exchanged for small prizes and candy. The material rewards for the two-month study cost about $80. In the beginning, the points or tokens could be exchanged for back-up reinforcers close to the time they were earned. The period of time between earning tokens and spending them was gradually increased, however, until there was as much as a four-day delay between earning and redeeming tokens. The teacher was also instructed to make encouraging comments about appropriate behavior during the token program. She also rewarded approximations to desired behavior at the beginning of the program, gradually requiring greater similarity to the target behavior across the study. Inappropriate behavior was generally ignored.

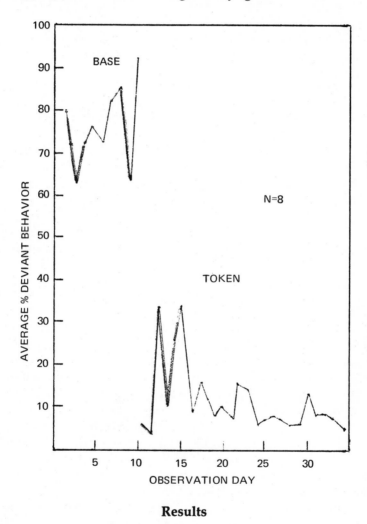

Results

The Figure shows the percent of deviant behavior observed during Baseline and experimental periods. Although Baseline levels were very high, implementation of the token procedures produced an immediate and marked decrease. The pattern was similar in all nine children observed.

Abstract 32

Behavior Modification of Children with Learning Disabilities Using Grades as Tokens and Allowances as Back-Up Reinforcers

Hugh McKenzie, Marilyn Clark, Montrose Wolf, Richard Kothera and Cedric Benson (University of Kansas), *Exceptional Children*, 1968, 34, 745-753.

A school behavior modification program that involves parents.

Although token economics has often been supported as an effective agent for effecting behavioral change, the additional burden its operation places on teacher-time and school budgets is sometimes difficult to justify. The authors of this study have designed a project using grades as tokens, thereby requiring little additional teacher-education and time. Accumulation of tokens is rewarded through parent-dispensed allowances. In this way, parents are also involved in the academic progress of their children.

Method

SUBJECTS AND SETTING: Eight students from a learning disabilities class were selected for the study. They ranged in age from 10 to 13 and had been classified as minimally brain-damaged, since they performed within a retarded range, although ability tests indicated that they were capable of higher achievement.

PROCEDURE: Children were taught predominantly through programmed instruction and were given weekly assignments. In each academic area assigned, children were required to complete all previous work before proceeding with new work. Work that was incomplete by week's end was reassigned as new material the next week.

Baseline: The system in use already provided a number of consequences for appropriate and inappropriate academic behavior. Recess, free time activities, special privileges (running school errands, line leaders, monitors), teacher attention, and eating lunch with the rest of the school rather than alone, were all contingent on completed work assignments. In addition, weekly grade sheets were sent home with the children for their parents to sign. Parents were asked to positively reinforce A's and B's, accept C's and express some concern over incompletes ("That's too bad you didn't finish all your work in reading this week."). Feedback was provided to the teacher in terms of the consistency of her application of consequences.

Pay For Weekly Grades Period: Parents were asked to provide allowances contingent on specific grades. For example, an A might be worth 50¢, a B worth 25¢, a C worth 5¢ and an Incomplete might result in a fine of 50¢. This was to be the only money available to the child to be used to spend on items that the child personally valued, such as movies, horseback riding, and dolls.

Results

Figures 1 and 2 present data for the percentage of designated time spent attending to reading and arithmetic, respectively. The median rose from 68% during Baseline to 86% during the pay period for reading. Similarly, the median level of attention to arithmetic was 70% during Baseline and 86% for the pay period.

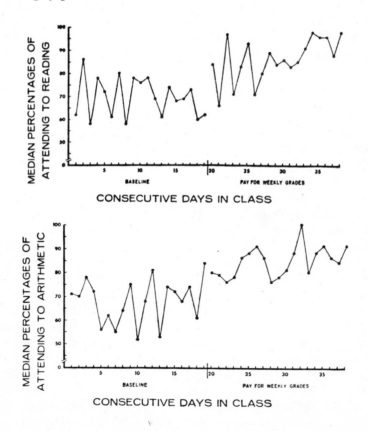

Abstract **33**

Disruptive Behavior and Reinforcement
of Academic Performance

TEODORO AYLLON, DALE LAYMAN, and SANDRA BURKE
(Georgia State University), *Psychological Record*, 1972, *22*,
315-323.

Improving academic performance reduces disruptive behavior.

Disruptive behavior has been a common focus of behavior modification
studies. Most have attempted to modify the unwanted behavior directly by
use of reinforcement or punishment. The study described here attacked the
problem indirectly by restructuring the academic environment of the
classroom and by rewarding academic behavior.

Method

SUBJECTS AND SETTING: The study took place in a classroom for 13
educable, mentally retarded children in an elementary school. The students
were considered the most unmotivated and troublesome in the school, and
four of these were selected as the most disruptive in the class. All four were
boys. I.Q.'s ranged from 72 to 80.

PROCEDURE: Disruptive behavior, such as being out of seat, making noise,
and talking out loud without permission, were observed using a 10-second
time-sampling procedure. Academic behavior in reading and mathematics
was also measured. Accurate answers to comprehension questions from
assigned stories served as a reading measure. Mathematics behavior
involved performance on a written test after the mathematics lesson.

Reinforcers. During experimental phases, the students could earn tokens
which were used to purchase a wide variety of privileges and toys. Initially
(for 10 days), students were permitted to spend their tokens as soon as they
completed both academic tests. Later, tokens were exchanged only after
lunch.

Experimental Phases. After three days of Baseline, the teacher introduced
a new instructional procedure and the token reinforcement system.

Each reading and mathematics instruction period (30 minutes) was divided into four, short, instruct-test periods. The teacher gave a set of assignments or some instruction and then presented a test. Students earned points for performance on the test. For the first four days only, mathematics work was reinforced, then only reading work was reinforced for the next three days. Finally, mathematics was reinforced for three days and then reading for nine days. During the last nine days, tangible rewards (candy) were phased out and replaced with normal classroom privileges or activities.

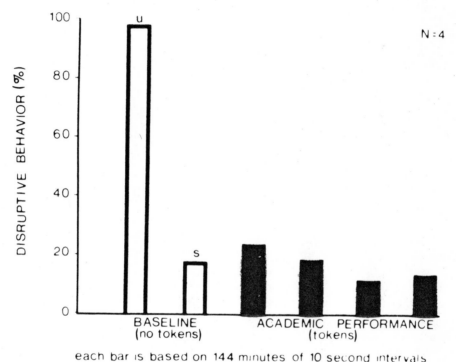

each bar is based on 144 minutes of 10 second intervals

Results

The Figure shows the average percentage of disruptive behavior during each phase of study. The data indicate disruptive behavior decreased when academic instruction in the classroom was restructured and academic performance was rewarded.

Additional data indicated that all four students increased the amount of work completed in reading. Mathematics performance also increased sharply when reinforcement was applied. In addition, the levels of work tended to remain well above Baseline rates, even when reinforcement was not contingent on academic work in the subject area.

87

Abstract 34

But What Happens When You Take That Reinforcement Away?

DONALD DICKINSON (University of Tennessee), *Psychology in the Schools*, 1974, *11*, 158-160.

A follow-up of classroom behavior modification.

Early behavior modifiers were sometimes ridiculed for thinking that simply providing tangible rewards would actually make a difference in the amount children learn. Later, however, after hundreds of studies showed tangible rewards did indeed affect learning, some critics became concerned with what happens after the rewards end. Will children continue to learn, or will they learn less because they are no longer rewarded?

Method

SUBJECTS AND SETTINGS: Fifty students who had participated in a token reinforcement program while they were in the fifth and sixth grades were compared to 218 students in nearby schools who had not been in reinforcement programs.

PROCEDURE: Data were obtained at the end of the eighth grade, two years after the token system ended. The special program involved the use of tickets as tokens, which could be redeemed for a variety of privileges and toys. They were earned for attending to work, completing assignments, and behaviors such as participating in discussions. Individualized instruction was also used extensively.

Reading scores on the Metropolitan Achievement Test at the end of the sixth grade were used as a covariate when reading scores at the end of the eighth grade were compared. The number of students on the honor roll and the number referred to the principal's office for disciplinary problems was also determined.

Results

Test data indicated students who had been in the reinforcement program made significantly greater gains in reading during the two years after the reinforcement program ended than did the group that had regular instruction. The reinforcement group also had a higher percentage of students on the honor roll and a lower percent sent to the office for disciplinary problems.

Abstract **35**

Teachers' Communications of Differential Expectations for Children's Classroom Performance: Some Behavioral Data

JERE BROPHY and THOMAS GOOD (University of Texas, Austin), *Journal of Educational Psychology*, 1970, 61, 365-374.

The impact of teacher expectation on teacher-student interaction.

In 1968 two psychologists, Rosenthal and Jacobson, published an interesting and controversial piece of research. Essentially, they provided false information to the teachers of several groups of children. Teachers were told that certain students in their classes had been identified as "late bloomers" by a special test, and that these students would do especially well that year. Actually, the test was an ordinary ability test, and the "late bloomers" had been selected randomly. However, the data suggested that the students identified to the teachers as "late bloomers" actually achieved at better-than-expected levels. They interpreted this as evidence of a "Pygmalion" or teacher-expectation effect. The study described here investigated the question of what specific differences in the behavior of teachers may account for this effect.

Method

SUBJECTS AND PROCEDURE: The study was conducted in four, first-grade classrooms in a small Texas school district. Two observers recorded the behavior of the teachers and preselected children for two afternoons and two mornings. The four teachers were asked to rank the children in their class in order of achievement. Since the classes were made up of homogeneous groups in terms of achievement, these rankings were considered indicators of the teachers' expectancies about the children. In each class, three boys and three girls high on the ranking, and three of each sex low on the ranking, were chosen for observation.

Teachers were not aware that their own behavior was being recorded; in addition, they were under the impression all children in the class were being observed as part of a study of the classroom behavior of children with different levels of achievement.

The observation system used focused on the interaction between the teacher and individual children. A large number of different types of behavior were coded. The number of opportunities to interact (e.g., when it was the child's turn in a reading group), the number and type of questions asked by the teacher, the quality of the child's response (correct, incorrect, no response), and the type of feedback given by the teacher (praise, criticism, rephrasing the question, and so forth) were all recorded.

Results

Analysis of variance procedures were used to interpret the data. The results indicated significant differences on most measures across classes, suggesting that teachers differed in the level and distribution of the types of interaction studied. In addition, high-expectancy children sought out the teacher more, asked her questions more frequently, and were more likely to show her their work and initiate interactions with her.

There were no overall differences between high- and low-expectancy groups in terms of teacher-initiated interactions. The low group, however, particularly the boys in that group, received significantly more teacher criticism. In fact, boys, regardless of group, were higher than girls on teacher-initiated contacts. Of the interactions between the teacher and boys in the low group, 32.5% involved criticism by the teacher, while the corresponding figure for high boys was 13.3%; for low girls, 16.2%; and for high girls 8.3%.

The highs produced more correct answers to questions and fewer incorrect answers than lows, had fewer problems in reading groups, and made higher scores on achievement tests given at the end of the year.

Perhaps the most important finding was that teachers consistently placed more demands on the highs and praised them more often for correct responses. Even though lows answered questions correctly less often, the likelihood of their being praised when they were right was less than for the high group. They were more likely to be criticized for incorrect responses, however. In addition, teachers were more likely to make an effort to get a high student to give the correct answer after an error, through rephrasing the questions or giving cues. Errors by lows more often resulted in simply supplying the answer or calling on another child. Teachers failed to give feedback of any sort only 3% of the time to highs and 15% of the time to lows.

Abstract **36**

Assessment of "Motivated" Reading Therapy with Elementary School Children

BONNIE CAMP (University of Colorado Medical School) and
WILLIAM VAN DOORNINCK (Eastside Neighborhood Health
Center), *Behavior Therapy*, 1971, 2, 213-222.

Evaluation of an inexpensive remedial reading program.

Although the public school system spends a great deal of instructional time during the first few years of school teaching the skills of reading, most schools still have a number of children who experience major academic difficulties because of poor reading skills. Remedial programs to deal with the problem are often expensive and trained professionals to staff them are difficult to find. This study describes an alternative, the use of nonprofessional aides as tutors.

Method

SUBJECTS AND SETTING: Sixty-six children were referred from schools in an economically-depressed section of Denver. They were third to sixth graders who were reading two or more years below grade level, but who were not retarded. The children were randomly assigned to an experimental and a control group.

PROCEDURE: Children in the experimental group were tutored two to three times a week for 30 minutes by a neighborhood aide or by college-student volunteers. The tutors were given training in the tutoring method used. The SRA Reading Lab was used in the tutoring session. Children did two types of reading. First, they studied the new word lists for a story and were awarded tokens for correctly reading the words. When they correctly read all the words on the list, they read the story itself, and were also awarded tokens for successful reading. The tokens were exchangeable for money. The average student in the study received 14 hours of tutoring. The control group received no special training.

Results

Data on seven matched pairs of children, one of whom was in the control group and one in the experimental group, were used to evaluate the effects of the tutoring. Three types of pre-posttest data were obtained. Before and after the tutoring period, the children were tested on 100 words chosen at random from the vocabulary list of the SRA Reading Lab. They were also tested on 100 words from the vocabulary lists of several primary textbook series, and they took the reading, spelling, and arithmetic sections of the Wide Range Achievement Test. The experimental group made significantly more gains on the two vocabulary lists but did not differ significantly on the achievement test.

Abstract 37

The Effects of Principal-Implemented Techniques on the Behavior of Pupils

RODNEY COPELAND, RONALD BROWN, and R. VANCE HALL (University of Kansas and Kansas City Public Schools), *Journal of Applied Behavior Analysis,* 1974, 7, 77-86.

Novel use of the school principal.

The role of the principal in a school is often defined as two-pronged—handling the administrative details of operation, and dealing, usually through the application of punishment, with discipline problems. This study presents three experiments that show how a principal can be more positively involved in the educational work of the school. One of the experiments is described below.

Method

SUBJECTS AND SETTING: The study was conducted in an inner-city school with about 750 students. In the study described here, two third-grade classes, with 36 and 38 students respectively, were the subjects. The first class was the most advanced, and the second the least advanced, of the third-grade classes in the building.

PROCEDURE: The target behavior was completion of arithmetic problems on a specially prepared set of six sheets of 100 problems. The problems all involved addition, some requiring carrying. During Baseline, the experimenter entered the classroom each day, handed out one of the six math-sheets, and asked the students to complete as many probems as they could in a five-minute period. The scores of each student were posted on a chart in the room. After 13 days of Baseline, the principal began coming to Classroom 1 twice a week and, in front of the class, praising each student who had improved his or her addition score from the previous day. He also named and praised the five students who made the highest scores. The principal also indicated he would return and that he hoped he would be able to name and congratulate more students the next time. The procedure took about three minutes. After six more Baseline sessions, the same procedure was implemented in the second class.

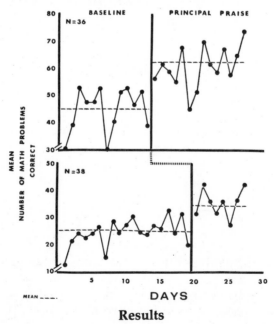

Results

The authors used a multiple Baseline design as shown in the Figure. When praise and recognition by the principal was instituted, the mean number of problems completed correctly increased in both classes.

93

Abstract **38**

The Effect of Self-Recording on the Classroom Behavior of Two Eighth Grade Students

MARCIA BRODEN, R. VANCE HALL and BRENDA MITTS (University of Kansas), *Journal of Applied Behavior Analysis,* 1971, 4, 191-199.

Changing behavior through self-control.

The vast majority of research related to changing student classroom behavior involves the use of an external agent of control such as the teacher, or other students. This study focuses on the effects of self-recording and, to a great extent, self-control, in increasing study behavior.

Method

SUBJECT AND SETTING: Liza was an eighth-grade student who was inattentive and achieved low grades in history class. Data were recorded at the end of each 10-second interval throughout the 40-minute history period. Behavior was classed as either "study" (attending to teacher-assigned tasks) or "non-study" (out-of-seat, inappropriate talking, doing nonhistory-related work).

PROCEDURE: **Baseline.** Throughout the study, a school counselor saw Liza twice a week, beginning in Baseline. No experimental procedures were initiated during this seven-day period.

Self-recording. On the eighth day, the counselor defined study behavior and gave Liza a slip of paper with three rows of ten squares, instructing her to record her study behavior "when she thought of it." A "plus" (+) indicated that she had been studying, while a "minus" (−) indicated that she had not.

Baseline 2. No self-recording materials were provided from Day 14 to 18.

Self-recording 2. Slips were given to Liza again and she was instructed as before.

94

Self-recording Plus Praise. In both previous self-recording conditions, the counselor praised Liza for the number of pluses she had earned. During this condition, Liza's history teacher was asked to praise Liza's appropriate study behavior whenever possible, in addition to the self-recording and counselor praise already in effect.

Praise only. The history teacher was instructed to continue praising Liza. No slips for self-recording were given.

Baseline 3. Teacher attention as well as counselor feedback and self-recording slips were discontinued.

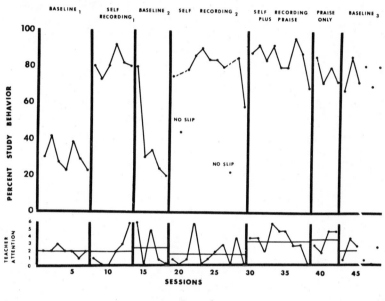

Results

Data for percent of study behavior is presented in the Figure. The first two Baseline periods indicate a low rate of study behavior, averaging about 30% of Liza's time. During all self-recording phases, percent of study time increased to a mean of at least 75% and, when teacher praise was included, averaged 88%. When self-recording slips were withdrawn but teacher attention was maintained, study behavior was observed at a mean rate of 77%. In the final Baseline period, the effects of self-recording and teacher and counselor praise appear to have generalized, since there is very little decrement in study behavior. The three unjoined points of the last Baseline phase represent follow-up data at three one-week intervals.

The graph in the bottom portion of the Figure presents the number of times per class that Liza's history teacher attended to her. Data for the two praise conditions (Self-recording Plus Praise and Praise Only) indicate that the amount of attention paid to Liza was greater when the teacher was instructed to praise her.

95

Abstract 39

The Effects of Loud and Soft Reprimands on the Behavior of Disruptive Students

K. Daniel O'Leary, Kenneth Kaufman, Ruth Kass, and Ronald Drabman (State University of New York at Stony Brook), *Exceptional Children*, 1970, *36*, 145-155.

Punishment of behavior need not be obnoxious.

Most behavioral approaches to disruptive behavior in the classroom stress the use of positive reinforcement for appropriate behavior and the importance of ignoring undesirable behavior. In some cases, however, the disruptive behavior that is being ignored does not go away. This study evaluated two methods of responding to undesirable behavior.

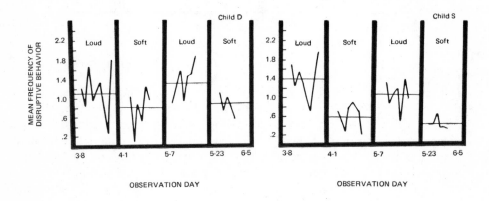

Method

SUBJECTS AND SETTING: Two children, both boys, in a second grade classroom, were studies. Each was very disruptive during class. During the study, their behavior was observed using a 20-second observe, 10-second record procedure. Nine kinds of disruptive behavior were recorded, including out-of-seat behavior, aggression, noise, and time off a task. Observations were made daily for about 20 minutes.

PROCEDURE: During an initial Baseline period, the teacher was asked to handle the children as she normally would. Generally, that involved the use of loud reprimands for disruptive behavior.

Then the teacher was asked to use soft reprimands for disruptive behavior. Instead of speaking in a loud voice, so that all the children heard the reprimand, she spoke softly so that only the child being corrected heard her. Two more phases, one of loud reprimands and a final one of soft reprimands, completed the study.

Results

The Figure shows the frequency of disruptive behavior for both children across the study. Mean level of disruptive behavior was consistently higher when loud reprimands were used.

In a second experiment (not described here), the authors found substantially the same results, although there was some indication that soft reprimands may actually increase disruptive behavior for a few children.

CHAPTER IV

Behavioral Counseling

Abstract **40**

Self-Observation as an Agent of Behavioral Change

STEPHEN JOHNSON and GEOFFRY WHITE (University of Oregon), *Behavior Therapy*, 1971, 2, 488-497.

The effects of observing our own behavior.

Most of the research in behavior modification is concerned with the efficient use of some form of consequences. But there is another side to the field. More than any other therapeutic system in psychology, it emphasizes the collection and use of precise, objective data during the course of treatment. Can the collection of data, in and of itself, produce beneficial effects? This study concerns itself with just that point by examining the effects of having college students record their study behavior.

Method

SUBJECTS AND SETTING: Ninety-seven students enrolled in an introductory psychology course participated in the study. They were given some course credit for their participation and were told that if they dropped out they would lose the credit and receive a small penalty.
PROCEDURE: Students were randomly assigned to one of three conditions,

with equal numbers of men and women in each group. One group received instructions on how to self-observe their study behavior. They received a packet of preaddressed post cards which contained a printed form for data recording. These were mailed in daily, or were given to the experimenter during class. The instructor, however, did not see the cards, and students were given code numbers to preserve anonymity.

Normally behavioral studies record how often (frequency) or how long (duration) a behavior occurs. Study behavior, however, is not one behavior but a class of several different types of behavior which are not equally important or effective. In recognition of this fact, the authors instructed the students to observe the amount and type of studying they did each day. Using a list provided by the experimenter, the students then assigned each type of behavior a point value based on the amount and type of studying that occurred. For example, reading a page of text was worth three points. The number of points was totaled each day and recorded on the post card.

Another group was given instructions similar to the group observing study behavior. The second group's target behavior was dating, however. A third group was told that more people had volunteered for the experiment than were needed at present, and that another opportunity would be given to them later.

All students were told that the purpose of the study was the investigation of the amount of time and energy students spent in certain activities. They were told that they would not have to study or date more or less than usual. If students failed to return the cards, they were contacted by phone.

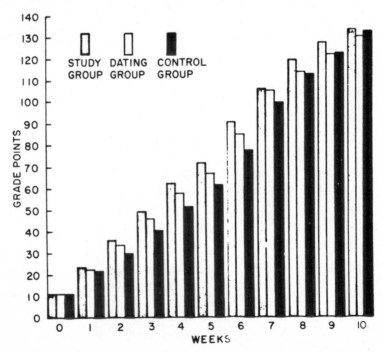

Results

The introductory course in which the study was conducted used a personalized system of instruction and required completing a number of small assignments across the semester. The final grades for the course were uniformly high for all three groups, as the course was designed to produce a large number of A's (80% of the students received A's). When the points earned by week six of the ten-week course were compared across groups, however, analysis of variance indicated that the group who observed study behavior had significantly more grade points than either the dating observation group or the control group (see Figure). Thus, they reached their goal more quickly than the other groups. In addition, there was a correlation of .61 between points earned in class and points recorded on the cards for study behavior, indicating that more study behavior was associated with higher grades.

Abstract **41**

A Learning Theory Approach to Group Counseling with Elementary School Children

WILLIAM HINDS (Michigan State University) and HELEN ROEHLKE (University of Missouri), *Journal of Counseling Psychology*, 1970, *17*, 49-55.

A group program for helping problem children.

The great majority of behavior modification studies conducted in educational settings have been carried out in the classroom. In fact, behaviorists have traditionally emphasized the need to work in the "natural" environment of the student rather than in artificial settings such as the counselor's office. This study differs from traditional operant practice by focusing instead on what can be done in a special or artificial setting, in this case a biweekly group counseling session.

Method

SUBJECTS: Forty elementary school children from grades 3, 4, and 5 were referred by their teachers because of behavior problems in school. Students from each of the four classes used in the study were randomly divided into groups balanced for age. Eight groups with five subjects each were formed, four groups in control conditions and four in experimental. Children in three of the control groups simply remained in their classes while those in a fourth attended sessions with the counselor, but did not actually receive any treatment.

PROCEDURE: Experimental groups attended biweekly sessions of 30-40 minutes for ten weeks. The sessions were run by two counselors, one male and one female.

After a two-day period that allowed the children to adjust to sessions and to videotape equipment, treatment was begun. Treatment involved the use of systematic reinforcement to shape the child's behavior toward adaptive responses and to extinguish inappropriate behavior. The Table presents a summary of the treatment program and its sequence. The children were told they could earn points enabling them to play games. Specific target behaviors were identified for each child, and counselors explained that as the children behaved appropriately points they earned would be recorded by the counselor on a hand counter. Each child was briefed on the kinds of behaviors for which he could earn points. For example, a quiet, withdrawn child was told that he could earn points for talking, while a hyperactive child earned points for sitting still and not interrupting.

After all children earned the specified number of points set for them they could vote on which game would be played for the remainder of the session (usually 10-15 minutes). Over the ten sessions, emphasis was gradually shifted from point reinforcement to social reinforcement, and schedules of reinforcement became more intermittent.

Results

Before treatment began, the behavior of the children in their classroom was videotaped. Eight 15-minute samples of general classroom behavior and two 15-minute samples of small group behavior were taken. This procedure was repeated the week after treatment ended. Videotapes were scored for eight types of Interfering behaviors (lack of attention to classroom activities, physical activity not related to classroom activity, nonparticipation, restricted class participation, verbal behavior not related to classroom activity, negative interaction with peers and teachers, submission in small groups, and domination in small groups). Eight types of Adaptive behaviors were also scored (attention to activities, concentration, participation, appropriate interaction with teachers and peers, and small group behaviors such as initiating interactions with others, not interrupting or dominating others, and supporting others and paying attention.

The counseling sessions themselves were also videotaped and scored.

Differences between the experimental condition and the control group who attended sessions but did not receive systematic treatment were examined, using the Mann-Whitney U test. Before treatment, there were no significant group differences, but by week four, at week ten, and at termination of counseling, the number of Interfering behaviors showed significant decreases, and the number of Adaptive behaviors showed significant increases for the experimental condition.

In addition, no significant differences were found between experimental and control groups on precounseling classroom behavior observations, while the experimental groups were significantly better than controls in both adaptive and interfering categories after counseling.

Table 1
Counseling Sequence

Unit	Activity	Contingency	Reinforcers	
1	Discussing stimulus stories	Earning 6 points each	Points and games	Fixed ratio
2	Group discussions (topics of choice)	Earning 6 points each	Points, verbal approval, games, and tokens	Fixed ratio
3	Group discussions	Earning 10 points each	Points, verbal approval, games, and tokens	Fixed ratio
4	Group discussions	Earning 20 points each	Points, verbal approval, games and tokens	Fixed ratio
5	Role playing of classroom scenes	1 point every 3 minutes or all accumulated points are lost	Points, verbal approval, and games; negative reinforcer—loss of points	Fixed interval/& fixed ratio
6	Role playing continued	1 point every 1 minute or all accumulated points are lost. Total of 20 points each and lost 1 point for each interfering behavior emitted	Points, verbal approval, and games; negative reinforcers—loss of accumulated points and loss of point for interfering behavior	Fixed interval/& fixed ratio
7	Group discussions	1 point anytime during 3 minutes	Points, verbal approval, and games	Variable interval
8	Group discussions	1 point anytime during 3 minutes	Points and verbal reinforcement by peers	Variable interval
9	Positive video	No contingencies	Verbal reinforcement only	Intermittent reinforcement
10	Role playing	No contingencies	Verbal reinforcement only	Intermittent reinforcement

Abstract **42**

Effects of Covert Modeling and Model Reinforcement on Assertive Behavior

ALAN KAZDIN, (Pennsylvania State University), *Journal of Abnormal Psychology*, 1974, *83*, 240-252.

Standing up for one's rights: two training approaches.

Observing a model is a technique that has been used extensively in training a variety of new behaviors. Covert modeling, however, or imagined performance of appropriate behavior, has received very little attention. Developing such a technique carries special promise, however, because of the negligible cost and time requirements involved as compared to other forms of modeling. Also, the imagined modeling can be more easily tailored to individual needs. In this study, the researcher looked at covert modeling as a possible training technique for assertive behavior with people who were genuinely interested in learning to be more assertive.

Method

SUBJECTS: Twenty-three females and 22 males who responded to an advertisement for free, assertive training and met the screening requirements were the subjects. Screening methods included attaining below-cutoff scores on several self-report assertiveness measures and on a behavioral role-playing test which was also the major dependent variable. Subjects included professional and business people, laborers, university students, and unemployed persons.

Behavioral Role-playing Test: This task involved responding to pre-recorded situations in which assertiveness was appropriate. For example, one scene involved being served unacceptable food in a restaurant. Ten pairs of situations were used, and each subject listened and responded to one of each pair in the pretest. Posttesting included responding to the same situation and to the alternate situation as a measure of generalization. A rating scale to measure assertiveness was developed which ranged from "not at all assertive" (1) to "very assertive and forceful" (5).

PROCEDURE: Subjects were randomly assigned to one of three experimental conditions or to a no-treatment control condition. They were also randomly assigned to one of four therapists (two female and two male clinical psychology graduate students). All subjects in the three experimental conditions were trained to clearly imagine situations (unrelated to assertiveness) that included a person like the subject (model) prior to the beginning of treatment.

No Treatment (N=11). These subjects were informed that they could not be scheduled for training immediately, but would receive it later. In fact, they were treated when the study terminated.

Covert Modeling Plus Reinforcement (N=12). In the first session, subjects were given five scenes to imagine; in the remaining three sessions ten scenes were presented (all but the control subjects received this number in this sequence). A scene involved 1) a description of the simulus setting for assertiveness, plus a person (model) much like the subject whom the situation involved, 2) an assertive response by the model, and 3) a desirable outcome resulting from the model's assertiveness. These scenes were imagined for 15 seconds following the subject's signal to the therapist that the image was clear.

Covert Modeling (N=11). These subjects were instructed to imagine the first two parts of the scene, i.e., the description and the assertive response, but they did not imagine a successful outcome.

No Modeling (N=11). Subjects in this condition were instructed only to imagine a scene in which assertiveness was appropriate.

Follow-up. One measure of the effect of the treatments on actual assertive behavior in the natural environment was a telephoned request to each person in the study, asking that the subject volunteer to work three hours in a hospital. If the subject refused, a sequence of appeals was made until the subject had either refused five times, or had agreed. If the subject agreed, he or she was informed that someone would call back to confirm the time. All subjects were later debriefed by letter.

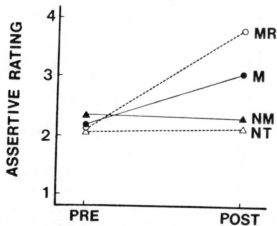

Mean assertive rating of responses to the behavioral role-playing test before and immediately after treatment for model (M), model-reinforcement (MR), no-model (NM), and no-treatment (NT) groups. (Adjusted posttest means are from the covariance analysis.)

Results

Generally, covert modeling and covert-modeling-plus-reinforcement produced significant improvements in assertiveness over no treatment and no modeling on the self-report and behavioral role-playing measures. The measure of anxiety used, however, did not indicate differences between the modeling-alone group and the control group. Changes in assertiveness tended to be greatest for the covert-modeling-plus-reinforcement group, although there were no significant differences between that group and the modeling-alone condition.

The Figure shows ratings on the behavioral assertiveness measure before and immediately after treatment for each group. Follow-up data showed covert modeling and covert-modeling-plus-reinforcement groups were superior to no modeling controls on self-report and behavioral role-playing measures.

Abstract **43**

Contingency Counseling by School Personnel: An Economical Model of Intervention

W. Scott MacDonald, Ronald Gallimore, and Gwen MacDonald (University of Hawaii), *Journal of Applied Behavior Analysis*, 1970, 3, 175-182.

Modifying behavior through cooperation between school and community.

A major difficulty with almost any form of therapeutic intervention is the number of hours required to implement therapy by highly trained personnel. Few schools, for example, can afford to hire enough counselors and school psychologists to provide direct services to all the children who have serious problems. In this paper, an alternative to expensive and highly trained counselors is illustrated: trained adults who had daily contact with students acted as "mediators" in the natural environment.

Method

SUBJECTS: Six students were identified as chronic nonattenders by a school counselor. Although the students were enrolled in a "special motivation class," their truancy from school had increased during the school year. These students were ninth-graders and, before collection of Baseline data, had attended school an average of 30% of the time. During the previous year, three of the students had quit school early in the spring, but returned to school again in the fall.

PROCEDURE: A program to encourage school attendance was supervised by the school counselor and the attendance counselor (a local parent).

Mediators. Community people who had already developed a relationship with the student were selected for each of the six subjects. When they agreed to help, the attendance counselor contacted them and helped each mediator develop a behavior modification program for the student. Individual mediators worked out contracts or "deals" with their student which specified a reinforcer that could be earned by the student if he attended school regularly. Reinforcers were different for each student, but included access to a pool hall, the use of fancy clothes, money, weekend privileges, and time with a girl friend.

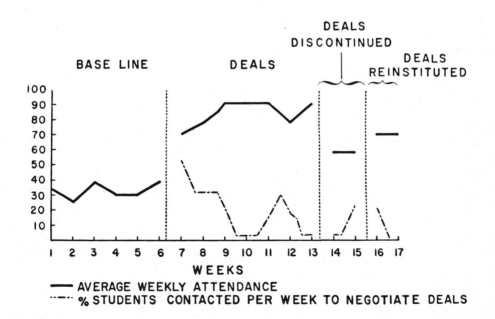

───── AVERAGE WEEKLY ATTENDANCE
------- % STUDENTS CONTACTED PER WEEK TO NEGOTIATE DEALS

107

Results

The Figure shows the percent of students who attended school during four phases of the study. The Baseline level of attendance was very low. Rate of attendance increased when students were seen by the mediators to arrange "deals" during weeks 7 to 13 and 16 to 17. In the reversal phase (weeks 14 and 15), when the deals were not in effect, attendance decreased. Two replications of the basic study yielded similar results.

Abstract 44

Teaching Self-Control of Study Behavior

WILLIAM BENEKE and MARY HARRIS (University of New Mexico), *Behaviour Research and Therapy*, 1972, *10*, 35-41.

A behavioral alternative to cramming for college students.

Attempts to help students improve their study behaviors have generally concentrated on either increasing their motivation to study or on teaching them a particular set of study skills. In this study, both approaches are combined; and long-term, follow-up data on the effect of the treatment are collected.

Method

SUBJECTS AND SETTING: The subjects were college students attending the summer session. Of 53 who volunteered, 15 dropped out after the initial meeting. Of the remaining 38, 30 were assigned to the main treatment condition, which involved group meetings, while eight were given written lessons which they picked up from the experimenter's office. Age of subjects ranged from 18 to 51.

PROCEDURE: Subjects in the group condition met twice a week. The group leader presented the lesson for that day, discussed the study problems of the previous week, and encouraged them to study. Students who worked individually simply picked up their lessons, completed them, and returned them to the office.

The training involved a sequence of topics which were covered in 11 lessons:

Introduction. Students were given data sheets and asked to record their study behavior. They also made lists of reasons (reinforcers) for why they should study.

Stimulus Control. The principle of stimulus control was explained, and students were taught how to choose a place that was associated with studying (quiet, well lighted, no distractions) and not associated with behavior incompatible with studying (no TV present). They were then instructed to study most of the time in that setting and to avoid doing anything else there.

Positive Reinforcement. Subjects made lists of activities and stimuli that could be used to reinforce studying, and they were taught how to graph their progress.

SQ3R (Survey, Questions, Read, Recite, Review). Robinson's method of studying was presented over several sessions. His technique began with surveying the material to be read, then questions to be answered were developed. Once the material was read, the student recited answers to the questions and then reviewed what he had read. During this period, instruction in positive reinforcement was also continued. Students were taught to specify their goals, identify a reinforcer, and display their goals prominently in their study area. Both short-term reinforcers (after 20 minutes of study) and long-term reinforcers (after completing one week's assignments) were established.

Punishment. Use of aversive devices, such as fines, foregoing a pleasant activity, and performance of calisthenics and housework to punish the occurrence of behavior incompatible with studying, was explained.

Taking Lecture Notes. This lesson covered effective ways of taking notes on lectures, and included skills such as outlining, identifying major and minor points, and reorganizing notes after a lecture.

Examination Skills. The SQ3R method was applied to studying for examinations and several methods for dealing with test anxiety (e.g., relaxation) were covered. Common problems on both essay and objective examinations were discussed, and techniques for dealing with each problem presented.

Review. The final lesson was a review of the previous lessons.

109

Results

There were no significant differences between the group- and independent-study subjects in terms of amount of time spent studying per week. The average subject in the group condition completed seven of the 11 lessons, while the independent-study group completed an average of six. This difference was not significant, nor was a correlation between hours studied and lessons completed. A correlation between time spent studying and gains in grade point average for the three semesters following the study also was not significant, but there was a significant relationship between lessons completed and gains in grades. In addition, although the results were variable when looked at by semester, students who completed seven to 11 lessons improved their grades across the next three semesters more than either the group of 15 who dropped out or the subjects who failed to complete more than six lessons. Improvement in grades was determined by comparing each student's grades in the two semesters prior to the study with those in the three following semesters. The gain in grade point average without concomitant increase in study time suggests that the treatment resulted in increased quality of study.

Abstract **45**

A Comparison of Four Behavioral Treatments of Alcoholism

ALLAN HEDBERG (Schick Hospital, Fort Worth) and LOWELL CAMPBELL, *Journal of Behavior Therapy and Experimental Psychiatry*, 1974, 5, 251-256.

Empirically evaluating treatment alternatives.

Although alcoholism is one of the major problems facing our society, the overall quality and quantity of research on treatment of alcoholism is very low. Even within the field of behavior modification, there have been few attempts to evaluate the effectiveness of the various forms of treatment available, and rarely has an investigator studied the relative effectiveness of several approaches in dealing with alcoholism.

Method

SUBJECTS AND SETTING: Forty-nine alcoholics referred to a mental health center were the subjects. Forty-six were males, the average level of education was 11th grade, and the mean age was 38.2. The average subject had been drinking for 17 years and drank five days a week. Most had tried unsuccessfully to change their drinking behavior.

PROCEDURE: All subjects were interviewed to determine their individual drinking history, their current drinking patterns, and the environmental antecedents and consequences of drinking. Each subject was asked to select a goal of either total abstinence or controlled drinking and was then assigned randomly to one of four treatment conditions. Regardless of the treatment, there were three hourly sessions per week for the first three weeks, followed by five weeks of one-hour sessions per week. During the next eight weeks, the sessions were biweekly, then monthly for the next two months. A six-month follow-up session was also held.

Systematic Desensitization. Fifteen of the patients received treatment based on Wolpe's systematic desensitization model. The underlying assumption was that drinking occurred because of anxiety related to specific aspects of the subject's life. The subjects were first trained in relaxation procedures. Then several hierarchies were developed. The hierarchies consisted of 10 to 12 items about which the subject was concerned. Common topics included authority relationships, marriage and family problems, and interpersonal anxieties. The specific items within each hierarchy were ordered from the most anxiety-provoking to the least anxiety-provoking. After being relaxed, the subject imagined the least anxiety-creating item (such as correcting the work of his secretary). Once he no longer felt anxious when imagining a particular item, the subject would be asked to imagine an item that was higher in the hierarchy. The process was continued until all items in the hierarchies were imagined without anxiety.

Covert Sensitiztion. This procedure, developed by Joseph Cautela, involved brief training in relaxation. Then ten scenes relevant to his drinking pattern were developed for each subject. Seven of the scenes were aversive (imagining the subject was in a bar, was about to take a drink, and vomiting into the drink) and three were "relief" scenes which had no aversive component. Essentially, the subjects were asked to imagine scenes associated with drinking, while also thinking about something very aversive. The relief scenes involved thinking of something *not* associated with drinking, while also thinking of something pleasant. The assumption underlying treatment was that pairing aversive thoughts with drinking would lead to avoidance of that response.

Electric Shock. A third treatment developed by M. D. Feldman and M. J. MacCulloch was studied. Their avoidance conditioning paradigm began with the selection of 15 slides depicting scenes associated with drinking and 15 slides not associated with drinking. During each session the 30 slides were shown to the subjects. They received a painful electrical shock each time an alcohol-related slide was shown, but were not shocked when other slide scenes appeared. Again, the assumption was that pairing an aversive stimulus (shock) with alcohol would lead to avoiding alcohol.

Behavioral Family Counseling. The fourth treatment consisted of a comprehensive counseling program for the alcoholic and his family, using a variety of behavioral techniques. Using the work of Richard Stuart and of Gerald Patterson as a framework, the therapists taught members of the family to reinforce each other appropriately. They were also taught basic principles of behavior modification, including positive reinforcement, negative reinforcement, and extinction procedures. Assertive training and behavioral rehearsal were used, and behavioral contracts for each family were developed. The contracts included a target behavior identified by each family member, a plan for changing the behavior, and a program to help achieve total abstinence or controlled drinking.

Results

To assess the effects, an Alcohol Questionnaire was administered before treatment and at the six month follow-up session, and through interviews with the subject, his spouse, and his therapist. In the behavioral family counseling treatment, 74% of the subjects attained their goal and an additional 13% were much improved. The next best treatment, systematic desensitization, had figures of 67% and 20%. Covert sensitization had 40% and 27%, while all except four subjects dropped out of the electric shock treatment before the fourth session, and only one of the four who remained actually improved.

Abstract 46

Reciprocity Counseling:
A Rapid Learning-based Procedure for Marital Counseling

NATHAN AZRIN, BARRY NASTER and ROBERT JONES (Anna State Hospital and Southern Illinois University), *Behaviour Research and Therapy*, 1973, *11*, 365-382.

Behaviorism's answer to "Dear Abby."

While the fact that more than ninety-five percent of the adult population is committed to a marriage relationship would seem to indicate that this is a desirable state, marriage is nevertheless an environment in which many social problems occur. The rate of divorce today is about one marriage in three, and about one out of four married couples is unhappy with their marriage. A comprehensive approach to marital counseling is presented in this study.

Method

SUBJECTS AND SETTING: Twelve couples who had either been referred by a college counseling service or who had responded to mailed solicitation for married couples participated in the study. Average duration of marriage was nine years, with a range of eight months to 31 years.

PROCEDURE: Reciprocity Counseling, the treatment program used for all couples, is actually a package of several different behavioral techniques. Table 1 shows the chronological sequence of treatment. Couples came for one-hour counseling sessions twice a week, and for the first three weeks the therapist simply helped the couple talk about their problems, but did not attempt reciprocity counseling. Throughout the seven weeks of counseling, each partner independently completed a Marital Happiness Scale (see Table 2) each day and returned it to the therapist.

Reciprocity Counseling began when the couple was asked to complete a "Current Satisfaction Procedure" which was designed to make the spouse aware of the reciprocity that already existed in the marriage. As a home assignment, each partner was required to list at least ten satisfactions the partner was currently providing the spouse, and at least ten the partner was currently receiving from the spouse. The lists were read aloud at the next counseling session, and any disagreements resolved. The emphasis was on specifying precise behaviorisms rather than general attitudes. In addition, the "Perfect Marriage Procedure" was used. Each partner wrote down at home the type of interactions (s)he felt would constitute her/his idea of a perfect marriage, regardless of how selfish or unreasonable it might sound to others. Regular feedback was also instituted by asking the couple to exchange Marital Happiness Scale forms each evening and to discuss each other's ratings. Feedback continued across the four weeks of reciprocity counseling. The couple was also taught to reinforce with praise any special or unexpected satisfactions provided by the spouse (Appreciation Reminder Procedure).

Session 1 of reciprocity counseling ended with the development of a Happiness Contract (see Table 3). The couple first specified a list of new satisfactions they would like to obtain from the other partner (Fantasy Fulfillment Procedure) regardless of how unreasonable they seemed. Once completed, the counselor went over each list and determined if the partner would agree to the request. If the partner agreed it was listed in the Happiness Contract. If initial agreement was not given (usually it was not) the counselor reached a compromise satisfactory to both partners.

The Happiness Contract included all the satisfactions agreed to by each partner and specified the consequences for not meeting the agreement.

113

Table 1. Method

Chronological Sequence

I. Catharsis counseling — first 3 weeks
    A. First week: Session 1
        1. Discussion of general information to clients
        2. Discussion of Marital Happiness Scale
    B. First through third week: Sessions 2-6
        1. Catharsis counseling procedure

II. Reciprocity Counseling
    A. Introduction (Session 6, last 15 min. after the last catharsis counseling session)
        1. 'Reciprocity Awareness Procedure' assigned for next session
        2. The 'Perfect Marriage Procedure' assigned for next session
    B. First week: Session 1
        1. Therapist discusses assigned Reciprocity Awareness procedure
        2. 'Feedback Exchange Procedure' initiated
        3. 'Appreciation Reminder Procedure' initiated
        4. Happiness contract for first three problem areas
           (a) Fantasy Fulfillment Procedure
           (b) Frequency Fulfillment Procedure
    C. First week: Session 2
        1. 'Happiness Contract' reviewed
           (a) Additional satisfactions suggested for first three problem areas
           (b) Incorporate additional agreements into Happiness Contract
        2. Assigned as home work the 'Fantasy Fulfillment Procedure—Home Assignment'
    D. Second week: Session 1
        1. Instruction in 'Positive Statement Procedure'
        2. Instruction in 'Sex Feedback Procedure'
        3. Incorporating agreements regarding second three problem areas into Happiness Contract
           (a) Fantasy Fulfillment Procedure
           (b) Frequency Fulfillment Procedure
    E. Second week: Session 2
        1. Happiness Contract reviewed
           (a) Additional satisfactions suggested for first six problem areas
           (b) Incorporate agreements into Happiness Contract
        2. 'Fantasy Fulfillment Procedure: Minimal Counseling' assigned as homework for last three problem areas.
        3. Discuss Sexual Feedback Procedure
    F. Third week: Session 1
        1. Incorporate agreements for last three problem areas into Happiness Contract
           (a) Fantasy Fulfillment Procedure
           (b) Frequency Fulfillment Procedure
    G. Third week: Session 2
        1. Reviewing all agreements in Happiness Contract
           (a) Additional satisfaction suggested for all nine problem areas
           (b) Incorporate agreements into the Happiness Contract
    H. Fourth week: Session 1
        1. Review outcome on all nine problem areas
        2. Make any new agreements
        3. Told next session will be last one
    I. Fourth week: Session 2
        1. Review outcome of all problem areas
        2. Told about follow-up

Failure to provide a satisfaction generally resulted in the partner withholding all new and old satisfactions for 24 hours. The contract was discussed and updated as new satisfactions were agreed to. During the first week of reciprocity counseling, only problems in the first three categories of the Marital Happiness Scale were dealt with. Three more problems were dealt with during each succeeding week, until all nine areas were covered.

In the second week, the couple was taught how to make negative statements less aversive. For example, instead of saying, "That was a dumb thing to say," an alternative might be, "That may be true, but did you ever think of it this way?" They were also instructed not to respond to negative statements that did not include some positive component. A sex feedback procedure was also used in the second week. Each spouse completed a rating scale on sex behavior which was discussed in the next counseling session.

In the third and fourth weeks, the counselor gradually provided less and less guidance and direction as the couple applied the procedures described above to the second set of three problems, and then to the third set.

Table 2. Marital Happiness Scale

This scale is intended to estimate your *current* happiness with your marriage on each of the ten dimensions listed. You are to circle one of the numbers (1-10) beside each marriage area. Numbers toward the left end of the ten-unit scale indicate some degree of unhappiness and checks toward the right end of the scale reflect varying degrees of happiness. Ask yourself this question as you rate each marriage area: "If my partner continues to act in the future as he (she) is acting *today* with respect to this marriage area, how happy will I be *with this area of our marriage?*" In other words, state according to the numerical scale (1-10) exactly how you feel today. Try to exclude all feelings of yesterday and concentrate only on the feelings of today in each of the marital areas. Also try not to allow one category to influence the results of other categories.

	Completely unhappy							Completely happy		
Household responsibilities	1	2	3	4	5	6	7	8	9	10
Rearing of children	1	2	3	4	5	6	7	8	9	10
Social activities	1	2	3	4	5	6	7	8	9	10
Money	1	2	3	4	5	6	7	8	9	10
Communication	1	2	3	4	5	6	7	8	9	10
Sex	1	2	3	4	5	6	7	8	9	10
Academic (or occupational) progress	1	2	3	4	5	6	7	8	9	10
Personal independence	1	2	3	4	5	6	7	8	9	10
Spouse independence	1	2	3	4	5	6	7	8	9	10
General happiness	1	2	3	4	5	6	7	8	9	10

Table 3. Happiness Contract

Attached is a list of activities which I have typically done for my partner on a regular or frequent basis. A similar list of activities which my partner regularly does for me is also included. In addition to these current activities, several requests for improving our marriage, half of them mine and half of them my partner's are also attached.

My signature below indicates that the new behaviors which my partner has requested of me are acceptable to me and that I sincerely intend to comply with each of them as indicated. I further acknowledge that the enforcement procedure described below is acceptable to me and that I expect this procedure to be followed in the event that a request of mine or my partner's is not met.

> AGREEMENT ENFORCEMENT PROCEDURE: If one partner fails, by oversight or intent, to comply with any of his spouse's new requests on schedule, the offended partner will notify the offending partner of the omission and will make clear his intention to begin a sustained omission of *all* of the offending partner's current activities and new requests on the following morning if the initially omitted request has not been fulfilled by then.

It is my understanding that future new requests or changes in any existing requests by my partner will not be binding on me until I have formally agreed to them.

_____
Wife

_____
Date

_____
Husband

Results

The first Figure shows the average rating of overall happiness (item ten on the Marital Happiness Scale) during the two counseling phases and at a one-month follow-up for all 24 participants.

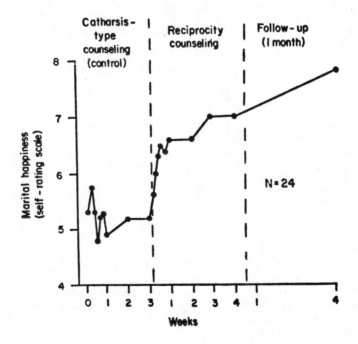

There was little change across the first three weeks, but when the reciprocity counseling procedure was introduced happiness increased and remained high through the follow-up. Twenty-three of 24 subjects reported a higher level of overall happiness during the last week of reciprocity counseling than on the day before it began.

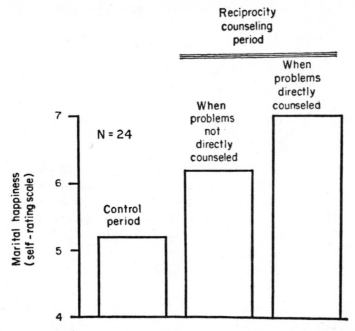

The second figure shows the changes in happiness reported for each of the nine problem areas. The average score for the three weeks of catharsis counseling (control) is presented beside the scores for reciprocity counseling. There was improvement in all nine problem areas. An additional analysis indicated that the introduction of reciprocity counseling produced an improvement in all nine areas when compared to the control period, and the problems directly counseled improved more than problems not specifically dealt with.

Abstract **47**

The Effects of Behavioral Counseling in Group and Individual Settings on Information-seeking Behavior

JOHN KRUMBOLTZ and CARL THORESEN (Stanford University), *Journal of Counseling Psychology*, 1964, *II*, 334-343.

Improving career planning through behavior modification.

A fundamental part of almost any type of counseling involves helping the client to obtain more information about some problem or decision. It is, for example, a major focus of career and educational counseling.

In this study, several methods of developing information-seeking behavior within a high school counseling setting are compared.

Method

SUBJECTS AND SETTING: The study was conducted at six suburban high schools, using 11th grade students who had volunteered for counseling about their educational and vocational plans. The six counselors who actually carried out the treatments were graduate students who had received training and practice in the methods they were to use prior to the study.

To form the treatment groups, two males and two females from each school were randomly assigned to one of the six treatment conditions. Four males and four females from each school were also assigned randomly to an inactive control group and to a reserve pool from which subjects could be drawn to replace any who dropped out.

PROCEDURE: Two major treatments (reinforcement and modeling) were studied in both individual and group counseling settings.

Individual Reinforcement Counseling. Under this condition, students were asked to discuss their thoughts about their future plans. The counselor praised or complimented any statements about obtaining more information (e.g., "I suppose I ought to find out how much college costs."). The counselor also provided some cues in the form of questions, pointed out specific things the students might do, and asked them to act on some of the ideas the students had developed during the interview. A second session one week after the first had a similar format.

Group Reinforcement Counseling. Students in this condition received the same procedures as above, but worked in groups of two males and two females instead of seeing the counselor individually.

Individual Model-Reinforcement Counseling. Again, the students were reinforced as described above, but before the discussions began they heard a tape of a counseling session in which a student made many comments about seeking information to help him make plans.

Group Model-Reinforcement Counseling. This was the same as group reinforcement counseling, except the students heard the tape at the beginning of the session.

Individual Control Film Discussion. This group saw a filmstrip and discussed it, but received no systematic reinforcement or modeling. They met for one session.

Group Control Film Discussion. This was the same as above except with a group of four.

Inactive Control. Students in this condition received no treatment.

Results

To determine what effect the counseling had on actual information-seeking, all the students were interviewed three weeks after the second session by an interviewer who was unaware of the group each student was in. Using a series of predetermined questions and a set of irrelevant buffer questions which disguised the purpose of the interview, the *frequency* and *variety* of information-seeking behaviors of the students were determined. In addition, to verify that these self-reports were accurate, three students from each school were randomly selected for verification. Each report of information-seeking they made was checked for accuracy by talking with people such as parents, relatives, friends or teachers. If, for example, they reported checking a book out of the library, it was verified with the librarian. Of 85 information-seeking behaviors, 79 were verified, six could not be confirmed, and none were invalidated.

An analysis of variance was used to analyze the data for both frequency of behavior and variety of behavior. Both the reinforcement and modeling reinforcement conditions produced more frequent and more varied information-seeking behaviors than did either control group. The model-reinforcement condition was more effective for males, while females had high levels of information-seeking behavior under both major treatment conditions.

Overall, there was no difference between group counseling and individual counseling, but a significant interaction suggested that for males model-reinforcement worked best in group settings, while reinforcement alone worked best in the individual condition.

119

Abstract **48**

Group Counseling with Nonverbalizing Elementary Students

DONALD TOSI, KENNETH UPSHAW, ANGELA LANDE and MARY ANN WALDRON (Ohio State University), *Journal of Counseling Psychology*, 1971, *18*, 5, 437-440.

Developing social skills in shy children.

The practising counselor may occasionally face a problem for which there are several potential treatment solutions, each with some research supporting its usefulness. Which treatment should be used? That is the sort of question this study addresses. Two procedures, social reinforcement and the Premack principle, are compared in a group counseling setting.

Method

SUBJECTS AND SETTING: Twenty-four reticent sixth- and seventh-grade students, who were referred by their teachers, served as subjects. To obtain a base rate of behavior before treatment, the children were observed for one hour a day for three days before treatment. These observations occurred in their regular classrooms. The behaviors measured included the number of times the student attempted to volunteer a response by raising his hand, and whether the student voluntarily gave a verbal response. In addition, the number of times the teacher called on the student after he volunteered was recorded.

PROCEDURE: After the baserate period, subjects were randomly assigned to one of four treatment conditions. Three counseling students were also assigned randomly, one to each condition. The actual counseling sessions involved one counselor and two students.

Social Reinforcement Condition. Children in this condition attended counseling sessions for 30 minutes and engaged in conversation throughout the entire period. They were immediately reinforced for their verbal responses with phrases such as "good," "that's wonderful," and "tell me more." Friendly gestures such as smiles were also used.

Premack Condition. The Premack hypothesis suggests that any high probability behavior can be used as a reinforcer for a behavior that has a lower probability of occurrence. Students in this group were initially told that if they engaged in conversation for five minutes they would be given 25 minutes of play time. Several games, such as Scrabble and Ping-Pong, and puzzles were available during that time. Discussions during the first five minutes were informal and the use of social reinforcers following verbal responses was minimized. The time for talking was increased by two minutes each session to a maximum of 15 minutes, while the total session was kept at 30 minutes.

Teacher Expectation Group. To control for the effects of teachers knowing that some children were being taken out of their classes for counseling, one condition involved taking children to a room where they saw a movie. There were no group discussions, and no systematic reinforcers for verbalizations were provided. Teachers were under the impression that this was a treatment group.

Control. One group of children simply remained in class.

Results

The measures taken before treatment were taken again over a three-day period, one week after treatment ended. Again, children were observed for one hour each day. Observers were not aware of which treatment the children received. The Figure presents the data. It was analyzed using a 3 × 4 analysis of variance. Both treatments and counselors were significant

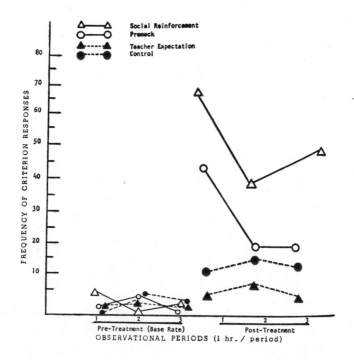

variables. The social reinforcement condition differed significantly from the control and teacher-expectation group, while the Premack condition did not. Premack and social reinforcement treatments did not differ from each other. However, both showed significant gains from pre- to post-treatment, while the teacher-expectation and control groups did not. In addition, one of the counselors was significantly more effective than the other two.

Abstract **49**

Effects of Practice, Instructions and Modeling on Components of Assertive Behavior

MICHEL HERSEN, RICHARD EISLER, PETER MILLER (University of Mississippi Medical Center), MIRIAM JOHNSON, and SUSAN PINKSTON (Veterans Administration Center, Jackson), *Behaviour Research and Therapy*, 1973, *11*, 443-451.

Identifying the active ingredients in an assertive training program.

A great many of the problems experienced by normal and hospitalized adults are caused by the individual's unassertiveness. That is, such people do not "stand up for their rights." The relative effects of several ways of helping people become more assertive were examined in this study.

Method

SUBJECTS AND SETTING: Fifty male psychiatric patients in a Veterans Administration Hospital were the subjects. They were selected from the hospital population because of their low scores on a simplified version of the Wolpe-Lazarus self-report measure of assertiveness. Five groups of ten were then formed, matched on age, years of education, assertive score, and psychiatric diagnosis.

PROCEDURE: The authors developed a Behavioral Assertiveness Test which involved having the subject role-play how he would act in a staged situation. The situations simulated commonly-encountered, real-life events which often require an assertive response. For example, one of the five situations involved being in a restaurant and ordering a steak cooked rare. When served, the steak is so well done it looks burnt. The subject then reacts to the situation. Another scene depicts a ball game at which the client finds that a woman in the seat next to the one for which he holds a reserved ticket has placed her coat on his seat and, when the subject is about to sit down, says to him, "I'm sorry, this seat is saved."

All subjects were given five situations from the Behavioral Assertiveness Test before and after the treatment sessions. Their behavior was then rated from videotapes on seven behavioral components of assertiveness: 1) duration of looking at the person who played the parts, 2) duration of reply, 3) loudness of speech, 4) the degree to which the subject complied, 5) the number of requests for new behaviors on the part of the other person, 6) the degree of affect in the subject's speech, and 7) the overall assertiveness of the response. Behaviors 3, 6, and 7 were rated on a five-point scale.

After the pretest, the subjects received one of five different treatment conditions:

Videotaped Model. Before the posttest, the subjects watched a videotape of a model (a male psychiatric patient) who behaved very assertively in the five situations. For four sessions across three days, between pre- and posttests, they observed the model after practicing responses to the scenes.

Instructions. Subjects were given specific instructions on how to behave, such as talk louder, specify how things should be changed, and look at the person when speaking. However, they did not see the model. This occurred for four sessions.

Instructions Plus Modeling. The two treatments above were combined.

Practice-Control. Subjects simply went through the scenes for four sessions without instructions or modeling.

Test-Retest. No contact occurred between the pre- and posttests.

Results

Separate analysis of variances were performed for each of the seven target behaviors. Modeling Plus Instructions was most effective in improving Duration of Reply, Affect, and Overall Assertiveness. Modeling Plus Instructions and Modeling alone were equally effective in improving Requests for New Behavior while Modeling Plus Instructions and Instructions were equally effective in improving Duration of Looking. Instructions produced the most changes in Duration of Looking, while Modeling most affected Compliance.

Group Play Therapy and Tangible Reinforcers
Used to Modify the Behavior of Eight-Year-Old Boys

PAUL CLEMENT (Fuller Theological Seminary) and
COURTNEY MILNE, *Behaviour Research and Therapy*, 1967, 5,
301-312.

Treatment of withdrawn children in groups.

Children's group play-therapy is widely practiced by child therapists as a means of altering the behaviors of their clients. Although it "feels good" to the practitioners, there is in fact very little research in the technique to test whether expected changes do occur. In addition, play therapy is a very loosely defined procedure and varies in focus from therapist to therapist.

Play therapy is defined operationally and specified treatment techniques, tangible and social reinforcers, are examined to discover if any objective difference in outcome for the children follows.

Method

SUBJECTS AND SETTING: Eleven boys with no major dysfunction (such as psychopathic behavior, perceptual handicaps, speech disorders) were selected as subjects. Measures for selection included the Bender-Gestalt figure drawings, responses to the Rorschach, a sentence completion test, and the Children's Manifest Anxiety Scale (CMAS). Mothers of the boys were also required to fill out the CMAS, a Q-sort, and a behavior problem check list (BPCL). In addition, the mothers judged their boys to be socially withdrawn and friendless, lacking in spontaneity and maladjusted but able to attend school regularly. The boys averaged eight years, ten months in age with an I.Q. of 100 and a range of 80-123. Therapy was conducted in a hospital setting once a week for 14 consecutive weeks.

PROCEDURE: The 11 boys were randomly assigned to a Token Group (n = 4), a Verbal Group (n = 4) or a Control Group (n = 3). Targeted behaviors, that is, the behaviors that were reinforced, were 1) walking toward another boy and/or 2) talking to another boy.

Token Group. Play therapy lasted for 50 minutes and involved the procedure suggested by Haim Ginott (*Group Psychotherapy with Children: The Theory and Practice of Play-Therapy*, McGraw Hill, 1961). Tangible reinforcers for the target behaviors were brass tokens which could be used to purchase small toys, trinkets and candy at the end of each therapy hour. These were dispensed on a variable-ratio, variable-interval schedule throughout the therapeutic sessions.

Verbal Group. This group was structured identically to the Token Group. It included verbal (social) reinforcement, but it did not involve tangible reinforcement. This group was considered to parallel typical play therapy for boys of the age included in this study.

Control Group. A therapist was not present in this condition. The boys were observed from behind a one-way mirror and were allowed to behave as they wished unless there was a chance of physical damage to another boy, the playroom, or the equipment. Intervention was required on one occasion.

Mothers' Group. Concurrent with the children's groups were guidance groups conducted for the mothers. These sessions did not involve counseling or psychotherapy.

Table
Summary of the Dependent Variables

Dependent variable (DV)	Index to DV	Person providing data	When measured
Productivity	Grades on report card	Teachers	Quarterly during academic year
Anxiety	CMAS	Ss ———— Mothers	Pre-therapy, 7th session, and 14th session
Social adjustment	Play room observations	Research assistants	Throughout each of the 14 play sessions
General psychological adjustment	Q-sort	Mothers	Pre-therapy, 7th session, and 14th session
Problem behaviors	BPCL	Mothers	Pre-therapy, 7th session, and 14th session

125

Dependent Variables. (See Table.)

Behavioral recording (social adjustment) used a time-sampling technique. An observer observed and recorded each *S* for twelve one-minute periods taken at four-minute intervals.

Results

The data were analyzed by single-factor and two-factor analyses of variance. Productivity and anxiety showed no significant effect due to treatment, contrary to what is typically expected from a psychotherapeutic procedure. Although mothers' evaluations of their sons suggested that the boys' behavior had improved during and after treatment, objective measures contradicted this finding. An important aside is that mothers' evaluations are typically used in clinical settings to verify treatment effectiveness. These data strongly suggest that these evaluations are not reliable and should themselves be the topic of research, in order to determine their relationship to actual behavior.

However, the token group did demonstrate improvement in social play, in talking to other boys in their group, in nearness to other boys, and in their behavior problem checklist scores. Members of the verbal group increased their number of statements to the therapist and in their proximity to other boys in the group. Their social play, however, decreased. The control group showed no change in all variables investigated.

Abstract 51

The Modification of Interview Behavior
by Client Use of Social Reinforcement

JUDITH CONGER (University of Illinois), *Behavior Therapy*, 1971, 2, 52-61.

Turning the tables: client modification of counselor behavior.

The effect of the therapist on a client is a common topic of research. But what about the effect of the client on the therapist? Can clients systematically modify the behavior of the therapist?

Method

SUBJECTS AND SETTING: The subjects were 30 graduate students taking courses in counseling or social work who agreed to participate in a study of "short-term interviewing techniques." They were told they would interview "real clients." Actually, they interviewed one of two graduate students who played the role of an unhappy, anxious, mildly-depressed person. Each "client" was interviewed by 15 subjects.

PROCEDURE: Each interview lasted about 30 minutes, and the subjects were told the purpose of the interview was to make some formulation about the client's problem areas.

For the first nine minutes, the client reinforced every third interaction made by the interviewer. This Baseline phase was followed by an 18-minute period in which the client reinforced every occurrence of the target behavior. For half the subjects, the target behavior was a present-tense verb, while the target for the other half was a past-tense verb. Reinforcement consisted of eye contact, smiling, leaning forward, increased volume of voice, and expression of interest and agreement (e.g., "Yes, that's an important point," or, "I've thought a lot about that.")

Results

The number of past- and present-tense verbs used in the Baseline and conditioning phase was determined for each subject. A ratio of the occurrence of the target verb class and the nontarget class in Baseline and conditioning phases was used. An analysis of variance indicated there was a tendency for the treatment to affect the behavior of the interviewer in the predicted direction.

Abstract **52**

Application of a Token System in a
Pre-Adolescent Boys' Group

JAMES M. STEDMAN (University of Texas Medical School at
San Antonio), TRAVIS PETERSON (Community Guidance
Center, San Antonio) and JAMES CARDARELLE (Department
of Welfare, Minneapolis), *Journal of Behavior Therapy and
Experimental Psychiatry*, 1971, 323-29.

Modifying aggressive behavior through contingent reinforcement.

Counseling groups can be operated on a number of different theoretical
models, ranging from psychoanalytic discussion groups in which the goal
is to work out the repressed problems from early childhood that are interfering with current adjustment, to humanistically based "here and now"
groups in which the goal is to help people learn to deal more effectively with
life by carefully attending to the manner in which they behave in the group
itself. This study reprsents an innovative use of a behavioral technique,
token economy, tailored to the needs of a group counseling situation.

Method

SUBJECTS AND SETTING: The group included eight boys, 10 to 12½ years of
age, who spent an hour in the session each week. Both aggressive and
withdrawn boys were in the group, although the general tone of the group
was one of hostile, aggressive behavior. The boys were having difficulty at
home and at school. Two of the boys were selected for special attention
because of their disruptive behavior. One was an 11 year old who attended
a special education class. He was often verbally and physically aggressive in
the group and at school. The second was 12½ years old and exhibited very
erratic and changeable behavior, ranging from extreme politeness to
aggressive outbursts.

Sessions began with a brief discussion of the plans for the session, and
the group then moved into an activity.

PROCEDURE: The experimenters developed a list of behaviors that would
be rewarded during the sessions. The list shown in the Table was developed cooperatively by the boys and the therapists. In addition, the two

boys selected for special attention were observed on two behaviors. For one, the behaviors were physical aggression and threats, and verbal aggression, while the target behavior for the second was verbal and physical interruption of conversations. At the beginning of the token program, a list similar to the Table was given to each group member and discussed in the session. The program was implemented the next week. Tokens, 1¼-inch steel washers, were awarded for appropriate behavior during the session. Some behaviors, such as one and three were reinforced as they occurred, but most others were reinforced at fixed time intervals (at 10, 30 and 45 minutes). Students who failed to receive tokens at those times due to an inappropriate behavior were so informed, and the behavior was described.

Table
Schedule for Earning Tokens as Positive
Reinforcement for Children in Group Therapy

I. Beginning Group
1. Come to group (1 token)
2. Stay in waiting room until group starts (1 token)
3. Good behavior in the waiting room prior to the group (1 token)
4. Come to place where the adult group leaders are and stay there (1 token)
5. Take part in group decision about today's activity (1 token)

II. Cooperation in Group
1. Participate and try in group activities—sports, discussions, hikes (1 token at beginning, middle and end of group session)
2. Act like a friend—do not hit, pinch, call names or hurt others (1 token at beginning, middle and end)
3. Try to help people be friends and get along—do not stir up one against another (1 token at beginning, middle and end)
4. Stay with the group (1 token at end)

III. Cooperation In Group Discussion
1. Listen to others—don't hog the time (1 token at beginning, middle and end)
2. Talk about the problem—don't act silly, shout, hit others (1 token at beginning, middle and end)
3. Make helpful comments to the other boy about his problem (1 token at beginning, middle and end)
4. Raise hand (1 token at beginning, middle and end)

IV. Behavior Ouside Group (as indicated on school report card)
1. Same conduct grades as on previous report card period
   A, 5 tokens
   B, 4 tokens
   C, 3 tokens
2. Any improvement in conduct grades (20 tokens)
3. Academic grades—same and show you are trying (10 tokens)
4. Academic grades—improved
   A, 5 tokens per grade
   B, 4 tokens per grade
   C, 3 tokens per grade

Decisions on how many tokens to award were based on a concensus of the therapists. Bonus tokens were also awarded occasionally for outstanding behavior.

The tokens could be spent for three types of behaviors: 1) the right to return to the next session (10 tokens), 2) attendance at a "party" during the last ten minutes of the session (5 tokens), 3) and field trips selected by the group (costs varied).

Results

The behaviors of the two target students are shown in the Figure. Both decreased the number of inappropriate behaviors when the token reinforcement was instituted. No data was taken on the remaining six boys in the group, but subjective impressions indicated their behavior improved, and several favorable reports were received from their school.

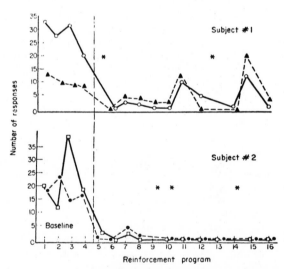

Occurrence of deviant behavior for two test subjects (⊘ Physical aggression or threatening gestures; ▲ Verbal aggression; ☐ Verbal interruption; ● Physical interruption; ★ Child absent for session).

CHAPTER V

Behavior Therapy

Abstract 53

Systematic Desensitization
as a Counterconditioning Process

GERALD DAVISON (State University of New York at Stony Brook), *Journal of Abnormal Psychology*, 1968, 73, 2, 91-99.

A study supporting Wolpe's theoretical explanation of systematic desensitization.

Systematic desensitization (SD) is a procedure developed by Joseph Wolpe, a South African psychiatrist. Several steps are involved in SD. First, the client is deeply relaxed. Sometimes drugs are used to help the patient relax, but many therapists use adaptations of Jacobson's progressive muscle relaxation methods. The client may be asked to concentrate on relaxing a particular portion of his anatomy and to progressively relax more and more parts. Sometimes the client is asked to alternatively tense and relax muscles until all the main muscle groups of the body are relaxed.

Once relaxed, the client is asked to imagine scenes from a hierarchy of anxiety-evoking or upsetting scenes, beginning with the weakest and proceeding up the hierarchy to the most upsetting scene. For a person afraid of riding elevators, the least upsetting scene might be approaching a building in which there is an elevator and the most upsetting scene might be imagining actually riding in an elevator in a tall building. The client progresses from one scene to another only when he does not lose his relaxed state. Wolpe assumed that if clients can be heped to imagine scenes progressively more and more like the scenes that upset them, without becoming anxious or tense, clients would no longer be afraid of those situations in real life.

A number of studies have shown that systematic desensitization works, but there is a considerable amount of controversy around the questions of *how* it works. Wolpe felt that pairing a response that is antagonistic to being anxious (being relaxed) with the stimuli that are associated with anxiety tended to weaken or suppress the bond between the stimuli and anxiety. This is called *counterconditioning*. Counterconditioning requires the contiguous association of graded, anxiety-provoking stimuli with responses, such as relaxation, which are incompatible with anxiety. However, it is possible that the effectiveness of SD is not based on counterconditioning but on some other factor. For example, perhaps relaxation alone is beneficial, regardless of whether it is actually paired with the feared stimulus. Or perhaps helping the clients order their fears in hierarchies and imagine them sequentially is the beneficial component of the treatment. Finally, perhaps talking with another person who is concerned and interested in the problem accounts for the success of SD. This study addresses the question of whether counterconditioning is a necessary condition for successful SD. All treatment was done individually.

Method

SUBJECTS AND SETTING: Twenty-eight female volunteers in an introductory psychology class reporting fear of nonpoisonous snakes were the subjects. They took a pretreatment avoidance test which involved entering a room in which a live snake was kept and getting as close to the snake as possible. Any subject who actually picked up the snake was excluded from the study. The behavior of the remaining subjects was observed on a 13-point scale which indicated how close they actually approached the snake. The subjects were also asked to tell the experimenter how anxious they were feeling, using a 10-point scale at each of the 13 points. The avoidance test was repeated after treatment. Eight subjects were assigned to each of three experimental conditions by matching them on the pretreatment tests. Eight were assigned to each of three treatment conditions and four to a control condition.

PROCEDURE:

Systematic Desensitization. One group was trained in deep muscle relaxation, using a 30-minute tape. The subjects then developed a hierarchy of snake scenes, ranging from scenes such as "picking up and handling a toy snake" and "standing in front of the cage, looking down at the snake through the wire cover" to "barehanded, picking up the snake." While relaxed, they were asked to imagine the least upsetting scene. When they clearly imagined the scene for 15 seconds without signaling to the therapist that they were anxious, they moved to the next most upsetting scene. A maximum of nine 45-minute sessions was required to progress through the hierarchy.

Pseudodesensitization. The same relaxation procedure described above was used, but subjects were relaxed and asked to imagine scenes from their childhood ("You are about five years old, and you are sitting on the floor looking sadly at a toy that you have just broken."). Snake-related scenes were never used. Each member of this group was *yoked* to a matched member of the SD group. The number of sessions, number of scenes given each session, and the duration of imagining each scene for this group was determined by the amount of time of the matched SD subject.

Exposure to Hierarchy. Subjects in this group made a hierarchy of snake-aversive stimuli and were yoked to members of the SD group. They imagined the sequence of scenes but were not taught relaxation and were not asked to relax.

No Treatment Group. Four subjects simply took the pre-and post-treatment avoidance test.

Results

Analysis of variance and t-tests on the data showed that only the SD group made significant improvements in approaching the snake from pre-to posttests. No other comparisons were significant. Similar results were reported for the data on the subjects' reports of anxiety in the test situation. A counterconditioning explanation of SD was thus supported.

Abstract 54

Two-Year Follow-up of Systematic Desensitization in Therapy Groups

GORDON PAUL (University of Illinois), *Journal of Abnormal Psychology*, 1968, 73, 119-130.

Long-term effects of systematic desensitization.

Follow-up studies that evaluate the effects of treatment during an extended period of time are very rare. In this study, a treatment program (group desensitization) was evaluated over two years. Previous research had indicated positive effects at the end of treatment.

Method

SUBJECTS AND SETTING: Subjects were all male college students who, before treatment, had been very anxious in social, interpersonal, or evaluative situations such as public speaking. There were four groups of ten males who had received group desensitization, individual desensitization, insight-oriented psychotherapy, or attention-placebo treatment. An additional ten subjects were used as controls. They were untreated and were matched with the group desensitization group. An additional 22 untreated controls were considered in some data analyses. Median age was 21. All students were enrolled in a public-speaking course.

PROCEDURE: Before treatment, a battery of personality and anxiety scales were administered during class. The scales were completed one week after subjects' first speech. Subjects in their respective groups then received the treatments described above, and a posttest consisting of the pretreatment scales and self-ratings of improvement was administered.

Table
Percentage of Cases Showing Significant Change from Pretreatment to 2-Year Follow-Up

Treatment	Significantly "Improved"	No Change	Significantly "Worse"
Focal treatment (Speech Composite):[a]			
Group desensitization	80%	20%	—
Systematic desensitization	89%	11%	—
Insight-oriented psychotherapy	50%	50%	—
Attention-placebo treatment	50%	50%	—
Untreated controls	27%	73%	—
Focal treatment (SR-Exam):[b]			
Group desensitization	70%	30%	—
Systematic desensitization	44%	56%	—
Insight-oriented psychotherapy	25%	62%	13%
Attention-placebo treatment	20%	70%	10%
Untreated controls	9%	81%	—
All other comparisons (five scales):[c]			
Group desensitization	38%	60%	2%
Systematic desensitization	42%	58%	—
Insight-oriented psychotherapy	30%	65%	5%
Attention-placebo treatment	24%	68%	8%
Untreated controls	22%	71%	7%

Note.—$N = 11$ for controls, 10 for group desensitization and attention-placebo, 9 for systematic desensitization, 8 for insight. Due to small expectancies in cells, chi-squares were computed with the following grouping: Both desensitization vs. Insight + Attention-Placebo vs. Controls, $df = 2$. Classifications derived by two-sided .05 cutoffs on each change score.

[a] $x^2 = 9.91$, $p < .01$.
[b] $x^2 = 4.16$, $p < .15$; Fisher exact probability for group desensitization versus all others, $p = .003$.
[c] $x^2 = 5.89$, $p < .06$.

After two years the subjects were again contacted. The test battery was given again, along with several behavioral questionnaires. Grades in school two years after treatment were also obtained.

Results

Data were obtained on 100% of the treated subjects and 69% of the untreated controls. Subjects who had had two or more contacts with a psychological helper during the follow-up period were excluded from the data analysis. No subjects were excluded from the group desensitization group, or attention-placebo group, but the insight group lost two, the individual desensitization group one, and ten were excluded from the untreated controls.

Data obtained two years after treatment, through self-report inventories, indicated the improvements in terms of decreased anxiety in social and evaluative situations which were noted just after treatment were either maintained or greater at the end of two years.

Data on grades, obtained before and after treatment, had indicated the group desensitization group improved their grades, while the controls had lower marks. Two years later the pattern was the same as indicated in the Figure. In addition, 90% of the group desensitization group was successful academically (graduated or in good standing) while only 40% of the control group was successful.

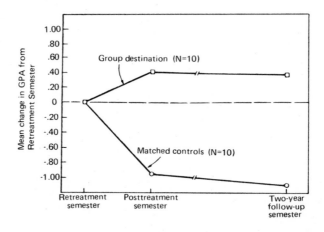

The Table presents a summary of the data in terms of the percentage of cases in each group that improved, did not change, or became worse. The data thus reflect the degree to which treatments were beneficial, as well as the possibility that some treatments could have been detrimental. Two measures that focused on the specific target of treatment, speech anxiety, were used—the speech scale on the S-R Inventory of Anxiousness and a speech anxiety scale developed by Paul. All other measures were considered as indicators of symptom substitution; that is, the possibility that improvement in speech anxiety might lead to the emergence of another symptom in a different area. As shown in the Table, both group and individual desensitization procedures produced higher percentages of improvement than the other conditions. There was no indication of symptom substitution in any of the behaviorally-treated groups.

Abstract **55**

Subjective Variables and Treatment Effects in Aversion Therapy

DAVID EVANS (University of Calgary), *Behaviour Research and Therapy*, 1968, *6*, 1-5.

A follow-up study of failures in aversion therapy.

Few behavioral studies have paid much attention to the clients who are treated unsuccessfully with behavioral methods. The focus has been, instead, on reporting the successes. This study obtained follow-up data on a group of exhibitionists who were treated with aversion therapy. Those successfully treated were then compared to the unsuccessful clients in an effort to identify important variables that influence outcome.

Method

SUBJECTS AND SETTING: Subjects were 20 exhibitionists referred by psychiatrists to a private Behaviour Therapy Clinic in Toronto, Ontario. Ten subjects reported that they did not exhibit during a six-month, follow-up period after treatment (Successful group) and ten reported they did (Failure group).

PROCEDURE: The men in both groups attended therapy sessions once a week for ten weeks, and after interviews with a psychiatrist and a psychologist they received aversion therapy. Each client provided details of his exhibitionistic activities. From this information, a set of phrases was constructed for each subject which were used to help the client imagine his exhibitional behavior. Phrases that helped him imagine nonexhibiting, often normal, heterosexual behavior were also developed. Treatment consisted of seating the client in a comfortable chair and having him watch a screen on which the phrases were projected. When a phrase appeared, the client was to imagine the scene it described. If the scene was one that involved exhibition, he would receive a painful shock, through electrodes attached to his fingers, from three to six seconds after the phrase appeared. The shock ended when the client activated a switch that advanced the projector to the next phrase in which a normal scene was depicted. During each session 20 phrases depicting exhibition were projected, as well as 40 normal phrases. Shock always accompanied the exhibition phrases, and a normal phrase always followed an exhibition phrase. The intensity of the shock was adjusted each session by the client to the highest level he felt he could tolerate.

Results

There were no significant differences between the success and failure groups in terms of age, level of education, frequency of masturbation, frequency of sexual intercourse, or marital status. The results suggest exhibition occurs in addition to rather than as a replacement for other sexual behavior. The failure group had been exhibiting longer than the success group, however, and had done it more often than the success group. Failure clients also required more treatment sessions to report that they were no longer exhibiting and they no longer felt the urge to exhibit. Finally, failure clients included fantasizing about exhibiting while they masturbated more often than success clients.

Abstact **56**

An Experimental Investigation of the Implosion
Technique

R. J. HODGSON and S. J. RACHMAN (London University),
Behaviour Research and Therapy, 1970, *8*, 21-27.

A study of implosion therapy with negative results.

Two major behavioral approaches exist for dealing with fears and phobias.
The first, systematic desensitization, involves relaxing the concerned
individuals and asking them, while relaxed, to imagine progressively more
frightening scenes. With systematic desensitization, the person is asked to
think of a more stressful scene only after less stressful ones elicit little fear or
tension. Implosion, the second method of managing fears and phobias, is
based on a very different principle. Imploding involves exposing the client
to very strong fear-producing situations or imagined scenes. A person who
is afraid of insects, for example, might listen to the therapist describe a
scene in which thousands of bugs crawl into the room, crawl over the
person, and into his ears, nose, and eyes. The theory behind implosion is
that requiring people to imagine in intense detail the events or situations
that they fear will produce high levels of anxiety. Since they experience this
anxiety in a safe environment (the therapist's office) over an extended
period of time, however, the anxiety should extinguish. The research
reported here is designed to evaluate the effectiveness of implosion therapy
but it also examines alternative theoretical explanations for its effectiveness. The process assumed to underlie implosion is extinction, but the
notion of behavioral contrast could account for the data as well. That is,
implosion therapy could be so intensely anxiety-arousing that actual
experience may, in contrast, seem much less fearful.

Method

SUBJECTS AND SETTING: Fifty snake-phobic females were selected from a
larger pool of potential subjects. Selection was based on high scores on a
self-report test of snake avoidance and an actual test of snake avoidance, in
which the person was asked to enter a room in which a snake was housed,
approach its cage, pick up the snake, and then place it on her lap. The tests
were given before and after treatment, and each subject was rated on her

proximity to the snake. Most subjects were college students between the ages of 18 and 24. After pretesting, the 50 subjects were divided into five groups of ten, matched on pretest scores.

PROCEDURE: All subjects heard a 40-minute tape recording and were then asked to repeat the tests given before treatment. Five different tapes were used:

Implosion. This tape followed the standard implosion procedure. It described in detail scenes from seeing a snake in the distance to chewing and swallowing a live snake. If extinction is the factor that makes implosion work, a tape that deals with the feared object should be most effective.

Horror Images. Subjects heard 40 minutes of tape that described horrific scenes such as the following: "Imagine you are involved in a car crash; you see a woman without a leg. Now imagine that you see her amputated leg by the side of the road, oozing blood." If contrast underlies implosion, imagining scenes that are much worse than the actual feared situation should be most effective.

Control Tape. Subjects heard 40 minutes of pleasant scenes describing kittens in situations similar to those on the implosion tape.

Horror Images and Snake Images. Subjects heard 30 minutes of the horror tape, followed immediately by the last 10 minutes of the implosion tape. If the presence of high levels of anxiety while imagining the feared situation facilitates extinction, then the 30-minute horror tape should improve extinction.

Horror Images and Delayed Snake Images. This group heard the same tapes as the preceding group, but the 10 minutes of snake images were played to the subjects 24 hours after the horror tape. Extinction should be poorer with the delay.

Results

There were no differences between the groups on pretest measures. Although the groups reported fears differentially after treatment, these differences were nonsignificant statistically. In fact, the control group who heard a pleasant, relaxing tape about kittens made gains as great or greater than the treatment groups in approaching the real snake.

Abstract 57

Instrumental Conditioning of Diastolic Blood Pressure in Essential Hypertensive Patients

S. THOMAS ELDER and Z. ROSALBA RUIZ (Louisiana State University), HERDIS DEABLER, ROBERT DILLENKOFFER (Veterans Administration Hospital in New Orleans), *Journal of Applied Behavior Analysis*, 1973, 6, 377-382.

A study showing autonomic responses can be voluntarily controlled.

By the 1970s, use of both operant and classical conditioning procedures to modify behavior had become commonplace in many clinics and hospitals. Some behaviors, however, such as heartrate and blood pressure, were long considered outside the realm of behavioral technology because they were controlled by the autonomic nervous system and thus less subject to voluntary control. This study is one of several that indicates modification of blood pressure is not necessarily outside the realm of individual control.

Method

SUBJECTS AND SETTING: Eighteen male patients between the ages of 23 and 59, with essential hypertension or high blood pressure, were studied. All subjects were inpatients in a Veterans' Hospital and all were taking medication (central nervous system depressants), but not for essential hypertension. They were randomly divided into three groups of six.

PROCEDURE: On the first morning of treatment, each patient reported to the hospital laboratory and had his blood pressure taken. Blood pressure was measured every two minutes for 20 minutes, and the mean of the ten measures was used as the basal systolic and diastolic blood pressure.

That afternoon, treatment sessions began and were held twice a day for three days. Follow-up occurred one week after the end of treatment.

Control Group. Patients in this group were seated in a comfortable chair and had their blood pressure measured. They were instructed to attempt to lower their blood pressure by any means possible. Additional instructions included asking them to relax and to avoid thinking about personal problems.

Experimental Group 1. Patients in this group received the instructions described above. Like the control group, blood pressure was measured every two minutes over a 20-minute period. Where pressure dropped below the measurement obtained at the beginning of the session, a red light came on. If blood pressure remained low for several two-minute trials, the red light did not come on unless the pressure dropped further.

Experimental Group 2. This group was treated in the same manner as the first experimental group. In addition, verbal praise was given when blood pressure dropped. The experimenter said "good" if diastolic pressure did not increase, "very good" if it dropped five units, and "wonderful" if it dropped ten units.

Results

An analysis of variance on pretreatment diastolic and systolic blood pressures indicated no significant differences between the groups. There was a tendency for systolic blood pressure to decrease across both treatment and follow-up for the group receiving feedback (red light) and praise. None of the groups showed significant differences in systolic blood pressure; however, diastolic pressure, which is considered more important by many cardiologists, did decrease significantly across treatment. The feedback-and-praise group was superior to both the feedback-alone and control groups in the amount of change. The feedback-alone group, however, was significantly improved over the control group, who maintained high diastolic blood pressure measures. Follow-up data taken one week after treatment produced similar results.

Abstract 58

An Unsuccessful Attempt to Treat a
Tiqueur by Massed Practice

RONALD FELDMAN (Jewish General Hospital, Montreal) and JOHN WERRY (University of Illinois), *Behaviour Research and Therapy*, 1966, 4, 111-117.

A treatment failure, using massed practice.

Massed practice or negative practice is a method of behavior therapy recommended since the 1930s as a means of treating certain repetitive behaviors. Massed practice requires the person to repeat the undesired behavior again and again. It is supposed such practice builds up reactive inhibition, a Hullian learning theory concept used to describe a state analagous to fatigue, which is assumed to accumulate when the same behavior is performed repeatedly. In this study, massed practice was used to treat several tics.

Method

SUBJECT AND SETTING: The patient was a 13-year-old boy who had multiple tics of the face, neck, and head which developed about age seven. His parents were separated, and he had spent some time in boarding schools. Two of several tics were selected for treatment. The first, a head jerk, involved a sharp, lateral rotation of the head. The second, an eyeblink, was accompanied by some facial distortion.

PROCEDURE: The initial period of each weekly session with the therapist was spent discussing the patient's progress. When the patient seemed relaxed, occurrence of the two target tics was observed for 15 minutes. During weeks one to four, only Baseline measures were taken. Then during sessions 5-15 the patient was required to practice the head jerk tic for five

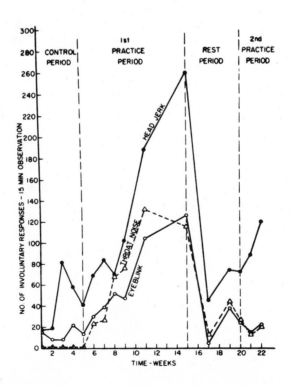

minutes during the session. He was also asked to practice at home three times a week for five minutes. The patient did not practice the tic at home for the first four weeks of treatment, but when the therapist assured the patient that the practice was beneficial, he consented. By week 16, however, the tics had become so severe that both the patient and his father were not inclined to continue. After a "rest period" from weeks 16 to 19, massed practice was instituted again, but only during the weekly session. The time spent practicing was increased to 15 minutes in weeks 21 and 22.

Results

The Figure shows the rate of occurrence of tics during the 15-minute observation period before treatment each week. The patient missed the session during the tenth week, and the therapist was on vacation during weeks 12 to 14. The results on three tics, a head jerk, an eyeblink, and a throat noise which reappeared after several months' absence during the first practice period, show that the massed practice actually produced an increase in both the practiced tic and the two tics not practiced. Treatment was discontinued after week 22, when massed practice again appeared to be making the tics worse instead of better. The reported occurrence of tics outside the therapy session generally followed the pattern shown in the Figure.

Abstract **59**

Programmed Relaxation and Reciprocal Inhibition with Psychotic Children

ANTHONY GRAZIANO (University of Bridgeport, Connecticut) and JEFFREY KEAN (NOMIC Child Development Center), *Behaviour Research and Therapy*, 1968, 6, 433-437.

Psychotic children can be trained to relax.

Researchers and therapists have typically viewed relaxation training as inappropriate for both psychotic and child populations. Psychoticism is generally considered to be precipitated by an "abnormal organic state," and those who are psychotic do not appear to respond in a sufficiently predictable and consistent pattern to allow such training. Children are viewed as having too limited an experiential history to be treated successfully with relaxation training. In this study, what would seem to be the impossible from the above theories is attempted. Psychotic children are treated with relaxation training. The rationale is that the children are habitually tense, which to some extent explains their sensitivity to ordinarily innocuous stimuli. If they can be trained through minimal steps to relax, then their anxiety reponses will be decreased in frequency, intensity and duration.

Method

SUBJECTS: Four children, three males and one female, aged five, six, nine, and six, who had been diagnosed as autistic, were selected as subjects. Relaxation training was instituted as the first step in a program that would include systematic desensitization later on (see Abstract 53 for more details on systematic desensitization).

PROCEDURE: Because the children had no behavioral referent for the concept "relax," it was necessary to begin very slowly and to expect minimal or no gains and to use social reinforcement ("good work," "good job") frequently.

Step 1: For three days prior to training, children were told that they would have "relax time."

Step 2: Children were instructed that it was "relax time" and that they were to put away their toys and lie on the mat. The lights were turned out, and the therapist told them soothingly to close their eyes and pretend they were in their nice, comfortable beds. This session lasted two minutes.

Step 3: For the next 104 sessions, the children were gently massaged by the therapist.

Any approximation to relaxation was verbally reinforced immediately, so that eventually relaxation was cued by instruction alone. The mean duration of training was 7.1 minutes a day for the 105 days.

Criteria For Relaxation: A child was considered trained in relaxation if he was cooperative, quiet, and visibly "loosened" on instruction for five consecutive sessions.

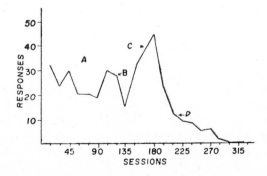

Results

The Figure presents data on frequency of excitement responses before and after relaxation training was begun. "A" represents the Baseline period of responses. "B" indicates the beginning of training. Although there is initially a decrease in excitement responses, when three of the children reach the relaxation criteria ("C"), there is in fact a notable increase in excitement responses. By the time the fourth child reached the criteria ("D"), however, there is a dramatic decrease in the frequency of excitement responses. Although training was considered complete after 105 sessions, excitement behavior was recorded for 195 more sessions. By session 300, all four children reduced their excitement responses to zero.

Abstract **60**

Brevital-Relaxation Treatment of Frigidity

JOHN PAUL BRADY (University of Pennsylvania), *Behaviour Research and Therapy*, 1966, 4, 71-77.

Behavioral treatment of sexual dysfunction, using drugs.

Conventional systematic desensitization generally consists of voluntary and aware muscle relaxation prior to proceeding through a hierarchy of anxiety-arousing scenes. These scenes range from very low to most arousing and are individually tailored to fit the particular person's problem.

This procedure can be modified, however, so that instead of being self-induced, the relaxation is drug-induced. This is in fact what was done in this study, which investigated a treatment for a highly refractory form of frigidity in married women.

Method

SUBJECTS: Five women, ranging in age from 17 to 30 years, who had been married from nine months to nine years, were treated. All reported intense negative reactions to sexual activity, and particularly to intercourse, varying from strong feelings of anxiety, disgust, or anger to actual pain at intromission.

PROCEDURE: Patients and their husbands were interviewed to obtain information concerning the nature and extent of the patient's sexual dysfunction and to explain treatment. Sexual activity during treatment was encouraged, but the participants were cautioned that it was very important to stop before the anxiety point. Following this interview, the patient and therapist met again to construct a hierarchy of sexual scenes. The following hierarchy was actually used for one of the subjects:

Typical Hierarchy Of Scenes For Deconditioning Frigidity

1. Being kissed on lips by husband
2. Same as above but with tongue contact
3. Breasts fondled while fully clothed
4. Undressing with husband in bedroom
5. Being kissed on lips while nude
6. Seeing husband with erection
7. Fondling of breasts while nude
8. Mouth contact with breasts by husband
9. Nude in bed with husband preparatory to coitus
10. As above with initial body contact
11. As above with kissing on lips and breast fondling
12. As above immediately before intromission
13. Intromission
14. Continuing coitus (ventral-ventral)

The subject then practiced imagining a scene. A neutral scene such as drinking a glass of water was used. The drug used was methohexital sodium (Brevital), a barbituate with an extremely short potency, diminishing appreciably in four to five minutes. In the first session, the subject was informed that she would receive a drug which would induce relaxation and freedom from tension. She was to facilitate its effectiveness by allowing herself to relax. At that time Brevital was injected. During the two-four minutes necessary for the drug to become most effective, she was told to be calm and relaxed. The subject was then told to imagine the first scene vividly and to lift her index finger if she felt any apprehension or uneasiness. The scene was visualized for about two minutes, and then the subject stopped and simply relaxed for one minute. The scene was then repeated for about three minutes and if there was no evidence of anxiety, the next scene was introduced, and so on. If there were signs of anxiety, the scene was immediately terminated, and the therapist judged whether progression through the hierarchy was too rapid or whether more Brevital was required.

During a typical 20-minute Brevital relaxation session, two or three scenes might be presented one to three times each. After the session, the subject rested for ten minutes and was then interviewed to determine whether she could vividly imagine the scenes. Remaining sessions were conducted much the same as the first, from one to three times a week, until all scenes had been presented.

Results

Four of the five women treated met the predetermined criteria for success. These criteria were: 1) the subject enters freely into sexual relations with her husband; 2) no pain or anxiety during sexual activity; and 3) sexual activity is reported as pleasurable, culminating in orgasm at least some of the time.

One subject terminated treatment after five sessions with no explanation.

Follow-up data were gathered from the four women in the form of subjective reports and indicated that all maintained improvement. The follow-up period varied from three to eight months.

All subjects were nonorgasmic prior to treatment. Reported increases in orgasm with intercourse ranged from 20% to nearly 100%.

Abstract **61**

External Validity of Laboratory Fear Assessment: Implications from Two Case Studies

JOHN LICK and THOMAS UNGER (State University of New York at Buffalo), *Journal of Consulting and Clinical Psychology*, 1975, 43, 864-866.

Questions regarding the validity of laboratory tests of fear.

Much of the research on the use of behavioral methods in the treatment of fears and phobias has used variations of the Behavioral Avoidance Test (BAT), as the criteria for success. The BAT (see Abstract 62) is a structured laboratory situational test which allows the client to approach the feared animal or object, which is usually placed in a cage or some other enclosure. This study questions whether changes in behavior on the BAT are good indicators of changes in behavior in the real world.

Method

SUBJECTS: Two clients, a 22-year-old female who was afraid of snakes, and a 45-year-old female who was afraid of spiders, served as subjects. The phobias of both clients were so severe, they interfered with their everyday living. The first client, for example, was prevented from going camping, could not walk in tall grass, nor engage in outdoor activities where snakes might be. The second client could not garden nor enter her attic or basement.

PROCEDURE: Both clients were given phobia questionnaires and a BAT. The snake-phobic client refused to enter a room which contained a caged snake, while the other client could only get within 15 feet of a harmless tarantula in a glass cage.

The questionnaires also indicated the two women had strong phobias.

After the pretests both clients received desensitization (see Abstract 62).

Results

After treatment the BAT was readministered. One client was able to walk up to the cage and pick up the snake with her bare hands. The other was able to touch the caged spider with a gloved hand. Posttreatment questionnaire data indicated both women reported less anxiety about being in the presence of snakes or spiders.

In spite of the positive results described above, neither of the women was able to do the things she reported being unable to do because of the phobia (e.g., camping, going into the attic).

As a further test of the degree to which the phobia had been eliminated, the therapist asked the snake-phobic client to stand 30 feet away from the cage. He then removed the snake from the cage and put it on the floor. The client trembled, screamed, and demanded the snake be returned to the cage. Similar results were obtained with the other client.

The authors concluded that for many clients improvement on the BAT, in which the behavior of the feared animal is predictable and controlled, in a situation in which the therapist assures them no harm will come to them, may not be correlated with improvement in the natural environment.

Abstract **62**

Relative Efficacy of Desensitization and Modeling Approaches for Inducing Behavioral, Affective, and Attitudinal Changes

ALBERT BANDURA, EDWARD BLANCHARD and BRUNHILDE RITTER (Stanford University), *Journal of Personality and Social Psychology*, 1969, 13, 173-199.

A comparative study of behavioral techniques.

It is contended that avoidance behavior is mediated through a two-process system. Although the behavior itself, avoiding, is an instrumental response, the initiator, emotional arousal, is classically conditioned and arises primarily in the central nervous system. In order to most effectively decondition fear, for instance, it would be necessary to treat both the physiological or emotional response and the instrumental behavior. Fear itself could be treated through training an incompatible response, relaxation, or through extinguishing it by repeatedly pairing the feared stimulus with a neutral outcome.

Three treatments were compared in this study: traditional systematic desensitization, symbolic modeling accompanied by relaxation training, and modeling with guided participation. In addition, because of the very little research conducted on the reationship between behavior and attitude change, this variable was investigated as well. Not all of the details of the entire study are reported here.

Method

SUBJECTS: Forty-eight subjects, five males and 43 females, who were considered snake phobic on the basis of self-reports and a behavioral avoidance test, were selected for the study. The behavior avoidance test demanded that the subjects complete a series of 29 graded steps, culminating in allowing a four-foot king snake to crawl on their laps. Those subjects who could lift the snake inside its cage were eliminated from the study.
PROCEDURE:
Pretreatment Assessment: In addition to the behavioral test of fear noted above, subjects rated, on a scale from one to ten, the intensity of fear they experienced as the response required was explained to them, and as they actually performed the behavior.

Attitudes of subjects were measured by two means. On a scale from one to six, in which one end indicated strong enjoyment and the other indicated strong dislike, subjects rated various possible encounters with snakes, such as being shown a film on snakes and visiting a reptile exhibit. A bipolar adjective checklist was also used, in which such pairs of contrasting adjectives as good-bad, interesting-dull and belligerent-peaceful were rated.

Subjects were also required to complete a questionnaire indicating origin of the phobia.

Treatment: Subjects were matched on behavior avoidance test scores and randomly assigned to one of four conditions, 12 to a group.

1) Systematic Desensitization: In this condition, deep muscle relaxation was paired with imaginal representations of snakes arranged in hierarchical order from least to most aversive. A series of 34 scenes made up the hierarchy. New scenes were not suggested until the subject could relax completely to the current scene.

2) Symbolic Modeling with Relaxation: These subjects viewed a graduated film showing children, adolescents, and adults interacting in progressively more threatening situations with snakes. The film was 35-minutes long and began with models handling plastic snakes and terminated with a large snake crawling over their bodies. Subjects were also trained in relaxation techniques and could regulate presentation of modeling stimuli. If the scene became anxiety-creating, subjects were instructed to rewind the film to the beginning of the sequence and reinduce relaxation. Subjects rated their fear responses on a ten-point scale, as in pretreatment.

3) Live Modeling with Guided Participation: Initially, subjects observed the experimenter model nonphobic behavior through a one-way mirror. After 15 minutes, subjects were invited into the room with the experimenter and the snake. The experimenter modeled intimate interaction with the snake and eventually aided subjects, through demonstration and joint participation, to perform progressively more threatening approaches to the snake. When subjects entered the room, the snake was in its cage, and it was then that actual joint participation began. Progress through the steps was at the subject's own pace.

4) Control: Pre- and posttreatment measures were administered but no formal treatment was instituted. To control for model sex effects, half the subjects in each of the three treatment conditions received treatment from a male and half from a female.

Treatment was scheduled twice a week and continued until subjects achieved terminal criterion (allowing snake to crawl on lap) or until 5.25 hours of treatment were completed. Average duration of treatment was two hours, 10 minutes for live modeling, two hours, 46 minutes for symbolic modeling and four hours, 36 minutes for systematic desensitization.

Posttreatment Assessment: All measures administered in pretreatment were readministered with the single change that half the subjects were tested with a corn snake rather than a king snake on the behavior avoidance test. This was done to determine the generalization effects.

Results

Subjects did not approach the king snake significantly more than the corn snake, nor did they rate their fear arousal differentially.

The Figure below presents the mean approach responses performed by subjects in each condition. Control subjects showed no significant improvement, while all three treatment conditions were superior to their pretreatment approach responses. There was no significant difference between systematic desensitization and symbolic modeling. Live modeling was significantly more effective than either of the other two treatments. In addition, 92% of the live modeling groups reached criterion, while 33% and 25% reached that criterion in the symbolic modeling and systematic desensitization groups, respectively.

To determine relative fear arousal before and after treatment, the mean level of fear arousal rated for approach responses before treatment was compared to the same subset of responses after treatment. Because there were more approaches after treatment, the pretreatment mean was also

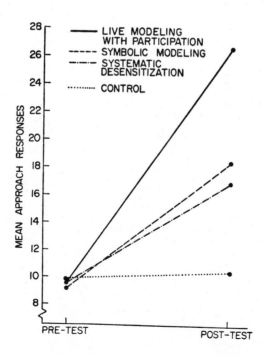

compared to the overall approach response mean after treatment. The first Figures below present results of both comparisons. On the left, the subset of approach responses attempted both before and after treatment are graphed. Simply being familiarized with the requirements resulted in less arousal of fear, as can be seen in the control group data. All treatment conditions resulted in significantly reduced arousal. There was no significant difference between the two forms of modeling, but both were superior to systematic desensitization.

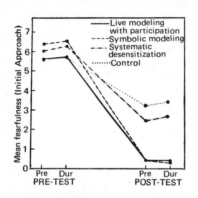 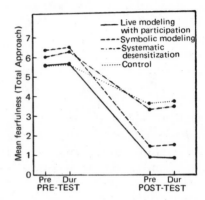

On the right, the data comparing the mean of all approach responses before and after treatment are presented for each condition. Control subjects did not experience significantly less fear. All treatment conditions did. As in the comparison between the subset of approach responses attempted before and after treatment, there were no significant differences between modeling conditions, but both were superior to systematic desensitization.

Attitude changes, as measured by the attitude scale and the semantic differential scale (adjective pair checklist), are graphed in the last Figures. Results for both measures were comparable and will be discussed together. The left Figure presents the attitude scale measure and the right Figure presents the semantic differential.

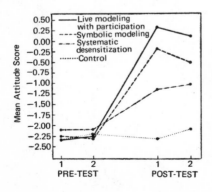 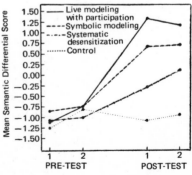

Information about reptiles given to all groups did not change attitudes significantly, as can be noted in the control group data. All treatment conditions significantly improved attitudes. Unlike the fear arousal comparisons, modeling with guided participation was superior to the other two treatment conditions. As in the fear arousal comparisons, symbolic modeling resulted in significantly greater attitude changes compared to systematic desensitization.

An interesting finding was that subjects in the treatment conditions administered by the female experimenter displayed greater changes on the semantic differential than those treated by the male.

A final result to be noted is that attitude change was positively correlated with behavior change.

Abstract **63**

Comparison of Smoking Treatments

LEWIS SACHS, HOWARD BEAN (West Virginia University) and JOSEPH MORROW (Indiana University, South Bend), *Behavior Therapy*, 1970, *1*, 465-472.

An experimental comparison of treatment alternatives using precise dependent measures.

Treatment of smoking is one of the most difficult and unrewarding endeavors for a psychologist to attempt. Generally, the data have indicated that neither behavioral nor nonbehavioral methods have been successful in terms of decreasing smoking. The authors of this study, however, contend that lack of differential effectiveness and little improvement may be more an artifact of the measurement procedure than of the treatments themselves. They have therefore compared a behavioral, a nonbehavioral, and an attention-control treatment, using more sensitive criteria for change.

Method

SUBJECTS: Although 49 subjects began the study, only 24 completed it, due partly to general attrition factors and partly to the behavior itself (some just did not want to stop smoking after all). Subjects were selected from volunteers who responded to a newspaper article and had a mean age of slightly less than 20.

PROCEDURE: Subjects were instructed to record their operant level of smoking. More specifically this was 1) the intensity of desire to smoke; 2) intensity of pleasure (both rated on a seven-point scale); 3) time; 4) description of the event, thought, or feeling prior to smoking; and, 5) a description of the pleasurable attributes of smoking. Subjects returned with their records in a week and were randomly assigned to one of three treatment groups. Each group met once a week for three consecutive weeks. Subjects were told at their last group meeting that they would be contacted in a month for follow-up evaluation. One therapist was assigned to the behavioral treatment group (covert sensitization), while a second was assigned to both the nonbehavioral (self-control) and attention control (placebo-attention) groups.

Covert Sensitization (n = 8). Using the "description of pleasurable attributes of smoking" as recorded in the first week, subjects were asked to rank order the reinforcing stimuli. In addition, they were given a list of 17 pleasurable components of smoking to rank according to both their initial reports of smoking and their "attributes," rating scale in terms of pleasure. After learning to physically relax (Edmund Jacobson, *Progressive Relaxation*. Chicago: The University of Chicago Press, 1938. Rev. ed., 1974), subjects were told to imagine the most pleasurable smoking sensation and pair it with imagined aversive scenes (for example, vomit). The therapist paired these verbally for the subject until the subject indicated he could do it himself. Subjects proceeded through the component hierarchy, pairing each item with an aversive scene ten times, beginning with the most and ending with the least pleasurable sensation. Subjects were instructed to follow the same procedure daily. The therapist spent an average of 20 minutes per session with each subject.

Self-Control (n = 8). Using the "description of the event, thought or feeling prior to smoking" as a discriminative stimulus, subjects were asked to rank these according to the difficulty of not smoking in the situation. Subjects were then asked to discontinue smoking in those situations, beginning with the condition that would be *least* difficult. They were not required to actually stop smoking, but rather to leave the situation if they were going to smoke. For example, if subjects wanted to smoke while reading, they could, but only if they left the reading situation until after they had smoked. The average duration of contact between subject and therapist per session was ten minutes.

154

Placebo-Attention Control (n = 8). Subjects were simply told that maintaining records of smoking behavior increased awareness and facilitated elimination or reduction of smoking. The therapist collected and commented on smoking records each week, verbally reinforcing complete records and statements of increased awareness. Therapist-subject contact averaged ten minutes per session.

Results

Data were analyzed by a 3 × 4 (treatment × time) analysis of variance. As indicated in the Figure, treatment for all groups had a cumulative effect, so that by Week Three each group showed a significant reduction in its operant level of smoking. Follow-up data, however, indicated significant treatment effects only in self-control and covert sensitization groups.

The Figure represents in absolute terms the operant smoking level of each subject before, during, and after treatment. A chi-square test indicated that the number of smokers who quit depended on the treatment condition. The effect of self-control treatment was significantly better than covert sensitization.

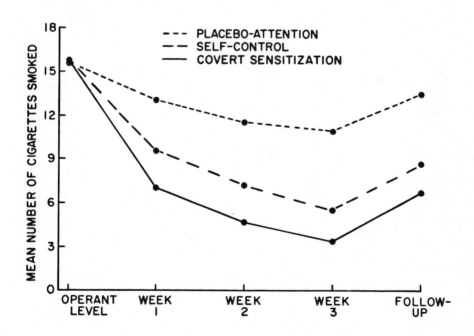

Abstract **64**

Operant Treatment of Asthmatic Responding
with the Parent as Therapist

JOHN NEISWORTH (Pennsylvania State University) and
FLORESE MOORE (Wilmington Special School District, Delaware), *Behavior Therapy*, 1972, *3*, 95-99.

A demonstration of asthma as an operant behavior.

Although asthma is generally considered a medical problem, its manifestations can sometimes be altered through the use of behavior modification, as illustrated by this study.

Method

SUBJECT AND SETTING: The subject was a seven-year-old boy who was diagnosed as asthmatic at the age of six months. Asthmatic attacks involving coughing, wheezing, and abrupt inspiration were frequent occurrences from that time onward, and required trips to the hospital emergency room. Medication and dietary restrictions had not alleviated the problem. At home the mother had a typical pattern of behavior. She frequently cautioned the child not to overexert himself, reminded him to

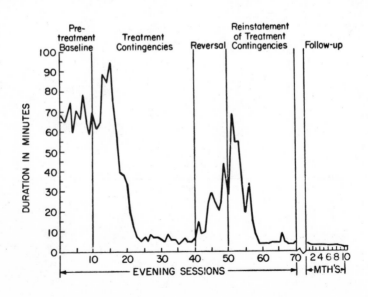

take medication, and was careful to keep him from eating restricted foods. The child received a great deal of attention and sympathy, particularly at bedtime, when wheezing attacks occurred.

PROCEDURE: Principles of operant conditioning were discussed with the mother, and she spontaneously suggested that her behavior might be reinforcing the attacks, while "nonasthmatic" behavior was rarely reinforced. Both the mother and father agreed to stop attending to the bedtime attacks and no medication was given. The child was put to bed in the usual manner (which included affectionate interactions between parent and child), but no further attention was given until morning. In addition, the child could buy his lunch at school instead of packing it when he coughed less during the preceding night than he had the night before.

Results

A ten-day Baseline of the number of minutes of asthmatic attacks at bedtime was taken before treatment began. As shown in the Figure, the attacks actually increased for the first few days of treatment, a common occurrence when extinction procedures are used, and then dropped to a very low level. The level increased during a reversal phase, when the parents reluctantly agreed to again give attention to attacks and provided lunch money noncontingently. Reinstitution of treatment produced another decrease, and follow-up observations across 11 months indicated stable, low levels.

Abstract 65

Behavior Therapy in the Home: Amelioration of Problem Parent-Child Relations with the Parent in a Therapeutic Role

ROBERT HAWKINS, ROBERT PETERSON, EDDA SCHWEID, and SIDNEY BIJOU (University of Washington), *Journal of Experimental Child Psychology*, 1964, 4, 99-107.

Short-circuiting child therapy: treating the parent.

When a parent and child are referred to mental health clinics, one common therapeutic procedure involves seeing both in weekly therapy sessions at the clinic, sometimes together and sometimes separately. This paper points out several problems with this procedure. A major difficulty is in the artificial setting, in which unbiased observation of both parent and child behavior is almost impossible. Another overriding problem concerns minimal evaluation possible when no objective-data measures are taken. The model presented here deals with those problems.

Method

SUBJECTS AND SETTING: The subjects were a four-year-old boy, Peter, and his mother. He was the third of four children in a middle-class family. The child was referred to a university clinic because he was extremely difficult to manage and control. Peter's mother reported she was unable to deal with his frequent tantrums, disobedience, destructive behavior, and verbal abuse.

PROCEDURE: Treatment consisted of two to three one-hour sessions per week, held at the subject's home. During that time Peter's behavior was observed as he moved freely about that part of his home, permitting unrestricted observation. Nine objectional behaviors, such as kicking, hitting, threats and derogatory statements, throwing objects, and pushing his sister, were observed, using a ten-second time-sampling procedure. If one or more of the nine behaviors occurred during any ten-second interval, it was scored for those behaviors. The number of times Peter and his mother spoke to each other was also recorded.

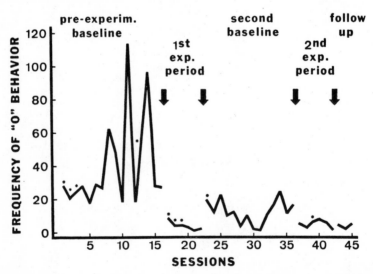

For the first 16 sessions (Baseline), behavior was observed, but no effort was made to change Peter's behavior or that of his mother. His mother was then told that the experimenter would sometimes give one of three signals during the observation period. Signal "A" meant she was to tell Peter to stop whatever objectional behavior he was performing. Signal "B" indicated Peter had not stopped the behavior, and she was to place him immediately in his room alone, with the toys removed. Peter was required to remain quiet and in his room for five minutes. Toys and other items of interest were removed before "time out" was used. "C" meant she was to praise him for some appropriate behavior. Signals were provided for six sessions. A second Baseline period of 14 sessions followed, in which no signals were used; signal warnings and "time out" were then reinstituted for six additional sessions. Twenty-four days after the last treatment session three additional one-hour follow-up observations were made. Between treatment sessions in which signals were used, Peter's mother was given no special instructions, but was free to use any of the techniques she learned.

Results

Peter's objectional behavior is shown in the Figure. When signals were used in the first experimental period, this behavior dropped to a low level. Peter's mother used time out several times during this period. On two occasions Peter broke the windows in his room. His cuts were bandaged unceremoniously the first time, and the glass cleared away. No injury resulted the second time, and the incident was ignored. During the second Baseline, objectionable behavior rose somewhat, but not to the original Baseline level, perhaps because Peter's mother reported difficulty responding to him as she had before learning to use behavior modification procedures. Objectionable behavior again dropped to a low level during the second experimental period and remained low at follow-up.

Abstract 66

Adverse Effects of Differential Parental Attention

EMILY HERBERT, ELSIE PINKSTON, M. LOEMAN HAYDEN (University of Kansas), THOMAS SAJWAJ, SUSAN PINKSTON, GLEN CORDUA, and CAROLYN JACKSON (University of Mississippi Medical Center and Millsaps College), *Journal of Applied Behavior Analysis*, 1973, *6*, 15-30.

Negative effects of a common behavior modification procedure.

Instructing parents to provide differential reinforcement for their children is a common, almost universal, part of behavioral parent-training programs. Generally, parents are told to ignore inappropriate behavior and to attend to and praise appropriate behavior. The effects of this procedure were evaluated in this study.

Method

SUBJECTS AND SETTING: Six mothers participating in parent-training projects and their children served as subjects. Mothers ranged in age from 27 to 44, with economic backgrounds varying from welfare recipients to upper middle-class. None of the six children was attending public school. Some had normal IQs while some were considered retarded. One was labeled autistic, another as learning disabled, while a third was described as very oppositional and disobedient.

PROCEDURE: The mother-child pairs were observed in a clinic setting four or five days a week, for 20 minutes. The mother and child sat at a small table and the mother was instructed to have the child do several preacademic and academic tasks (e.g., tracing letters, playing with toys, labeling colors). Observers, using a time-sampling procedure with ten-second intervals, recorded whether the child was attending to the task, emitting deviant behaviors such as arguing, screaming, hitting mother, or destroying items, or doing none of the above. Parental attention was also recorded, as well as whether it followed task-oriented behavior or deviant behavior.

The mothers were also given training in the use of differential attention procedures. The specific training varied from mother to mother, but written instructions, hand signals from an observer, and instructions given through a wireless microphone were used. The last approach involved

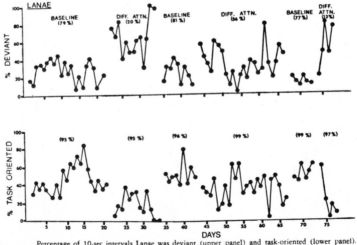

Percentage of 10-sec intervals Lanae was deviant (upper panel) and task-oriented (lower panel). The percentages of those behaviors followed by maternal attention appear in parentheses.

providing the mother with an FM radio with an earphone. The trainer then observed her interaction with her child from an adjoining room and provided instructions via a small, hand-held transmitter. The instructions and training generally involved having the parent ignore, turn away from, or walk away from the child when inappropriate behavior occurred. Appropriate behavior was to be praised.

Results

Data from one case are shown in the Figure. After a Baseline phase, the use of differential attention procedures produced an increase in deviant behaviors and a decrease in task-oriented behaviors. This pattern was consistent across two further shifts, from Baseline to differential attention phases.

Deviant behavior increased substantially in four of the six children when differential attention procedures were used by the mothers. Further, all children exhibited undesirable changes in some aspects of their behavior when differential attention was in effect. Four began assaulting their mothers, one rammed a pencil up his nose and bled profusely, one scratched herself until she bled, and another began dangerous climbing in the room. At home, one child became more enuretic, and another began urinating out his bedroom window, which faced a busy street.

The results suggest differential attention may not always produce beneficial effects.

Abstract 67

Effects of Token Economy on Neurotic Depression: An Experimental Analysis

MICHEL HERSEN, RICHARD EISLER (Veterans Administration Center), GEARY ALFORD and W. STEWART AGRAS (University of Mississippi Medical Center, Jackson) *Behavior Therapy*, 1973, 4, 392-397.

An interesting application of a token-economy procedure.

Individuals labeled neurotically depressed are those whose general behavior patterns are observed to be reduced in frequency and variety, and whose emotional responses are subdued or flat. From a behavioral viewpoint, a possible intervention would be to somehow stimulate an increased activity level, a condition that is incompatible with depressed behavior and shallow affect. Token economies have been used widely in institutional settings to treat a number of disorders, but to date there has been no direct test of their effectiveness with depression. This study examined the therapeutic influence of a token economy on the behavior of depressed people.

Method

SUBJECTS AND SETTING: Three hospitalized males experiencing recent losses and subsequent depression were selected as subjects. All were receiving drug therapy, as well.

PROCEDURE: Using an ABA reversal design, a token-economy program was established for the three subjects. Behavior measures were taken using the Behavioral Rating Scale (Williams, Barlow and Agras, 1972) by nursing assistants unfamiliar with the hypothesis. Three categories of behaviors, talking, smiling and motor activity, were rated for their absence (0) or presence (1) using a time-sampling technique.

Baseline: A token system was instituted in which subjects were awarded tokens for appropriate behavior, such as assuming minimal responsibility and maintaining personal hygiene, in a work setting off the ward or in occupational therapy. Tokens during this phase had no extrinsic value, however, and privileges were issued noncontingently.

Token Economy: Tokens in this condition represented a point system. Privileges were now contingent on a predetermined accumulation of points.

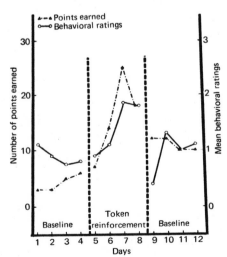

The second Baseline replicated the first. The second token-economy phase was not instituted because one subject was discharged and changes were made in the medication given the other two subjects.

Results

As indicated in Figures 1 and 2, the behaviors of subjects one and two were clearly affected by the token program. During both Baseline conditions, subjects accumulated fewer tokens and were engaged in fewer nondepressed behaviors (talking, smiling and motor activity). When privileges were contingent on accumulating tokens, however, these subjects participated much more actively. Data from subject three (Figure 3) does not show such a clear relationship. Although the subject definitely emits many more nondepressed behaviors during the token reinforcement phase, the first Baseline suggests that he was already improving in that direction.

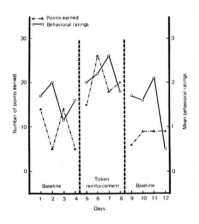

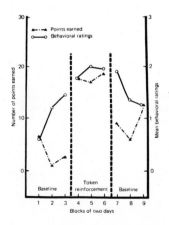

Abstract **68**

A Comparison of Tangible Reinforcement and Feedback Effects on the WPPSI IQ Scores of Nursery School Children

JERRY WILLIS (University of Western Ontario) and BEN SHIBATA, (University of Guelph) *Aportaciones al Analysis de la Conducta* (Comocho, Inesta, and Ruiz, eds.) Mexico City: Editorial Trillas, 1974, 454-475.

Raising I.Q. scores through token reinforcement.

Intelligence tests are often used as though the I.Q. scores obtained from them were direct measures of innate ability. This study assessed the effect of two modifications of the testing procedures on I.Q. scores.

Method

SUBJECTS AND SETTING: Thirty preschool children, 20 boys and 10 girls, in a day nursery for working-class parents, served as subjects. Ages ranged from three years, three months, to six years, six months.

PROCEDURE: All subjects were administered the Wechsler Preschool and Primary Scale of Intelligence (WPPSI) under the conditions specified in the test manual. They were then assigned to three retest conditions. The three groups were balanced for sex, age, and pretest I.Q.

Control Retest. Children in this group were readministered the test under standard conditions.

Feedback. Children in this group were informed of the correctness of their response. The examiner placed a pegboard in front of the child and explained that a peg would be placed in the board each time the child made a correct response. Four times during the test the children removed the pegs, counted them with the help of the examiner, and took a break from testing.

Reinforcement. The third group also received feedback as described above. In addition, four times during testing the children were able to take the pegs into an adjacent room and purchase small toys and edibles.

Results

An analysis of covariance using pretest I.Q.s as the covariate indicated significant differences between the three groups. Further analysis indicated that the Reinforcement group had significantly higher I.Q. scores than the other two groups. No other differences were significant. The results are graphically illustrated in Figure 1.

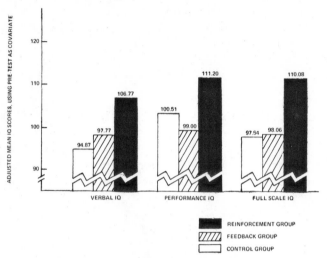

Figure 2 shows how the children in the groups would be classified by the pre- and retest. The pattern of classification remained stable for the control and feedback group. In contrast, the reinforcement group pretest scores indicated that half the group was either retarded or "dull normal," while retest scores placed all children in the average to very superior categories.

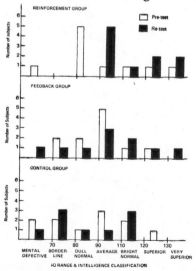

165

Abstract **69**

A Behaviorally-oriented, Didactic-Group Treatment of Obesity: An Exploratory Study

PHILIP BALCH (University of Arizona) and A. WILLIAM ROSS (University of South Carolina), *Therapy and Experimental Psychiatry*, 1974, *5*, 239-243.

Losing weight behaviorally.

Although there are hundreds, perhaps thousands, of weight-loss programs, few of them have ever been subjected to careful research evaluation. In fact, many of the studies that have been conducted used as subjects our old standby, college students, who were only mildly overweight. This study evaluated a behavioral weight-loss program in which a more typical subject sample was employed.

Method

SUBJECTS: Thirty-four females who responded to a newspaper advertisement served as subjects. All were overweight, averaging 35.3% over their ideal weight. Average age was 39.

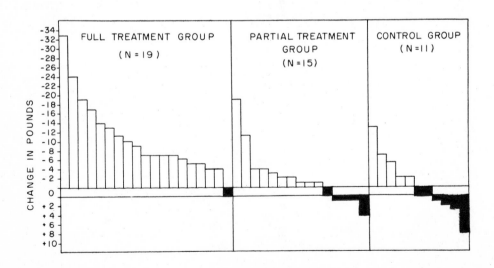

PROCEDURE: One group (Full Treatment) of 19 completed a nine-week treatment program based on *Slim Chance in a Fat World* (Richard B. Stuart and Barbara Davis, 1972, Research Press). Participants heard lectures on the problems of obesity and learned to record their daily food intake and their daily exercise on a special chart. They set goals in terms of the amount and type of food they would eat at each meal and the amount and type of exercise in which each participant engaged. They also selected reinforcers which they awarded themselves if they reached their goals.

A second group (Partial Treatment) of 15 was made up of people who attended up to six meetings (they averaged 3.5) but who dropped out before completing treatment. The final group (Control) was made up of 11 people who wanted to participate but could not attend because of scheduling difficulties.

Results

The pretreatment weight and obesity levels of the three groups were not significantly different. As the Figure shows, however, the Full Treatment group lost substantially more pounds than the other two groups.

Six weeks after the treatment ended this group had lost an additional 3.3 pounds per person.

Abstract **70**

Relative Efficacy of Self-Reward, Self-Punishment, and Self-Monitoring Techniques for Weight Loss

MICHAEL MAHONEY, NANCI MOURA, and TERRY WADE (Stanford University), *Journal of Consulting and Clinical Psychology*, 1973, 40, 404-407.

Evaluation of the components of self-control.

"Self-control" has become a popular topic of discussion and research. This study compared the effects of three aspects of self-control: self-reward, self-punishment, and self-monitoring on a common problem, obesity.

Method

SUBJECTS: Fifty-three subjects (48 female and five males) were selected from respondents to a newspaper ad. Average age was 40; average weight was 166 pounds, and the subjects were 13% to 130% overweight, with an average of 49%.

All participants had their physician's consent to participate, and none was enrolled in other weight-loss programs. The subjects were ranked according to level of obesity and then randomly assigned to groups.

PROCEDURE: All subjects paid a ten dollar deposit which was refunded at the end of the four-week treatment program. They were also given a booklet which described stimulus-control methods of weight loss. Five different variations of treatment were provided.

Self-Reward (N = 12). Subjects paid an additional $11.00, were asked to weigh in biweekly, and to keep a daily graph of their weight at home. They were also instructed to record the daily frequency of the following:

1. "fat" thoughts (discouraging self-verbalizations).
2. "thin" thoughts (encouraging self-verbalizations).
3. instances of eating fattening food or excessive intake.
4. instances of refusing fattening food or reducing food intake.

The $21.00 paid by each subject was considered 21 "shares" which could increase or decrease in value as the participants rewarded or refrained from rewarding themselves. At the biweekly weigh-ins, each person was given three shares, and it was recommended that participants self-reward themselves with two shares for a weight loss of one pound or more. The other share was to be rewarded if thin thoughts and instances of restraint (4 above) outnumbered nonadaptive behaviors (1 and 3 above).

When subjects did not reward themselves, their shares were added to the community pool and divided among the other participants. If subjects missed three weigh-ins, they were fined three shares for further absences.

Self-Punishment (N = 12). Subjects in this group were given the same program as the first group, except that instead of beginning with no shares in their account and accumulating shares by self-reward, they were given all 21 shares at the beginning of treatment and were instructed to punish themselves at each weigh-in for lack of weight loss and/or lack of behavior improvement.

Self-Reward and Self-Punishment (N = 8). Conditions for this group were a combination of the first two. Subjects began with no shares earned and could award or fine themselves up to three shares each weigh-in.

Self-Monitoring (N = 5). Conditions for this group were essentailly the same as in the first three groups, except that no additional deposit was required and no conditions of self-reward or self-reinforcement were used. The same bi-weekly weigh-ins were used, subjects were asked to record their behavior, and the same goals were suggested.

Information Control Group (N = 16). These subjects were given the booklet on weight loss but were not provided self-monitoring instructors, did not weigh-in biweekly, and did not self-reward themselves.

Results

Analysis of pre- and posttreatment weight indicated the self-reward group lost significantly more weight than the self-monitoring group, the self-reward and self-punishment group, and the control group. The self-punishment group was not significantly different from any group.

In all the groups that used either self-reward or self-punishment, there were frequent instances of inappropriate self-reward and/or failure to self-punish.

Thirty-one subjects were available at a four-month follow-up weigh-in. The self-reward and the combined group (self-reward and self-punishment) both lost a greater percentage of their body weight than the control group. The self-punishment group did not differ from the control group, and not enough subjects in the self-monitoring group were available for analysis. Over the four months the self-reward group lost an average of 11.5 pounds, the self-punishment group 7.3, the combined group 12.0, and the self-monitoring, 4.5. Controls lost 3.2 pounds.

Thus, self-reward may be a superior strategy given a choice between it and self-punishment or simply self-monitoring.

The authors also noted that in the self-reward group failing to self-reward when goals were not met (an appropriate behavior) was actually punished, because the subject's shares were divided among the other participants.

They suggested correction of this aspect of the system would result in more accurate self-reward.

Abstract 71

Behavior Modification and the Brat Syndrome

MARTHA BERNAL, JOHN DURYEE, HAROLD PRUETT and BE-VERLEE BURNS (University of California, Los Angeles), *Journal of Consulting and Clinical Psychology*, 1968, 4, 447-455.

Showing brattish behaviors can be learned and unlearned.

A brat is defined as a child "who often engages in tantrums, assaultiveness, threats, etc., which are highly aversive and serve to render others helpless in controlling him." Treatment is based on the assumption that brattish behaviors are learned and are maintained by the behavior of the child's parents.

Method

SUBJECT AND SETTING: Jeff was an eight-and-one-half-year-old only child attending a private school for the emotionally disturbed. Jeff was referred to an outpatient psychiatric clinic because of tantrums and physical attacks against his mother, teachers, and peers. At school he was demanding and often bullied or tattled on other children. He suffered from skin allergies and frequent respiratory problems; his behavior patterns included wetting the bed, odd speech patterns, and peculiar rocking movements. His measured I.Q. was above average, however, and he had a large vocabulary. Jeff's parents had experienced marital difficulties for several years and were separated when treatment began.

PROCEDURE: Jeff and his mother were seen in the clinic for five sessions. During those sessions, the therapist would discuss with Jeff's mother the treatment plan, give instructions, and replay parts of videotapes made during the previous session, to illustrate points or suggest changes. Then the mother joined Jeff, and they were videotaped for about 15 minutes. During taping, a brief tone was played over an intercom to signal the mother when she reinforced Jeff's abusive behavior. After taping, the mother was warmly praised for appropriate performance.

Pretreatment observations of the interaction between Jeff and his mother indicated she consistently responded to him in a weak, monotone voice, even when correcting him. In fact, she tried to pacify Jeff at almost any cost. Neither Jeff nor his mother expressed warmth or affection toward each other.

Several specific instructions were given to the mother during treatment, as follows:

First, she was taught to ignore Jeff's abusive behavior, including sulking and physical assault. Second, she was taught to emit a series of cues for Jeff which signaled that she did not approve of his behavior. If ignoring did not stop the behavior, she expressed anger through frowning and, with an angry tone of voice, told Jeff to stop the behavior. If the behavior still did not cease, she was instructed to spank Jeff. The therapist hoped that the mother's instructions to stop would become conditioned negative reinforcers because they were consistently followed by a punishment, spanking. The third set of instructions required the mother to identify positive behaviors emitted by Jeff, to respond with warmth and praise, and to tell him precisely what behaviors she liked.

Results

Videotapes of mother-child interactions made before (one session), during (five sessions) and after (one) treatment were scored for several behaviors, including abusive and obedient behavior by Jeff, and ignoring and affectionate behavior by his mother.

A time sampling procedure was used. The tapes were divided into 30-second intervals. Each interval in which a behavior occurred once or more was scored for that behavior. The data showed that Jeff's inappropriate behavior decreased markedly and obedience to commands increased from zero to 100%. His mother ignored 11% of his abusive behavior initially, but by the end of treatment she ignored 100% of it. She expressed no affection during the early part of treatment, while 20% of the post-treatment intervals included affection.

Treatment 2

In a subsequent series of treatments, the mother and Jeff were seen for two more sessions along with a nine-and-one-half-year-old boy, Albert, who often played with Jeff. The mother reported she could not handle Jeff when Albert was present. Observations in the clinic indicated she was not ignoring Jeff's abusive behavior and was not using the cues taught her. When Jeff became difficult, she would often turn to Albert and interact with him rather than with Jeff. In addition, she attempted to induce Albert to handle Jeff's problems. For example, she would instruct Albert to hit Jeff back to avoid dealing with Jeff's aggression herself.

The mother was given instructions on basic behavior modification, with examples from videotapes to illustrate concepts. Tapes were also reviewed, and the mother asked to stop the tape and describe a different manner by which problems could be handled. She was also praised for direct interventions with Jeff.

Results (Treatment 2)

Data from the videotapes again indicated major improvements in the target behaviors of both Jeff and his mother.

From one week before to eight weeks after treatment, Jeff's mother kept extensive records of occurrences of Jeff's abusive behavior at home. According to these data, abusive behavior decreased dramatically after treatment.

Abstract **72**

Teaching Adaptive Responses to Frustration to Emotionally Disturbed Boys

JOHN GEIBINK (University of Wisconsin), DONALD STOVER, and MARY ANN FAHL (Wisconsin Children's Treatment Center), *Journal of Consulting and Clinical Psychology*, 1968, 32, 366-368.

A positive alternative to punishment of aggression.

Aggression is a primary characteristic of children referred to psychological and psychiatric services. In most cases, these aggressive behaviors are responses to situations that are considered frustrating to the child. This study attempted to teach children in a residential treatment center alternatives to aggression when they faced disappointing situations.

Method

SUBJECTS AND SETTING: Six boys, ages 10 to 12, who were in a residential treatment center using behavior modification, served as subjects. Four were diagnosed as neurotic and two as schizophrenic. They had been at the center for an average of one year.

PROCEDURE: The experimenters and the cottage staff who collectively supervised the children developed a set of 14 common situations in which the children often acted aggressively. Two examples are, "Your favorite TV program is coming on, but the staff says you can't watch it"; and, "You're ready for your teacher to check your workbook, and he keeps helping another child with a very simple problem." Eight of the situations that could be easily observed in the center were assigned either to a training condition or to a control no training condition.

The six boys were randomly divided into two groups of three each. All children completed a "Frustration Questionnaire," which involved describing what they could do in the situations. They were also observed in each of the eight situations, and their behavior categorized as adaptive or not. The questionnaire and observations were obtained the week before treatment, after the first group received treatment the following week, and at the end of the third week when the second group completed its treatment.

Treatment consisted of teaching the boys five alternative ways of behaving in each of the four situations selected for treatment. The vehicle for instruction was a game similar to commercial games played regularly by the children. Each player began at a common starting point and threw dice to determine how many spaces he would move toward the end goal. Landing on some spaces resulted in the child receiving a response card that had an alternative response to one of the frustrating situations written on it. If the child later landed on a space that described that situation, he received a bonus or surprise if he could produce a response card that matched the situation. The boys played the games about four times, with a snack following the completion of each game.

Results

The small number of subjects precluded use of inferential statistics. Each group increased its number of trained responses to the questionnaire only after experiencing treatment. The mean number of adaptive responses given increased from 8.8 to 10.2, while inappropriate responses decreased from a mean of 3.2 per child for all four items to a mean of 1.2. Finally, the behavioral observations indicated that the social appropriateness of the responses increased for the four experimental situations, but not for the control situations.

Abstract 73

Programming Response Maintenance
after Withdrawing Token Reinforcement

RUSSELL JONES and ALAN KAZDIN (Pennsylvania State University), *Behavior Therapy*, 1975, *6*, 153-164.

Maintenance of positive gains after cessation of treatment.

Although there are a great many studies showing that token reinforcement can lead to improvement in a variety of behaviors, there are few data on the question of what happens after token systems are terminated. Basic operant principles would suggest that withdrawal of the reinforcing consequences for a behavior would lead to its extinction. This study raises the question as to whether extinction can be prevented by systematic application of treatment procedures geared to making the behavioral changes more durable.

Method

SUBJECTS AND SETTING: Four educable, mentally retarded children (two boys and two girls) attending a demonstration school on a university campus served as subjects. Their teacher reported that they frequently emitted undesirable behaviors in class, such as not attending to the lesson and moving about excessively. During the study the students were observed for 30 minutes in the morning, during a reading lesson, and for 60 minutes in the afternoon, during art or a discussion period. One observer was assigned to two students and would observe one student for 15 seconds and the other for the next 15 seconds. Two categories of behavior were measured: Movements (undesirable seat behavior, such as placing feet on the desk, rocking the chair, or engaging in repetitive body movements back and forth in the chair) and Posture (sitting slumped in the chair, or facing away from the lesson).

PROCEDURE: After a Baseline period which lasted 11 days for the morning sessions and 18 days for those in the afternoon, a token-reinforcement procedure was begun by the teacher. The teacher set a wrist timer, which rang on the average of every seven minutes in the morning (when a great deal of undesirable behavior occurred), and every 20 minutes in the afternoon. When the timer rang, each child who was behaving appropriately was given a token (a plastic chip), and receipt of the token was recorded on a large colorful chart on the classroom wall. Tokens could be used to purchase backup reinforcers such as free time, painting, recess, and access to toys and records. The variable interval-seven minute (VI-7) schedule used in the 30-minute morning session provided four opportunities to earn a token, while the VI-20 schedule in the 60-minute afternoon session provided three opportunities. Initially, each child was required to earn only one token during the morning to receive a backup reinforcer. Once reinforcement was earned, however, the child was required to earn one more token than on the previous day. Finally, each child was required to earn tokens every time the opportunity occurred. This phase lasted for 15 days in the morning and eight days in the afternoon.

Response Maintenance Programming. When the target behaviors had improved, two steps were taken to make the changes more durable. As the token system was removed, peer and teacher attention were programmed into the classroom routine. In addition, the use of tokens and their importance was gradually faded rather than being withdrawn abruptly.

To raise the interest of the other children in the class, the reinforcers awarded to the four target children were made available to all children during the afternoon sessions. All children were awarded tokens for appropriate behavior after the timer rang. This was not done in the morning session because the four students were reinforced in a reading group which included no other children. Children who received all the possible tokens came to the front of the class and were applauded by their peers and given verbal praise by the teacher. In addition, backup reinforcers were made intermittent. Instead of being available every day, they occurred on only three days each week. On days when no reinforcer was provided, the tokens were simply collected at the end of the day.

After five days of the response maintenance program, tokens were dropped completely, and the teacher announced, "You are all such good children, we no longer need tokens for you to behave like big people." She then told the class that if the four target students were "good all day" the class would receive a reinforcing event (a movie, ice cream, recess). No tokens were given to the four students, but the teacher continued to award praise on a variable interval schedule. In addition, each target child's behavior was announced at the end of the morning and afternoon sessions and they were individually applauded if they had a good day.

Results

The Figure shows the percentage of inappropriate behavior for the four children during the experiment. The initial token-reinforcement system produced a marked improvement in behavior. Over the next two phases, tokens were intermittently rewarded and then dropped completely, without the loss of improvement. Two follow-up periods, which covered twelve calendar weeks after the formal treatment program ended (including peer praise and group contingencies), indicated that the changes produced by the token system were maintained after treatment was withdrawn.

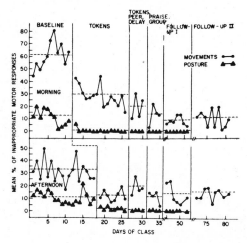

Abstract **74**

Setting Generality: Some Specific and
General Effects of Child Behavior Therapy

ROBERT WAHLER (University of Tennessee), *Journal of Applied Behavior Analysis,* 1969, 2, 239-246.

The effects of behavior modification outside the treatment center.

Does the use of behavior modification procedures in one setting affect behavior elsewhere? The question of generalization is the focus of this research.

Method

SUBJECTS AND SETTING: Two boys, Steve, age five, and Louis, age eight, were referred to an outpatient clinic by their teachers. The parents of both boys reported they were experiencing problems at home, as well. The boys were observed once a week in school and once at home. Steve's behavior was scored as either oppositional or cooperative for each 10-second interval of the 30-minute observation period. Louis' behavior was scored as either studying or disruptive. For both children, a 10-second interval was scored positively (cooperative or studying) only if behavior was appropriate across the entire interval.

PROCEDURE: After a five-week Baseline, the parents were trained to use behavioral methods to control behavior in the home. Reinforcement of appropriate behavior, ignoring of inappropriate behavior, and use of time out for particularly difficult behavior were emphasized. This training was subsequently provided to the teachers, as well. Throughout Baseline and treatment, the relevant behaviors of both parents and teachers were recorded.

Results

Training increased Steve's parents' use of behavior modification procedures during the phase following Baseline. Teacher use remained low until the fourth phase, when she was trained.

The data collected on Steve's behavior is shown in the Figure. Although home behavior improved when the parents were trained, there was no generalization to the school, and home behavior returned to Baseline levels when his parents stopped using the techniques. School behavior improved only after the teacher instituted treatment in the classroom. Similar results were obtained for Louis, as well.

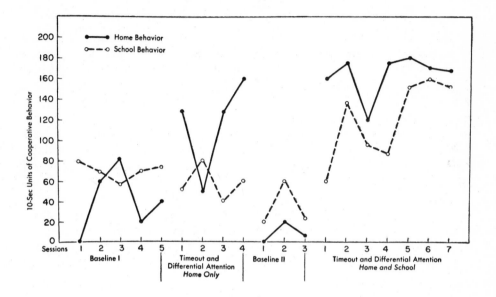

Abstract **75**

Strategy of Multiple-Baseline Evaluation: Illustrations from a Summer Camp

HENRY RICKARD and NANCY TAYLOR (University of Alabama), *Perceptual and Motor Skills*, 1974, *39*, 875-881.

A research design in which treatment does not have to be withdrawn.

The most commonly-used single subject requires the research design experimenter to remove the treatment for a short period after it becomes effective, in order to demonstrate that the target behavior "reverses" or returns to Baseline when the treatment is removed. Although popular, the reversal design is often difficult to use in applied settings for a number of reasons. Teachers and parents are frequently reluctant to stop treatment "in the interest of science" once behavior such as tantrums, self-mutilation, or fighting improves.

This study demonstrates the use of an alternative, the multiple-baseline design, which does not require removal of treatment.

Method

SUBJECTS AND SETTING: The research was conducted in a summer camp for emotionally-disturbed children. The campers were divided into groups according to age. Group 1 consisted of eight boys, ages 12 to 13; group 2 had eight boys, ages 13 to 15; and group 3 had nine girls, 8 to 13, and ten boys, 7 to 8.

PROCEDURE: The campers attended class five days a week throughout the seven-week camp and worked with programmed texts. Most students were assigned to reading or mathematics programs. Two teachers supervised the classroom and recorded the number of responses each student made to the text material.

Baseline. During the initial phase, classes were a uniform 40 minutes in length. Each group came to class at a separate time. Near the end of class, students took a brief, informal test of the work they had completed that day. If they scored less than 80%, they were required to complete the work again the following day.

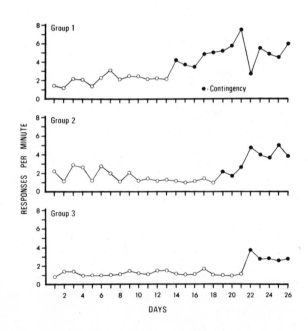

Treatment. A contingency-management approach was used. The children were told they could continue under Baseline conditions if they wished and remain in class for 40 minutes. Alternatively, they could make a verbal contract with the teachers to complete a specified amount of work (usually their Baseline level plus 10%) and leave class as soon as this was finished and they had passed the informal test with 80% or better. All subjects chose to contract work and leave early.

Results

A primary characteristic of the multiple baseline is the initiation of treatment at different times. As shown in the Figure, treatment was begun on day 14 for group 1, 19 for group 2, and 22 for group 3. The results indicate the treatment produced an increase in the first group when it was introduced, while the other groups remained at Baseline levels. As contracting was instituted in the remaining groups, their rate of response also increased.

Abstract 76

An Experimental Analysis of Feedback to Increase Sexual Arousal in a Case of Homo- and Heterosexual Impotence

STEVEN HERMAN and MICHAEL PREWETT, (Miami Veterans Administration Hospital), *Journal of Behavior Therapy and Experimental Psychiatry*, 1974, 5, 271-274.

Knowledge of results improves sexual functioning.

Few of us go through the day without receiving some form of feedback. Broadly defined, feedback is simply information we receive about the effects of our own behavior. Many jobs have built-in feedback systems. A secretary, for example, receives feedback when checking a letter for errors. If an error is missed, the secretary's employer may become a second, less immediate, source of feedback. Feedback is also the hallmark of programed instruction. Students make responses and then learn immediately whether their response is correct or incorrect.

In the present study, this rather commonplace technique is used in a very unusual way.

Method

SUBJECT: An adult male, age 51, was the subject. He had a history of homosexual behavior since the age of 13. He had always had difficulty maintaining an erection, however, during either homosexual or heterosexual contact. A short, unsuccessful marriage was never consummated. At the point of treatment he had difficulty maintaining an erection, even during masturbation, and seldom attempted any sexual activity.

PROCEDURE: Using a reversal design, the researchers evaluated the effects of providing the client with feedback about penile circumference as he attempted to achieve an erection. The client sat in a comfortable chair and watched a set of ten lights. As his penis became more erect, more lights came on. If it began to deflate, the lights went out, one by one. Each session during treatment consisted of four trials of feedback, each lasting about three minutes. The client was simply instructed to concentrate on getting an erection, and the degree of erection attained was measured by a special instrument which was clipped around the client's penis and attached to a polygraph. Thirty minutes after each session, penile erection was measured as the client watched slides of attractive nude males and females.

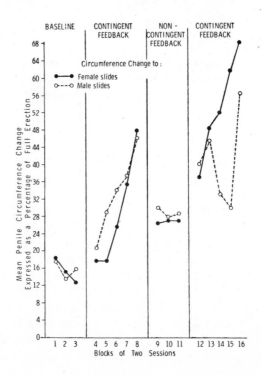

Results

The Figure shows the degree of erection obtained during the experiment as the client viewed the slides. Before feedback treatment began (Baseline) the level was below 20% of full erection. After feedback was begun, the percent of erection increased markedly. During a reversal phase, when the operation of the lights was not related to penile circumference, the trend reversed. Reinstitution of feedback produced an accelerating rate of erection.

During treatment the client also reported that he began to masturbate successfully, dated a female, and had two successful homosexual encounters.

Abstract 77

Fading to Increase Heterosexual Responsiveness in Homosexuals

DAVID BARLOW and W. STEWART AGRAS (University of Mississippi Medical Center), *Journal of Applied Behavior Analysis*, 1973, 6, 355-366.

Changing sexual preference without punishment.

Programs to modify sexual preferences have often relied on the use of aversive procedures. For example, efforts to change the preferences of homosexual clients have often paired slides of homosexual scenes with shock. When a heterosexual slide was shown the shock ceased.

The present study is an attempt to develop more positive procedures, based on the operant principle of fading.

Method

SUBJECTS AND SETTING: Three male clients who requested help in changing their sex-partner preference from male to female were the subjects. They were between the ages of 21 and 30, and had long histories of homosexual behavior. Treatment was conducted in a medical center.

PROCEDURE: Two types of data were collected. One, penile curcumference, was measured while the client observed a set of slides depicting homo- and heterosexual scenes. Using a specially constructed strain gauge which was placed around the shaft of the penis, the experimenters were able to measure the degree of erection.

The clients were also asked to record daily in a notebook the number of times they were sexually aroused by the sight of a female ("urges") and the number of times they had heterosexual fantasies or engaged in heterosexual behavior. All clients were seen individually.

Baseline. During the first six sessions no treatment was provided. Penile circumference, however, was measured in a "generalization" test session. The client chose slides of 30 male and 30 female which were most attractive or least unattractive to him. During the generalization session, the client saw for two minutes each three male and three female slides, randomly chosen from the sets of 30 selected previously. There was a minimum 30-second interval between each slide which allowed the penis to return to Baseline levels of erection. When treatment began, the generalization sessions were given the morning following afternoon treatment.

Fading. Clients were told that they would see slides of nude females and males to help them reorient their sexual preferences. Each client selected two slides, one male and one female, which he considered most attractive or least unattractice. Using two slide projectors, both slides were shown at varying levels of intensity.For all three clients fading began with the male slide shown at 100% illumination and the female at 0%. The intensity of the female slide was gradually increased while that of the male decreased. Figure 1 shows five of the steps from zero to 100% illumination for the two slides of one client. Sixteen steps were used in the study, and movement from one step to the next occurred when at any time during the two-minute presentation of each step penile erection reached 75%. If erection did not reach the criterion of 75%, the step was shown for additional two-minute periods until the erection occurred. Each daily session involved six two-minute periods.

Results

All three clients increased their degree of erection to the female slides and maintained at least 75% erection with the female slide illuminated at 100% and the male slide at 0%.

Figure 2 shows the generalization session, penile-circumference data for one of the clients. Response to female slides was low during Baseline and increased when the fading procedure began. When fading was discontinued for six days, and the client simply viewed one slide at 100% illumination for one minute and then the other for one minute, the response

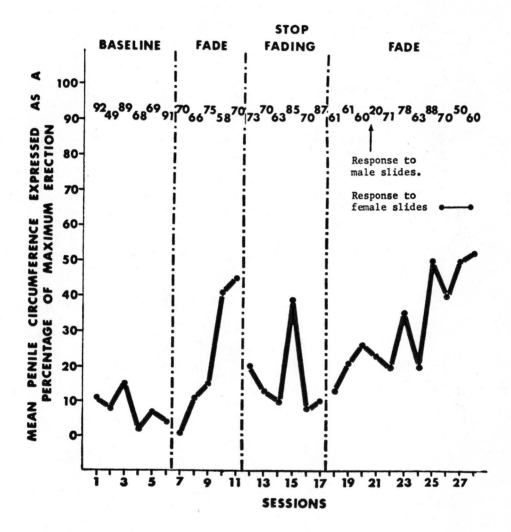

to the female slides decreased. It rose again when fading resumed. The other two subjects had similar patterns. Responses to male slides were generally high throughout the study, with little indication that they were decreasing. Urges and fantasy episodes of a heterosexual nature increased from .5 per day to above 2 per day for one client; another client reported no urges and fantasies during Baseline and a rate of 1.5 per day at the end of the treatment.

The third subject reported no heterosexual urges or fantasies during the study.

Follow-up showed varying degrees of success in changing sexual preference. One client reported continued strong homosexual arousal and was given a series of aversive treatment as well. He still did not approach women, and one year after treatment reported little contact with either males or females. The remaining two clients made heterosexual contacts and began having intercourse regularly. Both reported no homosexual arousal.

CHAPTER VI

Institutional Programs
of
Behavioral Change

Abstract 78

Mimosa Cottage: Experiment in Hope

JAMES LENT (Parsons State Hospital), *Psychology Today*, 1968, 2, 51-58.

A program to return retarded residents of institutions to the community.

A great many programs of behavior modification in institutions seem to be designed to help the person fit in the institution. The Mimosa Cottage Project is an excellent example of the opposite approach. Its developers identified and taught behaviors that would help retarded women fit in the community.

Method

SUBJECTS AND SETTING: Mimosa Cottage is an experimental residental unit at Parsons State Hospital, an institution for the mentally retarded with IQ's between 25 and 55. Seventy-one residents in three age groups (8-12, 12-16, 16-21) participated.

PROCEDURE: At the beginning of the study, research assistants observed the dress and behavior of people in the surrounding community in order to identify behavioral deficits many residents had. Four areas, personal appearance, occupational skills, social behavior, and academic skills, were selected for training.

The four areas were broken down into small, precisely-defined behaviors. The residents could earn tokens by participating in training programs designed to improve their skills in those areas. The token programs and the training itself were adapted to the level of the resident, so that younger or less capable residents had a simplified program, while older residents participated in a token program that required them to use the tokens as money and to become familiar with simple banking procedures. Tokens were earned for appropriate learning behavior and could be lost for inappropriate behavior.

Each of the general areas of training involved several subcomponents. For example, one area under personal appearance was concerned with wearing appropriately-fitting, coordinated clothes. Matching colors and patterns in clothes was one part of the training. Residents watched a movie in which many different combinations of apparel were presented. If they could not discriminate between appropriate and inappropriate combinations, they were given training in color and pattern matching and in selecting clothes appropriate to the season. The movie was administered after training as a posttest. Other areas, such as care of hair, posture, domestic skills such as sewing and cooking, heterosexual behavior, speech and language skills, and social skills, were taught in a similar manner.

Because generalization of improved behavior was a problem, it was often necessary to begin training in an artifical setting on simple tasks and gradually progress to more "real-life" training in the natural environment.

In addition to the general training programs used at Mimosa Cottage, individual behavior modification programs were developed to deal with particular problems (e.g., tantrums) of some residents.

Results

Figure 1 shows data from two years in seven general areas. During 1965-66 improvement occurred in most areas, except verbal and social behavior. Training programs were therefore revised and more attention to those areas was given during the next year. Improvement occurred in those areas during the second year, but at the expense of some other areas that declined. Several areas in which declines occurred were those in which the residents had reached high levels of skills, so that the decrease was not as serious as it might have been.

At the time the paper was written, twelve of the Mimosa Cottage residents had returned to the community.

Although the program cost $35,000 more per year than the regular hospital program, each resident who received training was able to live in the community, thus saving the taxpayer about $100,000 in cost of institutional care per patient.

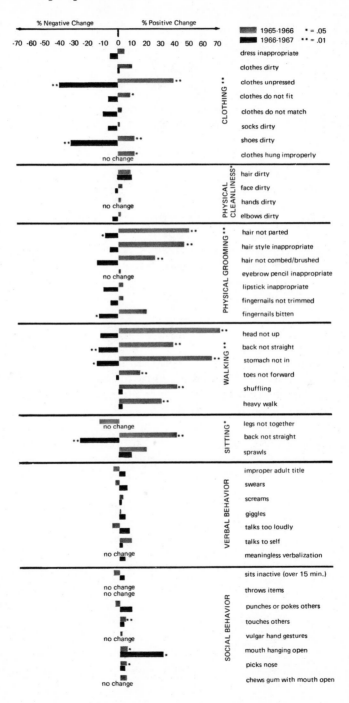

Abstract **79**

The Development of Socialization Skills in an Electively Mute Child

PHILLIP BLAKE and THELMA MOSS (Neuropsychiatric Institute, University of California, Los Angeles). *Behaviour Research and Therapy*, 1967, 5, 349-356.

Training a mute child in the fundamentals of speech.

Treatment of children who are autistic or severely disturbed is extremely difficult. A prime problem lies in developing effective teaching techniques; another area involves overcoming such behaviors as tantrums, crying, and rocking, in order to train adaptive skills. This study focuses on those problems in one electively mute child.

Method

SUBJECT: A four-year-old electively-mute girl who would make only four sounds, similar to babbling, and who imitated neither verbal nor non-verbal behavior, was selected as subject. She was often disruptive, emitting tantrum, crying, and rocking behaviors.

PROCEDURE: The experiment involved four stages: 1) Baseline occurrence of vocalizations in the subject's (Dolly) repertoire; 2) extinction of disruptive behavior; 3) shaping eye contact and following instruction; 4) training nonverbal behavior and two meaningful verbal responses. These stages overlapped.

Stage 1 (Session 1): Possible reinforcers and verbal behavior available to Dolly were assessed initially through use of a color organ. The lights of the organ flashed only when Dolly made sounds, at first crying, which gradually changed to verbal sounds such as "s" and "ah".

Stage 2 (Sessions 1-9): Because Dolly was very disruptive, it was decided to extinguish this behavior so that adaptive ones could be trained. Dolly was placed in a booth with a partition separating her and the experimenter. Her side was dark so that her only access to light was when the shutter between the experimenter and Dolly was lifted. For eight sessions the shutter remained closed until Dolly stopped crying. When Dolly stopped for a minimum of three seconds, the shutter opened, the experimenter said

"Hi Dolly!" and offered her some sugar-coated cereal. The shutter was lowered again when she began crying. In the ninth session, the procedure was repeated, except when Dolly cried, the experimenter said "Stop crying, Dolly." If she stopped within three seconds, the shutter remained open. Otherwise it was closed for 15 seconds.

Stage 3 (Sessions 10-20): In session ten, eye contact was shaped by reinforcing Dolly for it with a spoonful of ice cream. Dolly's half of the booth was dark; every 15 seconds the shutter opened and the experimenter said "Hi Dolly—look at me." If Dolly looked, she was rewarded; if she did not, the shutter was closed for 15 seconds. Sessions 11 through 20 focused on training handclapping and inducing Dolly to pull the experimenter's ear (these tasks conceptually involved initiating imitative behavior, social contact, and obeying commands). Both were accomplished through fading. At first, the experimenter moved Dolly's hands to the appropriate place (hands or ear) and rewarded her. Gradually, experimenter involvement was reduced. Sessions 12 through 20 also included reinforcing approximations to the appropriate use of the verbal response, "Hi!"

Stage 4 (Sessions 21-40): Dolly was reinforced for successive approximations to the word "eat." In session 40, all four responses that had been targeted were reviewed: "Hi!" "eat" (actually pronounced "ee" by Dolly), handclapping, and pulling on the experimenter's ear. From session 21 to the conclusion, "social" sessions were held outside the booth between the experimenter and Dolly.

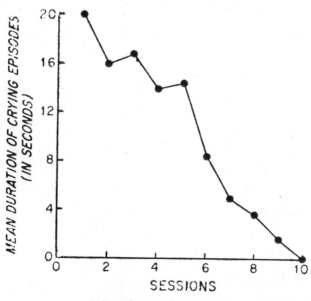

Extinction of operant crying.

Results

Dolly's crying responses are represented in the Figure above. By Session 10 they had been extinguished. The Figure below represents the number of responses Dolly made to the prompts for handclapping, ear pulling, and saying "Hi!" Handclapping shows a fairly steady increase, as does ear pulling, except in Session 14. Dolly was ill that day. The response "Hi!" increased rapidly and steadily. Finally, the rate of verbal responses, "Hi" and "ee" (eat), throughout the sessions, where these were the target behaviors. "Hi" showed a rapid and dramatic increase, while "ee" increased steadily and substantially to a total of 40 in 30 minutes.

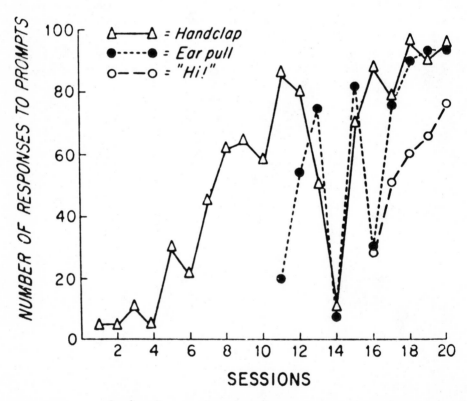

Imitative responses over twenty sessions.

Abstract **80**

Development and Evaluation of an Interpersonal Skill-Training Program for Psychiatric Inpatients

JEAN GOLDSMITH (Illinois State Psychiatric Institute) and RICHARD MCFALL (University of Wisconsin, Madison), *Journal of Abnormal Psychology*, 1975, *84*, 51-58.

A positive approach to rehabilitating psychiatric patients.

Training in social skills is a general therapeutic procedure in psychiatric hospitals, aimed at improving the participant's ability to handle critical life situations. Training techniques in this type of therapy utilize an educational approach. The rationale for this approach is the assumption that problems in handling life situations are due to a lack of mastering learnable skills, just as illiteracy is due to a failure to learn the skill of reading. This study is one of the few to include evaluation of the content of what was taught, as well as the methods used.

Method 1

The first phase of the study involved systematic development of the program to be taught. Through rating scales and personal interviews, outpatients in a psychiatric hospital described interpersonal situations in which they had difficulty (e. g., dating, having job interviews, relating to authorities, making personal disclosures, handling conversational silences). Then male inpatients in a psychiatric hospital rated each situation on a scale, indicating the degree to which it caused them difficulty. To obtain appropriate responses to the problem situations, eight male staff members of a psychiatric hospital listened to audiotaped presentations of the situations and then role-played how they would react. The eight responses to each of 55 situations were then rated in terms of effectiveness by five additional staff. Responses were considered effective if they were rated competent by four of the five judges. Forty-four of the 55 situations had at least one effective response. Each judge was also asked to specify why he felt a response was effective or ineffective. From these rationales, a set of principles governing effective behavior was derived. They stated both what behavior should occur and what behavior should not occur. The principles were used to coach subjects in the following section of the study and were also used as criteria for scoring responses.

Thus, this phase produced a list of problematic interpersonal situations, a list of effective responses, principles governing effective behaviors in these situations, and a scoring manual for evaluating responses to the problem.

Method 2

SUBJECTS AND SETTING: Thirty-six inpatients on a psychiatric ward of a Veterans' Hospital were randomly assigned to one of three treatment conditions.

PROCEDURE:

Interpersonal Skills Training: Subjects attended three individual one-hour training sessions over a five-day period. Fifteen minutes were spent covering each of 11 problem social situations, with 15 minutes of review at the end of training. Several training procedures were used, including behavior rehearsal, modeling, coaching, recording responses, playback, and corrective feedback. Each situation was dealt with using the following sequence:

1. The subject listened to a description of the problem situation and was coached about the principles of effective behavior in that situation.
2. He then heard a competent response by a male model, a review of the training, and a discussion of the likely consequences of different manners of responding.
3. The therapist then stopped the recorder and discussed the material with the subject. When the subject agreed to practice a response, the recorded situation was replayed, and the subject rehearsed a solution. When the response was played back, the subject and then the experimenter provided corrective feedback, indicating what could be improved. The rehearsal-feedback procedure was continued until both the subject and the therapist agreed that the solution was effective for two successive rehearsals.
4. Training then began on a new situation or on another segment of the same situation.

Pseudotherapy Control: Subjects in this condition attended the same number of sessions and heard the same audiotapes, but they were not given training in response alternatives. Instead, they were encouraged to explore their feelings and look for insights into why they had such feelings.

Assessment-only Control: These subjects received only the pre- and posttreatment assessments.

Pre- and Post-Assessment Instruments: One day after the last treatment session, each subject took the Interpersonal Behavior Roleplaying Test, which was also administered before the training began. The test involved role-playing responses to common social situations which were previously identified as difficult ones for this population. Assessment-only controls were tested for these subjects at the same point in time as those for a corresponding group member.

Subjects also completed rating scales which indicated how comfortable they felt generally, how they rated their social ability, and how comfortable they would feel in 55 problematic interpersonal situations.

Finally, each subject was given a simulated real-life situation in which he was asked to carry on a general conversation with a male stranger, who was a confederate of the experimenter. The confederate and the subject then rated the comfort and ability of the subject during the previous ten-minute conversation.

Results

There were no significant pretreatment differences among the groups. Posttreatment measures were generally in favor of the skill-training group. Self-report measures indicated they were more confident and evaluated themselves more highly. On the role-playing test, the skill-training group improved more than the two control groups, neither of which changed significantly. This improvement on the part of the skill-training group occurred in the 11 situations in which they were trained, as well as 11 in which they were not trained. Finally, ratings by the subject and confederate in the simulated real-life situation indicated the skill-training group was more comfortable and more skillful than either of the control groups.

Abstract **81**

Token Control of Pill-Taking Behavior
in a Psychiatric Ward

JOHN PARRINO, LEN GEORGE, and AUBREY DANIELS (Georgia
Regional Hospital at Atlanta), *Journal of Behavior Therapy
and Experimental Psychiatry*, 1971, 2, 181-185.

Reducing the amount of medication requested by patient.

Token systems have been used to increase many different types of
behaviors in psychiatric hospitals. In this study, however, the goal was a
reduction of a behavior—pill-taking.

Method

SUBJECTS AND SETTING: Thirty-eight patients (19 males and 19 females) in
a token-economy unit of a state mental hospital participated in the study.
PROCEDURE: Patients on the unit participated in a token-economy which
reinforced such behaviors as personal grooming and cleaning their rooms,
as well as behaviors selected individually for each person. Patients spent
the earned tokens on such privileges as weekend leave, television viewing,
and items from a "token store." The staff was concerned about the amount
of medication taken by many patients on an "as needed" basis. Many had a
habit of taking sleeping pills, minor tranquilizers, aspirins, and other
medication which the unit physician and unit staff agreed were unnecessary. This study was concerned with unnecessary medication only and did
not involve interference in the taking of any medication the patient's
physician felt was necessary, regardless of whether it was scheduled to be
given at regular intervals or at the request of the patient.

　　Baseline. The number of medications taken by patients on the unit was
measured for four weeks prior to institution of the token economy.

　　Phase I Token System: Eleven weeks after Baseline, a token system was
introduced. Patients were charged two tokens for medication requested
outside the four, regularly-scheduled, 30-minute periods for medication
each day. (The patients could earn a total of 16 tokens each day.)

　　Phase II Token System: For the next six weeks, patients were charged two tokens for medication requested at the scheduled times and four tokens for that requested at other times.

Phase III Token System: For the remaining three weeks of the study, all requests for medication cost four tokens.

Results

The Figure shows the number of medications taken during the study. The amount of medication taken was consistently higher for women patients than for men. Charging for medication produced a large drop in pill taking, with the lowest level reached in the token system that charged most.

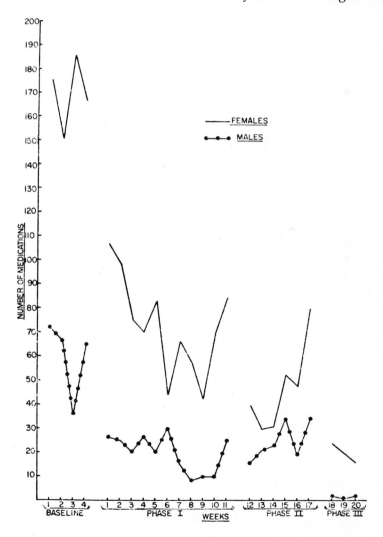

Abstract **82**

Restitution: A Method of Eliminating Aggressive-Disruptive Behavior of Retarded and Brain Damaged Patients

R. M. FOXX and NATHAN AZRIN (Anna State Hospital), *Behaviour Research and Therapy*, 1972, *10*, 15-27

Systematic use of relevant consequences.

The management of aggressive and destructive behavior is a problem common to many settings, including the home, the classroom, the wards of hospitals and institutions for the retarded, and facilities for offenders. Although punishment procedures such as electric shock and time out have been used successfully, the potential side effects of the available techniques (e.g., providing models for aggression) and the potential for misuse has limited their systematic application. In this study an alternative, restitution (sometimes called overcorrection), is proposed. Restitution involves restoring the environment to its original state, plus an improvement. Thus, a person who threw his meal on the floor of the dining hall would be required to clean up the mess produced and to leave the area cleaner than it was before the incident. When the problem is a disturbance in the psychological environment as opposed to the physical environment, the offender is still required to restore the environment to a "better-than-before" condition. For example, if a person is abusive and threatening, so that fear or anxiety is produced, the offender might be required to apologize and assure the people threatened that nothing will happen. He or she might then be required to reassure and apologize to other people present, as well. There are several advantages to the procedure: It fits the punishment directly to the undesirable behavior; it occurs immediately; and it requires the person to actually do something, rather than passively receive a punishment.

Method

SUBJECTS AND SETTING: Three case studies were presented in the original article, only one of which is reported here. The work took place in a unit of a state hospital and was carried out by the staff of the unit with the assistance of one of the authors.

The subject of the study described here was a fifty-year-old profoundly-retarded female, with an IQ of 16, who had been hospitalized for 46 years. She had several physical disabilities, including epilepsy and impaired hearing. Her speech consisted of one phrase, "I want to eat," which was repeated throughout the day. Since the age of 13 the patient, Ann, had been a major problem because she damaged furniture by throwing or upsetting beds, chairs, and tables. She was excluded from most ward and educational activities because of the problem. Many attempts to change her behavior through the use of time out, physical restraint, and even requiring her to upright the overturned furniture had been unsuccessful.

PROCEDURE: During an eight-day Baseline, Ann was verbally chastised for her problem behavior and required to restore the furniture to its original position.

After eight days, the restitution program began. When Ann overturned a bed, she was given a 30-minute restitution program. First, she restored the upset furniture; then she remade the bed completely and neatly; finally, she straightened up and pushed against the wall all the beds on the ward. If a table or chair was overturned, she righted it and then straightened all other tables and chairs on the ward, wiped them with a damp cloth, and emptied all the trash cans. If a table with food on it was overturned in the dining room, she was required to clean that entire room.

In addition to improving the physical environment, Ann was required to apologize to all those present on the ward when an episode occurred, because they were usually apprehensive because of her behavior. Generally, apologizing involved Ann nodding her head appropriately to questions,

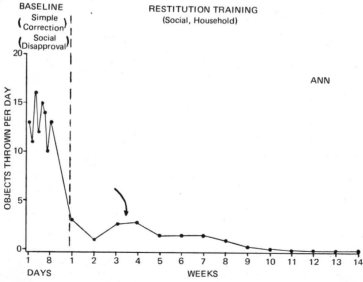

The arrow indicates a period when training was conducted improperly by one of the trainers.

197

because she had few verbal behaviors. The restitution program involved giving verbal directions to Ann, with no positive reinforcement such as praise. When she did not follow the directions, a procedure called *Graduated Guidance* was used. Essentially, it involved manually guiding Ann's limbs in making the desired behavior (e.g., making up a bed). Only the amount of pressure required to produce the desired movement was used, and guidance was gradually reduced, then removed, as Ann began to perform voluntarily.

Results

The Figure shows the number of objects thrown during the study. The rate was quite high during Baseline, but dropped quickly when treatment began. There were no objects thrown during the final month of the study.

Abstract 83

Reducing Aggressive and Self-Injurious Behavior of Institutionalized Retarded Children through Reinforcement of Other Behaviors

ALAN REPP (Georgia Retardation Center) and SAMUEL DEITZ (Georgia State University), *Journal of Applied Behavior Analysis*, 1974, 7, 313-325.

Emphasizing the positive.

Possibly the most humanistically acceptable method of decreasing self-destructive and aggressive behavior within an institution focuses on reinforcing behaviors incompatible with self-injury and with aggression. This cannot always be done (see Abstract 84 for other methods), however, because it requires a very small staff-resident ratio in order to be successfully effected. This study was conducted in a setting in which this was possible and that permitted an examination of the use of differential reinforcement of other than self-destructive or aggressive behaviors (DRO) in conjunction with other behavior modification techniques.

Method

SUBJECTS: Two subjects will be presented here. One subject was a twelve-year-old severely-retarded male, who emitted a high rate of aggressive behaviors (hitting, biting, scratching, kicking others). A second subject was a ten-year-old severely-retarded female, who was generally restrained by elbow splints so that she could not scratch her face.

PROCEDURE:

Aggression Study: This experiment was conducted in an activity room in which nine fellow residents and three staff members were usually present. A Baseline count of inappropriate aggressive responses and of appropriate responses (touching without hitting, kicking, biting or scratching) was tabulated. During Baseline, each aggressive response resulted in a 30-second restraint of the subject by the teacher. In phase two, a timer was set so that a bell rang if the subject was not aggressive during the interval, and he was then given an M&M candy (DRO). If he was aggressive, however, the timer was stopped, the subject was restrained for 30 seconds, and the timer was reset. The DRO interval began at five seconds for the first session of the phase and was graduated so that by session 12 the interval was 15 minutes. Phase one, Baseline, was replicated, followed by a replication of phase two. The single difference between phase four and phase two was that the DRO interval was gradually increased to 30 minutes.

Self-Injury Study: This experiment was conducted in an activity room of the cottage where the subject was a resident. Three staff and ten fellow residents were usually present. Because this subject wore elbow splints as restraints, Baseline consisted of ten five-minute segments in which alternatively the right restraint was removed, then the left, then both were removed. The teacher said "no" each time the subject scratched or picked at her face. Initially in phase two, the subject was taken to an adjoining room where the splints were removed. A DRO interval of one second was used in the beginning. After the timer bell rang, the subject was given bits of an M&M candy. If the subject scratched, the teacher again admonished "no," placed the resident's hand at her side, and reset the timer. By session 20, the interval had gradually increased to 120 minutes. At session 21, the subject was reintroduced into the activity room for increasing periods of time, so that in session 21 she spent two minutes in the activity room, and by session 56 she remained in the activity room for the entire 120 minutes. A reversal was not considered appropriate because of the possible damage to her face.

Results

The results for the experiment with the aggressive boy are presented in the first Figure (S-1). Baseline occurrence of aggressive behavior was generally very high, while the occurrence of appropriate touching behavior was almost zero.During the first treatment phase, aggressive behavior was reduced to almost zero. Appropriate behavior increased to a reliably higher rate. The effectiveness of differential reinforcement of appropriate behavior

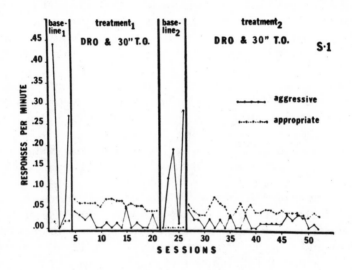

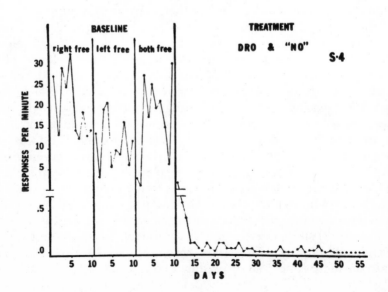

was clearly demonstrated in the next two phases. When DRO was removed, aggressive behavior again increased dramatically, and appropriate behavior simply did not occur. With reinstitution of treatment, the trends reversed; appropriate behavior was again reliably higher than Baseline, and aggressive behavior decreased.

Figure 2 represents the data gathered for the subject who scratched and picked at her face. Baseline occurrence of scratching was very high. The effectiveness of reinforcing behavior incompatible with face scratching is powerfully demonstrated in the sharp decrease of self-mutilating behavior from the outset of intervention.

Abstract 84

Manipulation of Self-Destruction in Three Retarded Children

O. IVAR LOVAAS and JAMES SIMMONS (University of California, Los Angeles), *Journal of Applied Behavior Analysis,* 1969, 2 143-157.

Positive Effects of Punishment.

Self-injurious behavior is a common problem in some institutions and with some types of clients, particularly autistic children. Drug therapy and warm, sympathetic attention are commonly used to deal with the problem, but there is little empirical evidence to suggest either procedure is effective. There is even evidence suggesting that the sympathetic attention provided increases the rate of self-injury. One alternative involves non-attending and therefore extinction of the behavior, and the immediate application of a punisher, shock, whenever the behaviors occur. This study evaluates these two techniques, extinction and punishment, in terms of their effectiveness in reducing self-destructive behavior.

Method

SUBJECTS AND SETTING: Three severely self-destructive children, considered the worst cases in their respective state hospital, were referred to the
program. There were two males, ages eight and eleven, and one eight-
year-old girl. Experimental treatment was conducted in hospital rooms
containing a bed, chest of drawers, a chair and a table.

PROCEDURE:

Extinction Study: Extinction involved the removal of all attendant
attention for a 90-minute period, during which the subjects were observed
in a special experimental room, equipped with a one-way mirror. Because
extinction is generally a slow process, which may begin with an increased
rate of responding, only the two male subjects were selected, since the
female subject already evidenced notable self-inflicted damage to her ears
and face.

One subject required such a lengthy extinction period that it was decided
to investigate possible factors maintaining it. Three sets of probe conditions were introduced: deprivation (DEP), satiation (SAT), and contingent
attention (REI). Deprivation represented a 24-hour period of confinement,
with no attention in the experimental room, as opposed to the scheduled
1½-hour period. Satiation involved constant attention, laughing with,
talking to, and tickling of the subject by an attendant, during a 24-hour
period. Contingent attention represented a period in which approximately
every third self-injurious behavior occasioned the arrival of a nurse, who
attempted to be warm and understanding.

Punishment Study: Although the situations in which the punishment
was instituted varied somewhat from subject to subject, the procedures

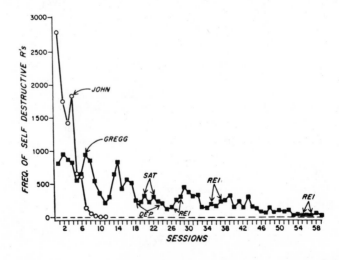

were similar. A baserate was tabulated for self-destructive behavior (hitting self), for whining, and for avoiding contact with an adult (for two subjects). Recording was usually done in two situations: one in which intervention followed immediately after Baseline stabilization, and a second in which intervention was delayed. In this manner, possible generalization of suppressed responding could be determined in a situation outside of the immediate treatment area. The punishment was a painful, but not burning or dangerous, shock contingent on self-injurious behavior. In the beginning, shock was delivered by only one experimenter to determine whether discriminations were possible for the subject.

Results

The results for the extinction study are represented in Figure 1. As can be seen, the number of self-destructive responses was extremely high in the 90-minute period, beginning at 2,750 for one subject (John) and 900 for the second subject (Gregg). Although John's response rate declined to zero in ten days, he hit himself almost 9,000 times during extinction. Gregg shows the same general pattern, although his self-injurious behavior did not begin as high and took much longer to eliminate. Deprivation (DEP), and satiation (SAT), did not appear to have a major effect on response frequency. Contingent attention or reinforcement (REI) for the first four probes did appear to have a noticeable effect, although this effect seemed to dissipate so that the fifth and sixth probes did not meaningfully alter the frequency.

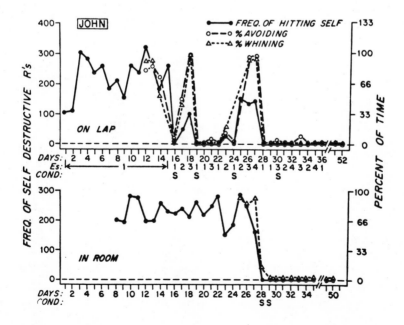

Figure 2 presents punishment study data from only one subject, but it is fairly representative of the three. John's base rate was very high in both recorded situations, sitting in a nurse's lap and in his room. When shock is introduced in session 16, an immediate decrease in all three behaviors, self-hitting, whining, and avoiding adult contact occurred, although shock was applied only to self-destructive behaviors. There was no generalization, however, as can be seen by the consistently high frequency of self-injury in his room, at the same time. One interesting finding was that all children eventually began to discriminate the experimenter giving the shock. At first, only the first experimenter shocked John, but when it was noted that the experimenter had become a discriminative cue for shock, another experimenter also shocked John. When John was also shocked in his room (session 28), self-destructive behavior decreased immediately and was maintained at a very low rate, almost zero, for the remainder of the recorded sessions.

Abstract 85

Vibration as a Reinforcer with a Profoundly Retarded Child

JON BAILEY (University of Kansas) and LEE MEYERSON (Arizona State University), *Journal of Applied Behavior Analysis*, 1969, 2, 135-137.

An initial step toward learning.

Where does a researcher begin with profoundly-retarded, blind and deaf institutional residents? How can progress be made when it is so very difficult to shape or maintain any sort of operant behavior? Where are the reinforcers? These are very real and important questions for anyone treating profoundly-retarded individuals. This study examined the effects of vibration as a reinforcer for bar-pressing behavior, a minimal but meaningful beginning for these individuals.

Method

SUBJECT: A seven-year-old profoundly-retarded, partially deaf, blind, mute boy, who was not toilet trained and could not walk or feed himself, was selected as subject. Phil weighed 27 pounds. He engaged in considerable self-stimulatory and self-injurious behaviors, such as sucking his fingers, rocking, slapping his face, and banging his head.

PROCEDURE: A padded lever was placed in his crib, which was connected to an industrial vibrator mounted under his bed, and to a frequency counter which tallied his responses. During Baseline, the number of lever presses was recorded. This phase lasted seven days. On the eighth day, the lever was connected to the vibrator and a counter. Vibration occurred for a six-second period; any response that occurred after the vibration period would initiate another six-second vibration period. After 21 days of this condition, the lever was disconnected and therefore no longer resulted in vibration.

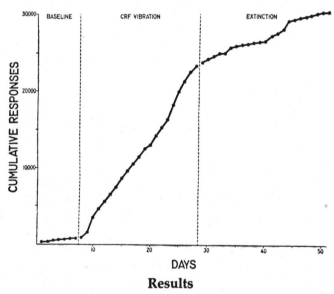

Results

The Figure represents a cumulative graph of lever pressing. During Baseline, bar pressing stabilized at about 135 a day, with a range of 30 to 300. When the vibration condition began, however, bar presses increased dramatically, averaging more than 1,000 responses a day, with a range from 700 to 2,000. Extinction resulted in a sharp decrease in responding. Within the first week, the average number of lever presses dropped to 400, and during the last week the response rate returned to Baseline frequency.

Abstract **86**

Effects of Goal-Setting and Modeling on Job Performance of Retarded Adolescents

SISTER JOANNE MARIE KLIEBHAN (The Cardinal Stritch College), *American Journal of Mental Deficiency.* 1967, 72, 220-226.

Comparing methods of improving work behavior.

Giving retarded individuals an opportunity to contribute to society through their work can be a very real benefit to both the individual and the culture, although there are practical problems that must be dealt with. This study focuses on the areas of quality and quantity in production, comparing two methods of improving job performance along these dimensions.

Method

SUBJECTS AND SETTING: Forty-eight male retardates attending a job training center were randomly divided into three groups. Mean I.Q. for the groups was about 59. Each of the three groups worked in the center's workshop at a different time. The experimental task involved affixing samples of tapes to pages in a salesperson's advertising booklet. This task included four steps: 1) matching the number on the roll of tape to the appropriately-numbered space on the page; 2) unwinding enought tape to cover the space; 3) pasting the tape on the page; 4) trimming off excess tape. The subjects worked on the experimental task 45 minutes a day, five days a week.

PROCEDURE: All subjects were verbally taught how to perform the task during the initial week of the study. The work was evaluated as *Inferior, Shop Average,* or *Superior.*

After the first week, the control group continued under the general procedure. In one experimental condition, *Expectancy,* the foreman counted the number of tapes affixed and evaluated them while the subjects watched. Each subject was then asked to specify how many tapes he expected to do the next day. This number was written down, and the subject was reminded of it before work the next day. In the second experimental condition, *Imitation*, a normal college student was assigned to the group. He served as a model for appropriate behavior. Subjects were told "Terry will show you how to do the task. . . He's doing a fine job . . . Watch him. . ." Attention was focused on the model throughout the five weeks during which the experimental conditions were in effect.

Results

An analysis of variance on the quantity of work produced yielded no significant overall differences between the groups. There was a significant change across weeks, with all groups improving. Further analysis showed that by the end of the fifth experimental week both the imitation and expectancy groups were performing at a higher rate than the control. The two experimental groups did not differ from each other, however.

A chi-square test was used to examine the quality dimension. This test indicated that the Expectancy group had significantly more products in the average and superior categories than either of the other groups. The Imitation group was significantly better than the control group.

Abstract 87

Some Experiments on Reinforcement Principles within a Psychiatric Ward for Delinquent Soldiers

JOHN BOREN and ARTHUR COLMAN (Walter Reed Army Institute of Research), *Journal of Applied Behavior Analysis*, 1970, 2, 29-37.

Treating a difficult population with token reinforcement.

Individuals hospitalized for behavior or character disorders have been particularly resistant to most treatment methods. In this study, a token or point economy was established in an attempt to modify the behavior of soldiers who had been referred because of their long histories of noncompliant and antisocial behavior. A series of experiments was conducted to investigate a number of variables, ranging from keeping fit to discussing personal problems. Three of the experiments are presented here.

Method

SUBJECTS AND SETTING: Twelve to 15 hospitalized delinquent soldiers, diagnosed as having behavior or character disorders, were the subjects. They were patients on a point-economy ward where points could be exchanged for privileges such as semi-private rooms, weekend passes, and coffee.

PROCEDURE: **Unit Meeting Attendance Study, Part A:** All patients were invited to attend a meeting at 8:00 A.M., where announcements and plans were made for the day. Although 20 points were given to all who attended, as many as 30% of the patients stayed in bed. In an effort to increase attendance, a ten-point fine was levied against all those who did not attend.

Results

Figure 1 represents the effects of punishment, the ten-point fine, on attending behavior. In Condition A, when 20 points were contingent, attendance varied between 70% and 100%. In Condition B, the fine condition, attendance dropped dramatically, varying between 60% and 0. Additional subjective feedback indicated that the patients were very hostile and after one week, Condition A was reinstituted. Attendance eventually increased almost to its Baseline frequency.

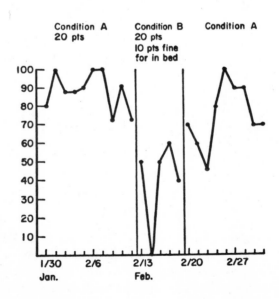

208

Unit Meeting Attendance Study, Part B: Five months later an alternative procedure was applied to the problem. By this time, attendance averaged about 40%, despite the 20 point contingency. Although the points contingent could have been increased, the economic inflation on the ward prohibited it, since privileges were easily accessible as it was. It was therefore decided to make all points earned through the day contingent on attendance at the meeting. That is, patients would not be awarded any points, regardless of their behavior, unless they had attended the meeting.

Results

Figure 2 represents the Baseline attendance (Condition C) with the 20 point contingency and the new intervention (Condition D) in which patients must attend in order to earn any points through the day. In the first week, attendance increased from a median of 38% to 63%, and by the last week attendance was approximately 87%.

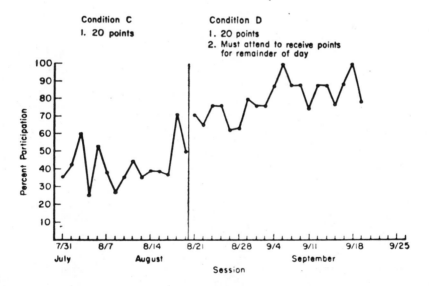

Personal Problems Study: In a class conducted by a psychiatric resident, problems discussed were classified into three categories: displaced (problem happened to someone else, was remote in time and place), personal (problem happened to patient, but was remote in time and place) and "here and now" (problem happened to patient recently). Because almost all problems discussed were displaced, it was decided to compare two methods of encouraging discussion of personal and "here and now" problems. In one condition, social reinforcement, the resident requested personal and "here and now" problems and verbally reinforced the group

209

when such problems were discussed. The second condition involved developing a point system which differentially reinforced the categories. "Here and now" problems were awarded ten points, personal, seven points and displaced, five points.

Results

Figure 3 presents the percent of problem situations described according to the two conditions. In the social reinforcement phase, a total of 25% of problems discussed fell into the "here and now" or personal categories, compared to a total of 65% in the point-reinforcement condition. Displaced problems constituted 75% of the situations discussed in the social reinforcement condition, and only 35% in the point reinforcement phase.

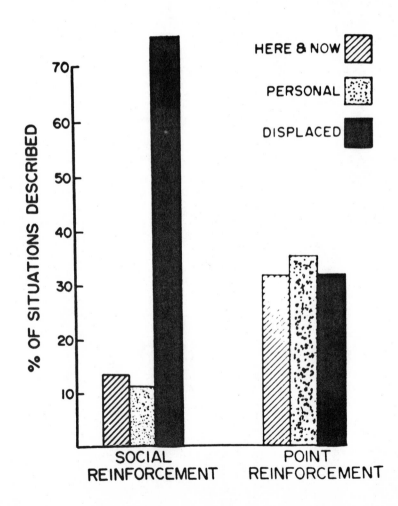

Abstract **88**

Following Up on the Behavior Analysis Model: Results After Ten Years of Early Intervention with Institutionalized, Mentally Retarded Children

STEPHEN SULZBACHER (University of Washington) and JOHN KIDDER (Ranier School), In *Behavior Analysis: Areas of Research and Application*,(Ramp & Semb, eds.). Englewood Cliffs: Prentice-Hall, 1975, 62-69.

Long-term benefits of behavior modification.

In the early 1960s, a small group of psychologists and educators cooperatively planned and put into practice one of the first behavioral classrooms at Ranier School in Washington. The work done at Ranier has had a major influence on the field. This paper is the first to report on the long-term effects of the program.

Method

SUBJECTS AND SETTING: Since 1962 the Programmed Learning Class at Ranier School has served about 100 institutionalized, mentally-retarded children. Children are referred to the class generally because their behavior is too disruptive in other classroom placements. The students work in programmed, educational material. They receive marks for successful completion of assignments which can be exchanged for rewards, and extensive use is made of peer tutoring. Students often score their own work and select assignments. Disruptive behavior is usually ignored by peers and teachers alike. Follow-up data was gathered on 52 children who attended the class full time for at least a year.

Results

Table 1 shows the disposition of the 52 students. Although the prognosis for independent living was poor for these institutionalized, retarded children, a large number are now living in community settings. Only two students were considered "failures"—likely to remain at the institution indefinitely.

Table 2 shows data from a comparison of the experimental group with an unmatched control group of 30 students. These data must be interpreted

Table 1
Summary of Current Job, School and Living Situation for PLC Students who Attended for at Least One Year between 1962 and 1973

Years of Attendance at PLC	N	Now Living in Community					
		Fully Employed	Sheltered Work Situation	Attending High School	Attending College and Working	Not in School and Not Working	Discharged (Records Unavailable)
6-8 years	10	—	2	2	1	—	1
4-5 years	6	1	3	—	—	1	—
2-3 yrstd	8	2	—	3	—	—	—
1 year	28	4	4	4	2	—	4
Total N =	52						

Years of Attendance at PLC	N	Still at Rainier School		Others	Disabled or Deceased
		Enrolled in PLC	Enrolled Community Oriented Pre-voc. Program		
6-8 years	10	3	—	—	1
4-5 years	6	—	—	1	—
2-3 years	8	2	—	—	1
1 year	28	2	6	2	—

cautiously, since the two groups may have been different in several ways (e.g., the experimental group may have had more behavioral problems), but the results generally suggest better outcome for the experimental group, who also had better reports from job supervisors and held better jobs. The authors suggested that although academic progress was a major goal of the program, the most important factors contributing to successful community adjustment may have been the improvement produced by the program in social skills, conversational skills, and in the ability to reliably and consistently complete assigned tasks.

Table 2
Comparisons of PLC Students with Matched Cohorts on Selected Indices of Subsequent Success

	PLC (n =)	Cohort (n =)
Percentage who are currently productively engaged (working or in school)	91.5	76.6
Percentage living in community	68.5	66.7
Percentage who live independently and are fully employed	13	10
Percentage who failed onplacement and were returned to institution	1.8	13.3
Percentage who have committed legal offenses	0	6.6

CHAPTER VII

Behavioral Approaches to Juvenile Delinquents and Adult Offenders

Abstract 89

Inducing Behavior Change in Adolescent Delinquents

ROBERT SCHWITZGEBEL and DAVID KOLB (Harvard University), *Behaviour Research and Therapy*, 1964, 1, 297-304.

A street-corner therapy for delinquents.

An important difficulty in altering behavior of socially delinquent individuals is finding them and enlisting their cooperation. The authors of this study confronted this problem innovatively and realistically by establishing a "storefront" research laboratory and offering delinquents a "job."

Method

SUBJECTS AND SETTING: The experimenters, a clinical psychologist, a social worker and a Jesuit priest, actively solicited boys from their "hang-outs," such as street corners and pool halls. The experimenter asked the boys to talk into a tape recorder on any subject they wished, while in a safe place (a restaurant), for payment of one dollar an hour. After the initial interview, appointments were made to continue the taping in the storefront labora-

213

tory. A control group of subjects was found through records of state correctional agencies. Subjects were matched on age of first offense (mean = 13.5), type of offense, nationality, religious preference (Roman Catholic), place of residence and total number of months incarcerated (mean = 15.1). The age range was 15 to 21, the average number of arrests was 8.2, only four of the 20 subjects had held a full-time job longer than six months, and only one had completed high school.

PROCEDURE: The principle techniques used were shaping and variable ratio positive reinforcement.

Attendance: Throughout the study, missed or late appointments were never punished. When an appointment was completely missed, the experimenter would allow several days to pass and then search for the employee in the last place of contact. Reluctance was overcome by a very gradual shaping procedure. For instance, one subject was met in the pool hall, then at the subway station nearest the pool hall, then at the subway station before the toll gate, then after the toll gate and with a reimbursement for the subject's fare, then at the exit near the laboratory, and finally at the laboratory itself. Throughout, the experimenter would sometimes buy a candy bar or cigarettes for the subject.

When the employee was late, something positive would be found on which to comment. For example, when a subject was an hour late, the experimenter would comment on how much better his performance was than last time, when he was an hour and a half late. He might even give the subject a bonus. It is important to note that no specified, predetermined schedule was identified, so that the experimenters could be flexible in handling difficulties as they occurred.

Interviewing: The taping task, assumed at first by the delinquents to be simple, proved more difficult than expected. Direction and tone of the interviews was shaped through small cash bonuses, verbal praise or unexpected privileges. For instance, expressions of personal feelings might be considered appropriate behavior which should be encouraged. Any reoccurrence of such behavior would be rewarded. Advice, even when requested by the delinquent, was not given.

Termination: Employment was terminated gradually by decreasing the number and time of taping as other part-time jobs were acquired. After nine or ten months, subjects left for full-time jobs, trade schools, or the armed services. A few had been incarcerated.

Results

The Figure is a graph of the attendance pattern of each subject. As can be seen, arrival time became dependable within 15 appointments. A three-year follow-up of the 20 experimental subjects and their controls showed a significant reduction in number of arrests and number of months incarcerated. Experimental subjects averaged 2.4 arrests compared to the control average of 4.7. The average number of months incarcerated for the experimental group was 3.5, while the control average was 6.9. There was no significant difference in recidivism.

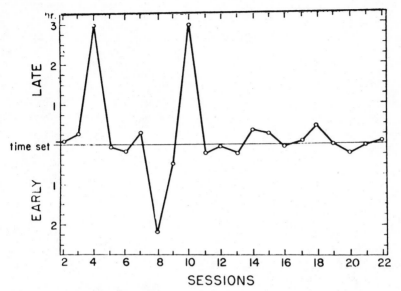

Arrival times of experimental subject S_2 for initial twenty-two meetings.

Abstract **90**

"Aversive" Group Therapy:
Sometimes Good Medicine Tastes Bad

ROBERT LEVINSON, GILBERT INGRAM, and EDWARD AZCA-RATE. (National Training School), *Crime and Delinquency*, 1968, 336-339.

An unusual use of therapy in a prison.

Attending group therapy is usually considered a valuable experience by the therapist, althought the patient or inmate required to participate may often describe it differently. The fact that some inmates in a federal institution for delinquents viewed "treatment" as a punisher was used in this study as a behavior modification procedure.

Method

SUBJECTS AND SETTING: Seventeen male adolescents in a penal institution, who had been placed in segregation at least once a month for three months, were the subjects.

PROCEDURE: Attendance at group therapy sessions, held once a week for an hour and a half, was made mandatory for subjects who met the requirements described above. They were required to attend until they met the exit requirement—three successive months without being placed in segregation. Placement in segregation meant the inmate had violated an institutional rule considered important by the correctional officer. Group therapy began with eight inmates, and as they left the group, new members were added.

Results

The Table shows the average number of misconduct reports on the participants before and after group therapy. Those who met the exit criteria (11) reduced the number from 4.0 to 2.3. Six inmates left for other reasons (transfer, work-release, end of sentence). They also reduced the number of misconduct reports written on them.

The therapist reported the sessions were somewhat aversive for both therapist and inmates. Almost every inmate stated as he left the group that it had done nothing for him. In response to the question, "Then why have you stayed out of segregation?" they often replied, "To get out of this damn group!"

Table
Average Number of Misconduct Reports Before
and after "Aversive" Group Therapy

| | Average No. Misconducts | | |
| | 6 Mos. Before | 6 Mos. After | Percent of |
Exit Criterion	(N = 13)		Change
Attained	4.0	2.3	—42.5
Not attained	5.8	3.3	—43.1
Total group	4.4	2.5	—43.2

Abstract **91**

Short-Term Behavioral Intervention with Delinquent Families: Impact on Family Process and Recidivism

JAMES ALEXANDER and BRUCE PARSONS (University of Utah), *Journal of Abnormal Psychology*, 1973, *81*, 219-225.

Behavioral intervention in the home environment of delinquents.

An alternative to treating the behavioral disorder of the individual is to treat the system in which it is found. This study offers a counseling package, short-term behavioral family intervention, which involves the entire family units of delinquent youth, altering the focus from individuals to a major source of their behavioral shaping, the family environment.

Method

SUBJECTS: Forty-six of 86 families referred by a juvenile court to a family clinic were assigned to the short-term behavioral family intervention program; 19 were assigned to a client-centered family groups program, 11 to a psychodynamic family program, and 10 to a no-treatment control. The sample included 38 male and 48 female delinquents, from 13 to 16 years old, who had been referred for running away, being declared ungovernable, habitually being truant, shoplifting, or possessing alcohol, soft drugs, or tobacco.

PROCEDURE: The major principle of the program centered on lack of reciprocity in family interaction. That is, an adaptive interaction pattern involved an equitable distribution of positive reinforcement throughout the family.

Short-Term Behavioral Family Intervention Program. The goals for therapy were 1) clear communication of substance as well as feelings; 2) clear presentation of "demands" and alternative solutions; 3) negotiation, with each family member receiving privileges for responsibilities assumed, to the point of compromise. These goals were to be accomplished by approximating predetermined "normal" or "adjusted" family living. In order to train these behaviors, therapists modeled, prompted, shaped, and reinforced approximations to the target responses.

A major component of training differentiated rules ("limits to regulate and control action and conduct") from requests ("asking behavior," in which the family member had the unrestricted option to say "yes" or "no"). A second major component was training in social reinforcement and in appropriate methods of increasing the clarity of the communication. Two additional components were applied to only some families. The manual *Living with Children*, Patterson & Gullion (Champaign, Illinois: Research Press, 1968) was assigned. And second, a token economy was instituted for some, since this demanded more precise specification of the desired behaviors.

The programs with smaller numbers of cases included the following:

Client-Centered Family Groups Program. A warm, empathic environment in which the therapist provided unconditional positive regard for his client-families comprised this group. This program covered the same period of time as the behavioral group. (19 cases.)

Psychodynamic Family Program. This group focused on the importance of insight as an effective change agent. (11 cases.)

No-Treatment Control. These families received no specific treatment but were tested five-six weeks after intake (as were all other groups). (10 cases.)

Dependent Variables. There were two major dependent variable categories, process measures and outcome measures. The process measures were developed to look at equality of family interaction, amount of silence (less silence was taken to mean greater family interaction), and number of interruptions. Interruptions were considered relevant because family members were trained to interrupt in order to clarify communication.

Table
Outcome Measures: Recidivism Rates for
Treatment and Comparison Groups

Condition	N	No. of cases of recidivism	No. of non-recidivism cases	% recidivism
Groups compared statistically				
Short-term family behavioral treatment	46[a]	12[c]	34[c]	26
Client-centered family groups treatment	19[b]	9[c]	10[c]	47
Eclectic psycho-dynamic family treatment	11	8[c]	3[c]	73
No treatment controls	10	5[c]	5[c]	50
Groups not included in statistical comparison				
Post-hoc selected no-treatment controls	46	22	24	48
County-wide recidivism rates, 1971	2800			51

[a] Includes 12 cases who dropped the program before completion.
[b] Includes 9 cases who dropped the program.
[c] Differences between samples: $x^2 = 10.25$, $df = 3$, $p < .025$.

218

Outcome measures involved rate of recidivism across all groups.

Results

Process measures indicated that short-term behavioral family intervention was significantly superior to the three other groups in terms of equality and amount of interaction.

The Table presents the data for recidivism, the outcome measure. As can be seen in the "% recidivism" column, behavioral family intervention resulted in only 26% recidivism, while no-treatment and client-centered groups averaged 50% and 47% respectively. Psychodynamic family therapy resulted in a 73% recidivism rate. The nationwide mean is 51% and a control group of matched subjects drawn from court records averaged 48% recidivism.

Abstract **92**

Modification of Delay Choices in Institutionalized Youthful Offenders through Social Reinforcement

JEROME STUMPHAUZER (Florida State University), *Psychonomic Science*, 1970, *18*, 222-223.

Manipulating consequences to encourage selection of long-term rewards.

Social reinforcement, verbal or nonverbal approval of one individual by another, is generally a powerful technique in modifying many types of behavior. This study investigated its effectiveness in altering the delay of gratification pattern of young adult offenders.

Method

SUBJECTS AND SETTING: Four 19-year-old male inmates of a correctional institution served as subjects.

PROCEDURE: Subjects were informed they would be presented with 100 choices between smaller but immediate rewards (e.g., 25¢ today) and larger but delayed rewards (e.g., 50¢ in three weeks). They were asked to choose carefully, because they would receive four of their choices but would not be told which ones until the task was completed.

Baseline. Twenty-five choices were presented, and the subject responses were merely recorded.

Delay Choice Reinforcement. Another 25 choices were presented. All delay choices were socially reinforced by the experimenter with either a "Good" or "Mm-hmm" comment.

Immediate Choice Reinforcement. Another 25 choices were presented. In this condition, immediate choices rather than delay choices were reinforced, as in the previous condition.

Delay Choice Reinforcement. This condition was the same as the second condition.

Results

The Figure presents the typical response pattern for all four subjects. During Baseline, the percent of delay choices was low but increased dramatically when reinforcement was applied. When immediate choices were reinforced, the percent of delay choices was drastically reduced. Delay choices increased dramatically when social reinforcement was again applied contingently.

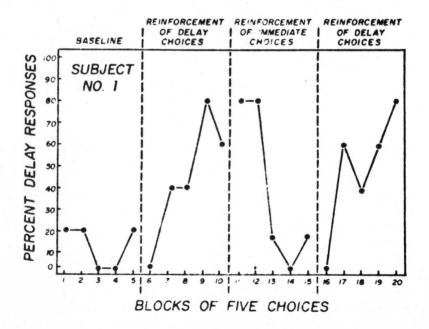

Abstract **93**

Increased Delay of Gratification
in Young Prison Inmates through
Imitation of High-Delay Peer Models.

JEROME STUMPHAUZER (University of Southern California Medical Center), *Journal of Personality and Social Psychology*, 1972, 21, 10-17.

Encouraging selection of long-term reward through use of high-status peers.

There appears to be considerable evidence in the literature suggesting that a major component of the socialization process, delay of gratification, has somehow eluded the young adult offender. A child's pattern of preferring immediate reward bears a striking resemblence to that of the young inmate. In earlier research this behavior in children has been altered successfully when either an adult or a child models an alternate behavior, choosing a greater reward whose receipt is postponed. This procedure was used to develop a program to modify the gratification behavior of young adults.

Method

SUBJECTS AND SETTING: Forty white 18 to 20 year-old new inmates in a correctional institution, who preferred immediate gratification (more than 70% immediate reward choices), were selected as subjects. The subjects were randomly assigned to the model treatment group or to the no-treatment control condition.

Models: Two older inmates (21 and 23) near discharge, with prestigious jobs (photographer and X-ray technician), participated in the study. Each served as model to 10 of the 20 subjects in the modeling condition. Two major dependent variables were used three times during the study. One dependent variable was four lists of choices (A, B, C & D) which varied in size and delay of the reward. For example, one item in list A might be a small candy bar awarded now, while another item in the same list might be a larger candy bar, whose award was postponed one week. The choice lists A, B & C were administered to the subject, while list D was given only to the models. Subjects were required to make 14 choices. In order to increase realism and improve motivation, a subject was actually given one of his choices at the experimenter-selected time (either immediately or delayed).

Because reinforcement alone might have an effect, only half the subjects in the control group and half in the experimental group were actually given one of their choices.

A second dependent variable was a money-saving questionnaire asking the subjects what they would do with varying amounts of money (25¢, $2, $20) added to their institution account.

PROCEDURE: All subjects were given the premeasure without modeling. Four weeks later, each of the subjects assigned to the experimental condition was called in with the model, whom the subject believed to be another subject. The position of the model was made clear to the subject through apparently casual questioning of the model about his occupation, age, and length of stay at the institution. When alternatives were given, the model chose to wait for a larger reward. Responses to the money-saving questionnaire were answered in such a manner that the subject could not see them. The model was then excused. Items on a second list were then displayed, and the subject was asked to choose. If he was in the *actual* reinforcement group, he received one choice in the assigned period, immediate or delayed.

Follow-up. A third choice list was presented to all 40 subjects four weeks later.

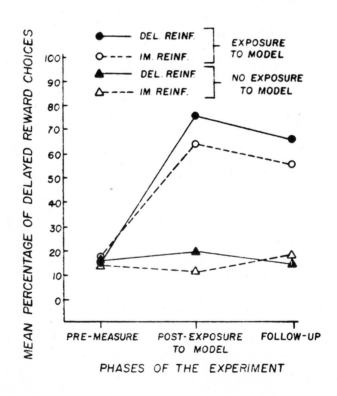

Results

A repeated-measure analysis of variance indicated that modeling had a highly significant effect on inmate choices, whether their reward was actually delivered immediately or was delayed. Follow-up data showed these results were maintained. The control group showed no significant change in the percentage of delayed choices. The Figure presents the percentage of delayed reward choices as a function of modeling and of reinforcement.

The money-saving questionnaire represented a generalization measure, because subjects did not know what the model chose to do. The modeling condition significantly affected the percentage of 25¢ and $2 that were saved, but had no differential effect on the number of $20 saved.

Abstract 94

Achievement Place: A Teaching-Family Model
of Community-based Group Homes
for Youth in Trouble

DEAN FIXSEN, MONTROSE WOLF, and ELERY PHILLIPS (University of Kansas), In *Behavior Change: Methodology, Concept and Practice* (Hamerlynck, Handy, Mash, eds.), Champaign, Illinois: Research Press, 1973, 241-268.

A community-based treatment program for problem adolescents.

Achievement Place may well be one of the most famous behavior modification programs in existence. Working with a difficult group, adolescent delinquents, predelinquents, and neglected youth, the authors developed a behaviorally-based living arrangement which attempts to modify the maladaptive behavior patterns of the residents.

Method

SUBJECTS AND SETTING: Achievement Place (AP) is a group home for six to eight youths who are experiencing problems in their home or in the community. It is staffed by a set of teaching-parents who operate the program and live with the youths. AP is housed in a large, older home which has been renovated. In this particular study, average age of the youths was 13. Most were far behind their peers academically, although their average IQ was 95. About 94% were classified as behavior problems in school. They averaged 2.2 police contacts and 1.9 court contacts before entering AP.

PROCEDURE: The three components to the AP program are as follows: 1) a point system (token economy), 2) the social behavior of the teaching parents, and 3) a semi-self government system.

Point System and Teaching Parent Social Behavior. The general goals of AP involve improving the youths' social, academic, and self-help skills. The residents are given specfic lists of behaviors for which they may earn or lose points. For example, under the category "Helping Others," the behavior of "bringing in luggage for guests" earned 300 to 500 points, while failing to "willingly help someone in need" resulted in a fine of 500 to 1,000 points. Other behaviors, such as doing jobs around the house, health-related tasks such as brushing teeth, school work, and a wide range of appropriate and inappropriate social behaviors, also produce points. The point system is set up so that the residents earn points for many routine behaviors which occur regularly, and lose points for undesirable behavior. Residents also can do special jobs to earn points. Thus a large loss of points can be made up by increased effort in another area.

Points were spent on a variety of privileges, such as snacks, TV time, allowance money, opportunity to avoid chores, visits home, and use of the recreation room, tools, telephone, and radio.

Awarding and taking-away points was one aspect of the social interaction between the teaching-parent and the residents. The teaching-parents systematically used positive social reinforcement for appropriate behavior and regularly provided feedback for the youths on their behavior. When negative feedback was given, the teaching-parent carefully explained the problem behavior, demonstrated a more appropriate way of behaving, asked the youths to practice the appropriate behavior, and gave positive feedback for doing so.

The boys moved through a series of phases in the point system. They began with an hourly point system in which points earned in one three-hour period could be used in the next three hours. They then moved into a daily and then weekly system. This progression required increasingly longer periods of work before reinforcement. The final phase was a merit system in which the resident earned all available privileges without any points awarded. This level approximated normal conditions, because only social feedback was used to maintain behavior.

Self-Government. A final aspect of the AP program was participation of the residents in establishing and enforcing the rules of AP. They learned how to cooperate in groups, how to lead, and how to develop and abide by rules through participation in self-government activities. The residents were not given the responsibility of establishing rules and enforcing them in the beginning. Instead, the teaching-parents modeled appropriate behavior and discussed the rules at Family Conferences after dinner. Gradually, as the youths gained more experience in managing their own lives, they took on more responsibility for governing themselves. The teaching-parents usually had veto power over decisions, but gradually relinquished more and more of the decision-making to residents.

Comment

The Achievement Place staff has conducted a large number of research studies on the program using within-subjects research designs. An example of one such study is given in Abstract 95.

Abstract **95**

Achievement Place: Experiments in Self-Government with Predelinquents

DEAN FIXSEN, ELERY PHILLIPS and MONTROSE WOLF (University of Kansas), *Journal of Applied Behavior Analysis*, 1973, 6, 31-47.

Democracy and delinquency: Using one to change the other.

Typically, a residential center for individuals labeled by society as in some way nonconformist is run according to predetermined rules, allowing very little input by the residents. Although there is a body of evidence supporting greater therapeutic effectiveness when residents feel some responsibility for their treatment, there has been little systematic investigation of the components involved. In this study at Achievement Place (see Abstract 94), an experiment was conducted to analyze some variables affecting participation in self-government.

Method

SETTING: Achievement Place (AP), a community-based group-home for six-eight boys, aged 12 to 16 years, who have been determined by the court to be delinquent, predelinquent and/or dependent-neglected, was the setting (see Abstract 94 for more details about the home). Briefly, the home is based on a token-economy system, in which privileges such as seeing a girlfriend, allowance, watching television, extra dessert, and avoiding some chores, are contingent on point accumulation. Prior to this particular experiment, a self-government system had developed in a bit-by-bit fashion, but had not been systematically investigated.

SUBJECTS: Seven AP residents, ranging in age from 10 to 16 years, participated in the study.

PROCEDURE: Particularly serious problems in AP were handled through a trial procedure which included participation by everyone. The trial procedure evolved around family conferences during the evening meal. Any person subject to a rule-violation penalty of more than 3,000 points could be introduced for peer evaluation by the teaching-parent. At this time, the person in question presented the circumstances surrounding the accusation and stated his involvement. Discussion was then opened to the other boys for further information relating to guilt or innocence. After discussion, a vote was taken. If the vote was not unanimous, minority dissenters were asked to support their position, more discussion followed, and another vote was taken. At that time, the majority opinion was followed. A "not guilty" verdict ended the trial. A "guilty" verdict, however, resulted in another discussion of appropriate consequences. The consequence would then be voted on and if there were dissenters the procedure as described previously would be followed.

Everyone could participate in discussion, but only peers could vote. The teaching-parent had the power to veto, although the boys could choose to override this veto if they were willing to accept the responsibility of their decision and consequences imposed.

Behaviors Measured. "Agreement" was defined as raising a hand to vote. When a second vote was required, results were tallied only from this vote. "Participation in discussion" involved suggesting alternatives or adding relevant information. Simply agreeing with another statement was inadequate behavior to be considered participatory.

Experimental Manipulation. The experimental manipulation included four conditions. The first was "Trial-set consequences" by which the person accused of rule violation was called to trial as noted above. The second condition, "Preset consequences," involved the teaching-parent applying a penalty prior to the trial. The trial then continued as usual, with the single alteration that the peers had the option of resetting the fine already made by the teacher-parent. In the third condition, "Unfair consequences probe," the teaching-parent applied a consequence that was ten times greater than would be fair. The fourth condition, "Preference probe," involved asking the boys in 12 of the 80 trials whether they preferred preset or trial-set consequences. Preference measures occurred for nine preset consequences and for three trial-set consequences.

Results

The Figure shows percent of participation occurring across trial-set and preset consequences condition; each was replicated once. As will be noted, participation consistently increased across the trial-set consequence condition and decreased during the preset consequence conditions.

Agreement to the trial decisions was almost always 100%. The Unfair consequences condition, which occurred twice, was rejected by all boys the first time and the second time, with only one out of seven agreeing. When discussed, however, the new consequence was unanimously agreed on.

The Preference data showed that when they were asked their preference during the preset consequence trial, eight of the nine times the boys preferred preset. Only one in nine times, therefore, did they prefer trial-set. When they were asked their preference during the trial-set consequences condition, three out of three times they chose trial-set consequences.

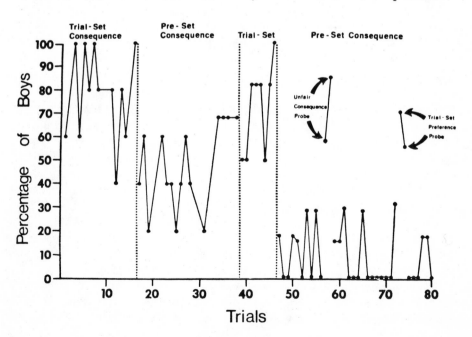

227

Abstract **96**

Intervention Package: An Analysis to Prepare Juvenile Delinquents for Encounters with Police Officers

JOHN WERNER, NEIL MINKIN, BONNIE MINKIN, DEAN FIXSEN, ELERY PHILLIPS, MONTROSE WOLF (University of Kansas), *Criminal Justice and Behavior*, 1975, 2, 55-84.

What do you say to a cop?

This study was originally titled "What Do You Say to a Cop?" Earlier studies suggest that about 70% of all youth could, at one time or another, be charged with a serious law violation. Research also indicates the behavior of a youth when he comes in contact with law enforcement officers is a major determiner of whether he is taken into custody or released. This study attempts to investigate the specific behaviors that influence the police officer's decision, and to train delinquent youth to behave in a manner that is likely to reduce the probability of being arrested.

Method

SUBJECTS: In the main experiment, six delinquent youths in a community group home volunteered as subjects. Several groups of policemen and community volunteers also participated in parts of the research.

PROCEDURE: In the initial part of the study, 15 policemen and 15 adolescent delinquents were interviewed to determine what behaviors each group felt affected prejudicial handling. Figure 1 shows the results of a questionnaire rating of the importance of such behaviors as presenting identification promptly; and a rating of how much effect the youth's behavior has on the officer's report; stopping the youth again; detention; and the ultimate decision of the courts. Both groups generally felt the behaviors listed were very important. In addition, officers felt behaviors such as looking at the officer, listening attentively, not interrupting the officer, and letting the officer know that he understands were highly desirable.

In the second part of the study, three delinquent youth were taught how to behave when they encountered police. Three other delinquents served as a control group and received no training. All six subjects were given

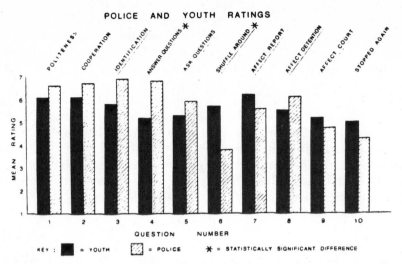

POLICE AND YOUTH RATINGS

KEY : ■ = YOUTH ▨ = POLICE ✳ = STATISTICALLY SIGNIFICANT DIFFERENCE

videotaped pre- and posttests in which they role-played being stopped by a uniformed policeman. The instructions for these tests and for the Baseline sessions told the youths to imagine that they were out walking alone after curfew when they were approached by a police officer who has stopped and questioned them before. The police officer was told to imagine that he was on patrol in a area where three burglaries had occurred that evening. He was told that it was past curfew when he approached the youths, whom he viewed as possible troublemakers. He was instructed to conduct his standard procedure.

Four behaviors were measured by the experimenters and taught during the training sessions which followed Baseline:

Facial orientation, which occurred if the subject's face was oriented toward the upper torso of the police officer or the person acting as a police officer.

Politeness in short answers, which involved following appropriate answers with some reference to the police officer's authority, such as "Sir" or "Officer."

Expression of reform, which occurred if the youth acknowledged he had been in trouble before and expressed an intention to "stay out of trouble."

Expression of understanding and cooperation, through comments that acknowledged the youth understood the officer's concern and was willing to cooperate with the officer.

Training consisted of three components: 1) instructions with rationale, 2) demonstrations, and 3) practice with feedback. The three experimental subjects were trained as a group, and sessions always began with the experimenters asking the youths whether they thought their behavior when interacting with a policeman was important, what the appropriate behaviors were, and what the consequences of various behaviors might be.

229

The behavior to be trained that day was discussed, and the experimenters provided a rationale concerning its importance. When a new behavior was trained, the previous behaviors were also discussed and reviewed. Subsequently, the experimenters demonstrated the behaviors in a simulated police-youth encounter. The youths were encouraged to discuss what they liked and disliked about the experimenters' behavior. Then, the youths practiced the behavior with an experimenter. The sessions were videotaped and played back so that the youths could get feedback and comment on each other's behavior. Training for each of the four behaviors usually took approximately 1½ hours, with the sessions spread over approximately three weeks. After training, the youths participated in posttraining sessions which consisted of an interaction with one experimenter acting as a police officer. Procedures were the same as Baseline.

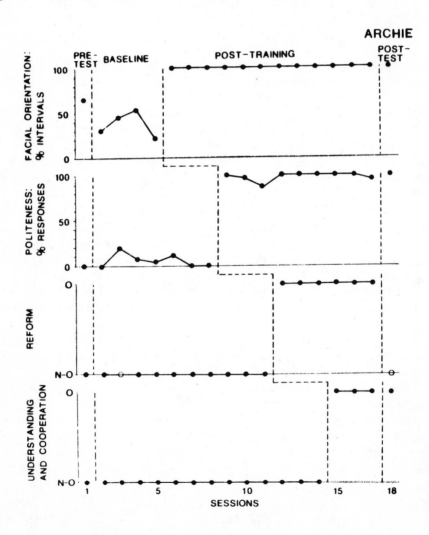

Results

Figure 2 shows the results of training for one of the subjects. The other two experimental subjects had similar increases in desirable behavior after training began. The dotted line on the graph indicates the point at which each behavior was trained. When compared to the control group, delinquents who were trained had significantly higher levels of the four behaviors. In addition, the relationship of the target behaviors to police and community ratings of the youth was evaluated by having five different police officers, five parents of delinquents, and five graduate psychology students rate the pre- and post-videotapes of all six youth. The data from this part of the study indicated the trained group was rated much more favorably on the posttest, while the untrained group made only slight gains.

Comment. The authors of this paper justify the procedures on the grounds that many adolescents who have come in contact with the courts are thereafter "labeled" as troublemakers, and thus are more likely to be detained, arrested, and charged by police, even when they have committed no further crimes. Some might argue that what the authors have done is provide the subjects with skills that will enable them to commit crimes again with less likelihood of being caught.

Abstract **97**

Training Predelinquent Youths and Their
Parents to Negotiate Conflict Situations

ROBERT KIFER, MARTHA LEWIS, DONALD GREEN and ELERY
PHILLIPS (University of Kansas), *Journal of Applied Behavior
Analysis*, 1974, 1, 357-364.

Making home a nicer place to be.

Early theories of delinquency and criminality emphasized innate or inherited tendencies toward antisocial behavior. In the twentieth century, however, the emphasis has shifted to an environmental view of criminality. Differences in the learning history of children and the manner in which problems are handled in the home are now considered major determinants of behavior, delinquent or otherwise. The authors here have attempted to train parent-child pairs in more appropriate negotiation skills, so that conflicts in the home are resolved more peaceably.

Method

SUBJECTS AND SETTING: Two mother-daughter pairs and one father-son pair served as subjects. Training was conducted in a windowless classroom containing tables and chairs, and videotape equipment.

PROCEDURE:

Behaviors Measured: Negotiation and agreement were the response classes measured. Negotiation was made up of 1) complete communication (each side communicated its position clearly and showed a willingness to negotiate); 2) identification of issues (explicit statements identifying the point(s) of contention were made); 3) suggestion of options (statements that suggested resolution were posed). Agreement consisted of 1) compliant agreement (one person agreed to the other's position); 2) negotiated agreement (an option was agreed on which could affect a compromise or a new alternative).

Home Observation: Each pair was observed in the home setting one week prior to classroom sessions, in which training was begun. Rates of negotiation and agreement were recorded while actual conflict situations were discussed.

Classroom Session: Each parent-child pair attended ten weekly sessions following the same procedural format: a) *pressession simulation*. Trainers provided a hypothetical conflict situation, required the parent and child to role-play opposing sides and then to reverse roles. No specific instructions were given, and simulation continued for five minutes unless resolved earlier. b) *discussion and practice*. Situations-Options-Consequences-Simulation (S.O.C.S.) was a standard procedure used in negotiating conflicts. A sheet listing a situation, response options, and possible consequences was handed out to the participants by the trainer, who then related all possible responses with probable consequences. Subjects then selected the most desirable consequence and, hence, responses most likely to lead to those consequences. Each subject practiced the desired option. In this experiment, typically the child began role-playing the youth in conflict and later switched to the parent role. c) *postsession simulation*. This condition replicated presession simulation. Subjects had the option of negotiating as they had been trained and could use "real-life" problems.

Training: A combination of instructions, practice, modeling, feedback and social reinforcement was used to shape behavior toward negotiation and agreement during the weekly sessions.

Design: A multiple Baseline across subject pairs was used to examine the effects of training on negotiation and agreements. All sessions were videotaped unless subjects specifically objected. Training began in the fourth week for one pair, in the fifth for another, and in the sixth for the third.

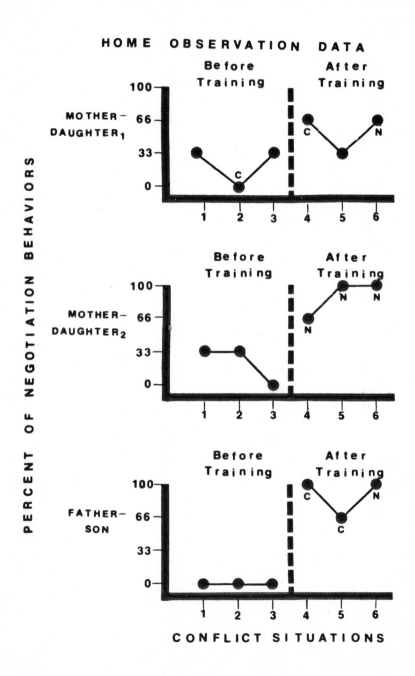

233

Results

The data for the percent of negotiating behaviors emitted by each parent-child pair during pre- and postsession simulation indicated all parent-child dyads increased negotiation behaviors over Baseline when training began.

The Figure shows generalization to the home, where actual conflict situations were dealt with. All subject pairs made substantial increases in the percent of conflict situations negotiated.

CHAPTER VIII

Community and Organizational
Applications

Abstract **98**

A Behavioral System for Group Living

L. KEITH MILLER and RICHARD FEALLOCK (University of Kansas), In *Behavior Analysis: Areas of Research and Application* (E. Ramp and G. Semb, eds.).Englewood Cliffs: Prentice-Hall, 1975, 73-96.

Communal living for college students.

There have been many books and papers written describing idealized communal living arrangements, and during the last century a number of attempts to develop such communities actually occurred in the United States. Most, if not all, failed, often because of behavioral difficulties between members of the commune

In this century, B. F. Skinner's novel *Walden Two* and the operant field of psychology have inspired many attempts to set up group-living environments. Token economies in mental hospitals and the Achievement Place program for adolescents in trouble are two familiar examples. This paper describes the development of a living environment for a more "normal" population—college students.

Method

SUBJECTS AND SETTING: The experimental living project is housed in a large three-story house which has 29 private sleeping rooms, a lounge, a large kitchen, a game room, and a shop. The house is owned by a nonprofit corporation whose board of directors is made up primarily of behaviorally-oriented faculty at the University of Kansas in Lawrence, where the house is located. Residents of the house are students at the university who agree to abide by the rules of the house and pay a fee for room and board. About half are female and half male. Each resident paid a $25 damage deposit and a $40 bond to ensure that he would abide by the rules of the house.

PROCEDURE AND RESULTS: Instead of evaluating the overall effects of the total living arrangement, the researchers have evaluated the usefulness of several of the different components of the communal living environment. The components and some of the results of the research is described below. Basically there were two major aspects of the system, worksharing and self-government.

Worksharing. In order for the house to operate and run smoothly, a number of chores were to be done regularly. These chores were divided into three subgroups: cleaning, food, and repairs. Altogether, there were about 100 jobs which occurred once a week. A list of these jobs was posted each Thursday, and members could sign up for any of them. There was no upper or lower limit on jobs, and members were free to select jobs that fit into their other committments (e.g., morning jobs only or weekend work only). All jobs were regularly inspected by a member who had a list of criteria that each job must meet. About once a week a reliability observer who was not a resident of the house made an independent check of the house to ensure that the work was being accurately observed and checked.

Members paid about $100 per month for room and board and could reduce their monthly payment by doing some of the chores. Each job was assigned a point value, based on the time required to complete the job and the desirability of the job. For example, two hours of cooking was worth 30 points because it was a popular job, while cleaning the grease from the oven, a very unpopular, one-hour job, also produced 30 points. Members could earn as many as 100 points a week for rent reduction, with each point worth ten cents. Thus, in a month, a person who earned the maximum points could reduce his rent by $40. Points earned above the 100 maximum were put into "savings" which could be drawn on in weeks during which the member did less than the maximum chores. Members could also borrow points from each other if they wished. Because some members who had points in savings would sign up for jobs and then not complete them, a $2 fine was levied against any member who signed up for but did not complete a job.

The Cleaning System. Jobs related to keeping the house clean and tidy were supervised by a coordinator who signed up for the job. The coordinator saw to it that the equipment was maintained and necessary supplies were available. Other members then signed up for the regular cleaning jobs which were inspected each day. Research conducted on the cleaning system indicated that providing points for doing the job, allowing the points to count toward rent reduction, and the daily inspection were all important components when the goal was accomplishment of the specified jobs.

The Food System. Evening meals were provided six nights a week. The system used preplanned menus which specified the dishes to be prepared and the items required. Jobs included cooking, serving, dishwashing, kitchen cleaning, inventory clerking, and food shopping. Members could change the menus by vote if the person suggesting the change provided a detailed menu. On a question, "How good is the food, considering the price, compared to a dormitory?" members rated it 6.2 on a 7-point scale.

The Repair System. This program was also run by a coordinator who was skilled in house repairs. This person identified problems and posted the jobs that needed to be done. A detailed checklist was also provided which precisely described what was to be done.

Self-Government. When the project began, there was no self-government component. The researchers specified the conditions under which the members were required to live, and there was no vehicle for members participating in the governing of the house. Although the house was clean, and good meals were provided, the members complained, rebelled, and lobbied for a voice in the operation of the house. The result was a system of self-government. Rules of the house, which were provided in a handbook, could be changed by a vote of 75% of the members present at a weekly meeting. Members received 15 credits for attending, and at least 75% had to be present for a quorum. The developers of the program were concerned about the possibility of members voting out some of the behaviorally-based elements of the system, such as worksharing. To acquaint members with the behavioral approach, they were required to take an introductory course in behavior analysis. It covered the application of behavioral principles to the everyday living situations of normal adults. The course was operated in a format similar to the personalized courses described in Abstract 98.

When asked whether they liked living in the house more than living in a dormitory, 18 of 20 residents indicated they preferred the house.

Abstract **99**

A Community-Reinforcement Approach
to Alcoholism

GEORGE HUNT andNATHAN AZRIN (Southern Illinois University), *Behaviour Research and Therapy*, 1973, *11*, 91-104.

Treating alcoholism by changing the environment.

Alcoholism is a major health problem. In the United States alone there are about ten million alcoholics, and problems associated with excessive drinking range from automobile accidents and lost productivity on the job to fatal diseases such as cirrhosis of the liver.

Alcoholism is one of several problems that are very difficult to permanently alter when treatment is within an institutional setting. It is easy to prevent the person from drinking while in the hospital, but the enforced abstinence of the hospital rarely generalizes sufficiently so that nondrinking is maintained in the natural environment. In an effort to program generalization, this study focused on increasing the patient's functioning in the community while alcoholism was being treated.

Method

SUBJECTS AND SETTING: The study was conducted in a state hospital for treatment of alcoholism which served a sparsely-populated, rural region of the Midwest. Sixteen male alcoholics were selected for participation and were divided into eight pairs of matched subjects. A coin toss then determined whether the patient would be assigned to a control group that received no special treatment or to Community-Reinforcement counseling. Both groups participated in the regular services of the hospital.

PROCEDURE: Community Reinforcement Counseling (CRC), the treatment used in this study, is actually a package of several different procedures. One underlying assumption of CRC is that drinking will decrease if it results in loss or suspension of reinforcers for the drinker. Another assumption is that increasing the number of reinforcers an alcoholic can obtain by not drinking will tend to discourage resumption of drinking.

The experimenters identified three general areas of living (work, family, and social life) and provided several programs to increase the number of reinforcers contingent on remaining sober.

Vocational Counseling. Patients without jobs were taught to write appropriate re̊sume̊s, were given instruction in finding a job, and were trained in job-interview skills. The counselor also arranged for transportation and accompanied the patient to his interview.

Marital and Family Counseling. The counseling program used is described in Abstract number 46.

Social Counseling. The experimenters assumed that drinking tends to exclude patients from many potentially reinforcing social interactions, so that the alcoholic's circle of friends is often limited to other problem drinkers. The patients were encouraged to establish social relationships with friends, relatives, and community groups in whose company drinking was unacceptable. They were also discouraged from interacting with friends who had a drinking problem.

Since the patient's history of drinking had often resulted in a very small circle of friends, a former tavern was converted to a social club where the patients could come with wives or friends for an evening. Drinking was not permitted.

Reinforcer-Access Counseling: In addition to the services described above, referrals were made to appropriate agencies if the patient experienced difficulties not addressed in the treatment package. Those having legal problems, for example, were referred to a lawyer.

If a subject did not have a telephone, newspaper, car, or television, the counselor helped him to obtain them. Installation charges and the first month's payment were sometimes paid for the patient, and he was expected to pay the remaining costs. This procedure gave the patient a more attractive living situation, provided needed transportation, and added reinforcers to the patient's environment that would be lost if drinking continued to be a problem.

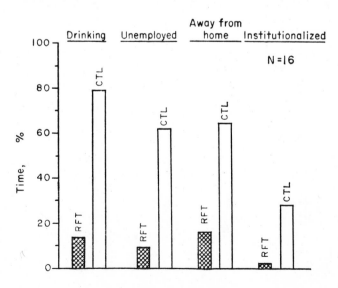

Results

After discharge from the hospital, a counselor visited the patient once or twice a week for the first month, and gradually decreased the amount of contact across at least six months.These visits were part of the therapeutic program, but they were also used to collect data in the form of self-reports and reports of family members on the patient's progress. The Figure shows the percent of days the control and treatment groups drank, remained away from home, were institutionalized, or were drinking. The differences, all in favor of the treated group, were significant (t-tests). The effects of treatment remained across the six-month follow-up. Patients in the CRC group made an average of $355 a month, while control group members made $190. In the CRC group, all patients except one discontinued regular drinking, while in the control group all patients except one continued to drink regularly.

Abstract **100**

Contingency Management in a Municipally-administered Antabuse Program for Alcoholics

STEPHEN HAYNES (University of South Carolina), *Journal of Behavior Research and Experimental Psychiatry*, 1973,4, 31-32.

A simple approach to the problem of dropouts in antabuse treatment programs.

Chronic alcoholism is a major problem in many large communities, with a sizeable percentage of law enforcement time and social-service attention directed at the problems and disruptions brought about by excessive drinking. Imprisonment, the traditional solution, has not been an effective means of solving the problem. Another approach, the use of antabuse, appears promising, but the high dropout rates that occur in many programs has limited its effectiveness. Antabuse, if taken regularly, reduces the intake of alcohol, because drinking after taking the drug makes the person very ill. This study describes a simple contingency system that was used to decrease the number of dropouts from the program.

Method

Individuals who had records of frequent arrests for public intoxication were given a choice of one year of antabuse treatment or the traditional 90-day jail sentence. Those who chose antabuse were required to visit the probation office of the municipal court twice a week and take the medication there. They were placed on probation for one year, and if they missed more than one or two visits their probation was terminated and they returned to jail to serve their sentence.

Results

At the end of the first year, 138 alcoholics had chosen the antabuse program, while only three chose the jail term. Sixty-six of the 138 were still taking antabuse at the end of the year, 35 had left town without permission, 17 had broken probation and returned to jail, 14 had left the community with permission (usually to take a job), three were hospitalized, and three were unaccounted for.

The arrest records of all those who remained in town indicated that they had had an average of 3.8 arrests during the year preceding the antabuse treatment, and only .3 arrests during the year they received treatment.

Abstract **101**

Conditioning Techniques in a Community-based Operant Environment for Psychotic Men

JOHN HENDERSON (Spruce House, Horizon House, Inc.) and PASCAL SCOLES (West Philadelphia Mental Health Consortium), *Behavior Therapy*, 1971, *1*, 245-251.

Between the hospital and the home:
A group-living environment for psychotic adults.

Until very recently, most treatment programs for psychotic adults involved state or private mental hospitals. The program described in this paper is an alternative setting in the community.

Method

SUBJECTS AND SETTING: Follow-up data presented on 21 residents who were assigned to Spruce House, a community-based, operant-environment for psychotic men, ages 18 to 55. Ten control subjects, who were sent to a state hospital, and nine who were sent to a city general hospital ,were also studied. Assignment to one of the three treatment alternatives was done randomly by an independent facility which had the initial contact with all residents.

PROCEDURE: Residents of Spruce House were involved in three types of programs: work habituation, social adjustment, and counter-symptom conditioning. Within each of these three areas a system of contingent reinforcement was used. In addition to social and primary reinforcement, tokens, called "grickles," were awarded, which could be exchanged for a variety of back-up reinforcers such as extra food, cigarettes, candy, telephone calls, passes, and merchandise.

Work Habituation. The work program operated six mornings and three afternoons a week, with four work-periods occurring in a typical work day. Available jobs were arranged in order of the amount of initiative or interpersonal skills required to perform them. Some of the jobs are listed in Table 1. Jobs that were higher on the list and thus involved more responsibility allowed the resident to earn more tokens. Consistent performance on a job led to "bonus" tokens after each work period, at the end of the day, and at the end of the week. Promotion to a more responsibile

Table 1
Partial Listing of Job Titles with Pay Rates and Bonuses

Job title	Maximum period pay+	Period bonus	Day bonus	Maximum day pay (inc. bonus)	Week bonus	Maximum 6-day pay (inc. bonus)
Kitchen steward	14	4	8	80	20	500
Headwaiter	12	4	6	70	15	435
Special projects foreman	13	4	9	75	15	465
Teacher[b]	10	5	5	—	15	—
Front office clerk	13	4	9	75	15	465
Kitchen aid	9	4	8	60	10	400
Messenger	8	4	7	55	10	340
Waiter	8	4	7	55	10	340
Special projects crewman	8	4	9	57	10	352
Janitor	7	4	8	52	10	322
Store clerk[b]	7	4	4	—	10	—
Floor waxer	6	5	6	50	18	310
Laundry man	6	4	8	48	10	298
Housekeeper	5	3	8	40	10	250

Table 2
Reinforced Social Behaviors and Associated Grickle Payments

Reinforced behaviors	Grickles awarded per occurrence	Maximum grickle reinforcement per activity		
		In facility[a]	Bridging[b]	In community
Nonsocial participation	1	4	2	4
Superficial conversation	2	6	6	6
Social involvement	3	9	12	12
Initiative or role modeling	4	8	12	12

[a] Activities include discussion groups, crafts, and games.

[b] Activities include role playing and "coed club" dances conducted wtihin the facility but with volunteers from the community participating.

[c] These activities are conducted at the YMCA and other in-community facilities.

job occurred when the resident earned the maximum available tokens for the job currently held—an indication the job had been done well. The hierarchical order of the jobs thus allowed the resident to begin with a job that was relatively simple and to proceed to more involved responsibilities as he demonstrated a capability for handling them.

Social Adjustment. Social activities were conducted three afternoons and six evenings a week. They included dances, athletics, field trips, role playing, discussion groups, crafts and games. Volunteers from the community participated in some activities, along with residents and staff. Tokens were awarded for four levels of social involvement, as shown in Table 2. More tokens were earned as the level of social involvement increased and as the involvement was more oriented toward the community and away from the facility. Residents were ranked once a week according to their work and social earnings, and privileges such as bedroom assignments and dining room seating were determined by the residents' ranking. Residents who showed substantial improvement could receive a special prize.

Counter-Symptom Conditioning. Problems peculiar to one or a few residents were handled through standard behavior modification procedures developed particularly for the individual resident. Examples are programmed instruction for residents who needed academic training and token reinforcement of "conversation" in a resident who was uncommunicative.

Results

Table 3 presents follow-up data on the three groups across the 18 months immediately following their release. Although Spruce House, the operant facility, kept its residents longer (initial hospitalization), these residents spent less total time in a facility (total hospitalization) and had fewer days of rehospitalization. They also spent more days in the community and more days employed.

Programs such as Spruce House can be operated for about 20 residents, with two or three staff members on each shift. Operating costs per patient are about three times greater than those reported by state hospitals and about half those reported by general hospitals.

Table 3
Initial Hospitalization, Rehospitalization, Community Tenure, and Employment during the Follow-up Period (549 Days) for Subjects from the Original Sample.

| | Facility of initial assignment | | | | | |
| | Operant (N = 21) | | State (N = 10) | | City (N = 9) | |
Variables	Days	%	Days	%	Days	%
Initial hospitalization (including transfers)						
Mean days	167		156		99	
% of follow-up period		30		28		18
Total hospitalization						
Mean days	180		249		202	
% of follow-up period		33		45		37
Time in Community						
Mean days	369		300		347	
% of follow-up period		67		55		63
Employment						
Mean days	125		42		99	
% of time in community		34		14		29
Rehospitalization	(n = 6)		(n = 5)		(n = 6)	
Mean days	45		178		154	
% of follow-up period		8		32		28

Abstract 102

Improving Job Performance of Neighborhood Youth Corps Aides in an Urban Recreation Program

CHARLES PIERCE and TODD RISLEY (University of Kansas),
Journal of Applied Behavior Analysis, 1974, *7*, 207-215.

Using reinforcement to improve the job performance of disadvantaged adolescents.

Although federal job training programs of the 1960s, which were geared toward disadvantaged adolescents and adults, provided money to pay those taking training, most funds were awarded in the form of salaries. That is, money paid the individual was contingent on his physical presence in the program, but not on what he actually did while there. This study focused on methods of improving job performance of a group of part-time workers in a neighborhood recreation program.

Method

SUBJECTS AND SETTING: Seven black adolescents serving as recreation aides through a Neighborhood Youth Corp (NYC) program were studied. There were three 14-year-old females, three 14-year-old males, and one 16-year-old male. All were paid $1.65 an hour by NYC and worked in a community recreation center in an economically-deprived area of Kansas City, Kansas. The center was open five days a week.

PROCEDURE: Initially, the trainees were told by the director of the center their job was "to help the kids, to teach the kids to play different games, and to supervise their play." After these instructions, the trainees spent most of their time playing games. Regular staff of the center then complained about the situation.

Several changes were made in the program in an effort to increase the job performance of the trainees:

Table 1
Brief Job Descriptions for Neighborhood Youth Corps Recreation Trainees

Recreation Supervisor:	For each time listed, record the number of persons in each activity area, and number playing, and the number of rule violations. Enforce immediately rule violations by writing the rule violated and the new program closing time on the blackboard.
Facility Supervisor:	Supervise program participants cleaning the center grounds and preparing the game room for recreation periods. Distribute passes for special recreation periods to those youths who correctly completed an assigned task.
Snack Bar Supervisor:	Operate a snack bar in the game room, inventory supplies, maintain a record of receipts for all purchases, and supervise cleanup periods in the snack area.
Tournament Supervisor:	Design and supervise daily tournaments for the younger program participants. Give a special recreation period pass to the winner of each period's tournament.
Participant and Rule Monitor:	Record names of participants in each activity area and minor rule violations not recorded by the Recreation Supervisor.
Hall Monitor:	Prevent participants from disrupting other on-going community center activities and graph data recorded by the other supervisors.

Table 2
Checklist of Staff Performance for 3:00 to 3:30 p.m. Time Period

Time	Staff	In Assigned Area?	Yes	No	Job Completely Done?	Yes	No
3:10	Rec. Supervisor	Recreation Room	—	—	Rec. room swept?	—	—
					Rec. room trash cans empty?	—	—
3:10	Par. & Rule Monitor	Recreation Room	—	—	Hallway, restrooms swept?	—	—
					Wastebaskets empty?	—	—
					Washbasins & mirrors washed?	—	—
3-3:30	Hall Monitor 1	In Hallway	—	—			
3:15	Rec. Supervisor	Recreation Room	—	—			
3:10	Snack Bar Super.	Behind Snack Bar	—	—	Kitchen swept?	—	—
					Wastebaskets empty?	—	—
					Counters & tables clean?	—	—
					Inventory done?	—	—
3:25	Tournament Super.	Small Games Area	—	—	Tournament set up?	—	—
3:30	Rec. Supervisor	Recreation Room	—	—	Closing time on blackboard?	—	—
					Rec. room doors open?	—	—

Job Descriptions. First, specific and objective job descriptions were prepared for each worker, and a daily checklist was developed from the descriptions. Brief job descriptions are shown in Table 1, and an example of a checklist is provided in Table 2. Each trainee was then regularly observed during his or her working day and his performance rated on the checklists. Time and number of observations per trainee each day varied somewhat, so that the trainees could not predict exactly when they would be observed. If a trainee was not performing a task appropriately, the observer informed him or her of the problem. The percent of tasks completed each day was posted beside the worker's daily sign-in sheet.

Threat to Fire. One week after the job descriptions were provided, the director of the center met with the trainees and told them he was still not satisfied with their work and threatened to fire anyone who did not improve.

Pay for Tasks Completed. At the end of the 11th day of the study, the director met with the trainees again and explained that the work was still not being completed. He indicated he did not want to fire anyone and outlined a new method of computing hourly wages. Instead of being paid for "clock time," they would be paid for "work time." That is, if the observations of their work behavior showed they completed only 50% of their tasks during a day, they would be paid for a half-day's work, even though they spent the entire day in the center.

Full Pay. After the 18th day of the study, the trainees were told that the observer who had been checking their performance had another job in the preschool next door and would not be able to observe their work in the future. They were told by the director that they were doing a fine job and were urged to continue the good work. He also indicated they would receive full pay during this period.

In essence, the conditions of the Full Pay condition were similar to those during the initial phase, Job Descriptions. Actually, the observer continued to check the workers' performances on "breaks" from his other job.

Pay for Tasks Completed. After the 21st day, the observer returned and began checking performance openly again. Trainees were paid according to the proportion of the jobs they completed. The study ended after 25 days, when the NYC program closed.

Results

The Figure shows the percent of tasks completed by each trainee under the various experimental conditions. Threatening to fire the trainees improved the performance of several, but the effects were temporary for a number of them. Basing pay on the tasks completed resulted in the highest levels of performance, and when the contingency was removed during the Full Pay condition, the percent of tasks completed dropped for all seven trainees. It rose again when the contingency was reinstated.

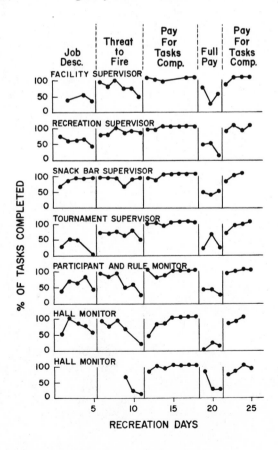

Abstract **103**

Increasing Rural Head-Start Children's
Consumption of Middle-Class Meals

CHARLES MADSEN, CLIFFORD MADSEN, and FAITH THOMPSON (Florida State University), *Journal of Applied Behavior Analysis,* 1974, 7, 257-262.

A behavioral approach to changing eating habits.

The absence of nutritious food for a well-balanced diet is a frequent part of the poverty cycle, even in developed nations. Improper diet has been associated with a number of psychological and learning problems. Through their attendance in Head Start, the children who were studied in this project had the opportunity to eat food that met their nutritional requirements. Observations in their homes indicated, however, that the type and style of preparation of the food was quite different from that provided at school. The result was a low rate of consumption of the Head Start food.

Since the food for Head Start was prepared in a central kitchen and trucked to the school, it could not be modified to make it more acceptable to the children. The investigators thus attempted to increase consumption of the available food.

Method

SUBJECTS AND SETTING: The subjects were 46 rural black children enrolled in a summer Head Start program. All children were from families with incomes below the poverty level; their mean age was six years, and they averaged four to six pounds underweight.

PROCEDURE: Parents were requested not to feed their children breakfast, because it was served at the school. The meal included items such as scrambled eggs, sausages, bacon, ham, toast, jelly, milk, juice, pancakes, and waffles. None of the items, except bread, was a normal part of their breakfast at home. Attendance averaged 35 children daily. Each prepackaged and sealed breakfast was weighed before eating. When the child finished eating, it was weighed again and the amount of food consumed calculated. Behaioral observations of eating behavior during the first 15 minutes of breakfast were also made. Each minute was divided into 15-second intervals. An observer then counted the number of children who

248

were eating during an interval, and at the end of the interval recorded the number on the data sheet. Two observers were used; each observed two tables of about seven or eight children.

Baseline 1. For four days, meals were weighed and behavior observed with no other changes in the breakfast routine.

Reinforcement 1. On the 5th day, the four teachers who worked with the children were instructed to circulate around the cafeteria, praising the children and giving sugar-coated cereal to those who were eating. They made comments such as "Sally, you're tasting those eggs this morning; that's very good, here's a treat!" In addition, all children who finished the entire meal were given a special reward (five small candies).

Baseline 2. On days 9, 10, and 11, the teachers were asked to behave in much the same manner as they did during the first Baseline. They walked about the room but provided no reinforcement for eating.

Reinforcement 2. During the last four days of the experiment the conditions were the same as in Reinforcement 1.

Results

The percentage of children who were eating during any 15-second interval was about 20% during the two Baseline conditions and 33% during reinforcement. The Figure shows a similar pattern in the percent of food consumed by the group. It was highest during reinforcement. The average child consumed about one fifth more food under the reinforcement conditions than under Baseline conditions.

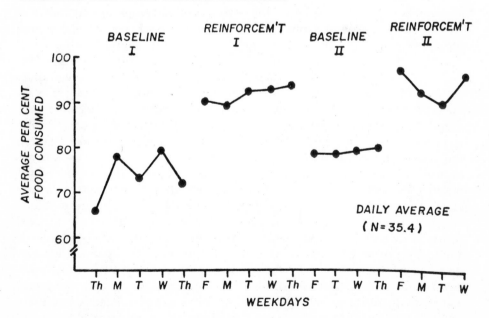

249

Abstract **104**

Job-finding Club: A Group-assisted
Program for Obtaining Employment

NATHAN AZRIN, T. FLORES, and S. J. KAPLAN (Anna State
Hospital), *Behaviour Reserach and Therapy*, 1975, *13*, 17-26.

Finding a job: A comprehensive job-search skills-training program.

The effects of unemployment range well beyond the obvious difficulties
involving morale and money experienced by the specific individual.
Unemployment has also been closely associated with problems affecting
the whole of society, such as high crime rates, alcoholism, and hospitalization. This study evaluated a comprehensive package of procedures designed to help unemployed adults find jobs.

Method

SUBJECTS AND SETTING: The project took place in a small college town of
about 30,000, which had a long history of above-average unemployment.
Clients were obtained from the state employment service, personnel
departments of large businesses, newspaper advertisements, and word-
of-mouth communication. Interested adults who wanted full-time employment and were currently unemployed were told that it involved daily
sessions. All clients who agreed to attend and who were not currently
receiving unemployment compensation were included. A rough estimate
of the employment probability for each client was obtained by considering
variables such as age, sex, race, education, marital status, type of position
and salary desired, dependents, and current financial resources. Clients
were then placed in matched pairs with a coin toss determining which
member of the pair received counseling and which was assigned to a control
group receiving no treatment. Clients attending less than four sessions
were dropped from the data analysis, as were their controls. In total, 60
clients, 28 males and 32 females, received at least five sessions of
counseling. Average age was 25, and average years of education was 14.
They had been employed for about six of the preceding 12 months.
PROCEDURE: Group counseling sessions were held daily, with the group
size ranging from two to eight. The first two sessions lasted about three
hours with later sessions one to two hours. A new group began about every

two weeks, and after two introductory sessions it joined the clients who had entered counseling earlier.

The counseling program had three major components: attending the group meeting, obtaining job leads, and pursuing leads.

The Group Meeting. The daily group sessions were used to train clients in appropriate job-seeking behaviors and to provide motivation. Each client was paired with a "buddy" who helped in all aspects of job hunting. Daily sessions also helped emphasize the full-time nature of the task of job finding. Areas such as dress and grooming were covered in the meetings, and each client's buddy was asked to comment on appropriateness of clothing and grooming. Clients were also encouraged to widen their range of positions to be considered and instructed to include information about their personal attributes, such as hobbies, interests, and so forth, on applications. Personal interviews and telephone contact with potential employers were encouraged, rather than exclusive use of application forms. They also shared transportation, because the city had no public transport; role-played interviews and telephone contact procedures; exchanged job leads, and provided mutual encouragement. During the meetings, additional attempts to encourage and motivate job-seeking included giving statistics and taped comments of former clients who had obtained employment. In addition, a letter to the client's family included suggestions on how it could help the client find a job.

Obtaining Job Leads. Several procedures for obtaining job leads were instituted. Each client shared leads which were not currently open to him; friends and relatives were systematically contacted; newspaper ads were scrutinized carefully and potential jobs followed up, even if the applicant was not sure every requirement was met. Former employers were contacted and asked about positions they had open or were aware of; businesses with jobs in the applicant's field were identified through the telephone directory and called by phone; client's placed "situations wanted" ads which described their job and personal qualifications (e.g., "likes to meet people"); finally, potential as well as former employers reporting no openings were asked to provide other leads and, in addition, were asked whether their names could be used in making the contact.

Pursuing Leads. Clients were taught how to write a résumé and were instructed to submit it at the time of initial contact with an employer. In addition, open letters of recommendation were obtained and provided at the initial contact. Clients were given extensive instruction and practice through role-playing in handling interviews and telephone contacts. They were instructed to ask permission of employers who had no openings at present to call back later. Clients also learned a record-keeping system which involved recording phone numbers, names, addresses, and outcome of contact. This facilitated later call-backs and sharing job leads. Finally, money, materials, and labor were made available to the clients to type résumés and letters, for postage, for photographs to be included with the résumé, and for specialized directories of local businesses and agencies.

251

Results

The average job-seeker who was counseled began full-time work in 14 days, while the control group averaged 53 days. The difference was significant using a Wilcoxin Text. Figure 1 shows the progress of the two groups in finding jobs during the first three months. The counseled group is clearly superior. Their mean starting salary was also higher, and, as Figure 2 shows, the counseled group tended to find a higher-level job than the control group.

Additional correlational data showed that those who attended the sessions regularly were more successful than those who attended sporadically.

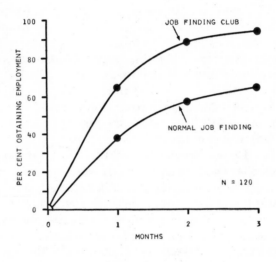

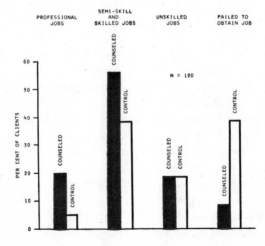

Abstract **105**

The Development of Anti-Litter Behavior
in a Forest Campground

ROGER CLARK, ROBERT BURGESS, and JOHN HENDEE (U.S. Forest Service and University of Washington), *Journal of Applied Behavior Analysis*, 1972, 5, 1-5.

Changing litter patterns through reinforcement.

Although there have been a number of national and local campaigns to reduce littering, the problem continues to grow. One study revealed, for example, that it costs about half a billion dollars a year to clean up litter along highways and in forests, parks, beaches, and other public places in the United States. Legal sanctions against littering, anti-litter propaganda, and the provision of garbage containers at convenient points are common but generally ineffective procedures. This study devised a reinforcement program to reduce littering in a camping area.

Method

SUBJECTS AND SETTING: Twenty-six children, ages six to 14, selected from seven families camping in a national forest, were the subjects.

PROCEDURE: The study was conducted during two successive weekends in August. Before each weekend, selected areas of the campground were "seeded" with litter such as paper bags, cans, nondeposit bottles, and deposit bottles. One hundred sixty pieces of litter had been previously planted and their locations marked on a map. The amount of planted and natural litter in the campground was counted each day by two observers who followed a predetermined route on Thursday to Sunday at about 4:30 P.M. and on Monday morning after most campers had left.

Baseline Weekend. On the first weekend, the experimenters simply counted the litter and then measured the level of litter in the campground over the weekend.

Experimental Weekend. On the following Saturday at about 10:00 A.M., one experimenter in a Forest Service uniform approached seven families and told the parents there was a litter problem in the area. He asked if their children would help. The children were told they could select a reinforcer for helping. The choice included a "Smokey Bear" shoulder patch or comic book, a Junior Forest Ranger Badge, a "Keep Washington Green" pin, or a box of chewing gum. Each child was a given a 30-gallon plastic bag and told in which general areas to look for litter. The ranger returned at 7:00 P.M. to pick up the bags and give the children their reward. No other contact with the families occurred, and the children were not observed or monitored during the day.

Results

The Figure shows the amount of litter in the campground across the two weekends. During the first weekend, the level of litter did decrease somewhat across the period, although there was still a large amount of litter in the campground on Monday morning. Deposit bottles were picked up most often, while paper bags and cans were less frequently placed in garbage receptacles. Data from Thursday and Friday of the second weekend show the level of all four types of litter was approximately the same as the preceding Thursday and Friday. After the incentive procedure was explained to the families, however, the level of all types of litter dropped to very low levels and remained there across the weekend. The experimenters reported the incentive procedure was enthusiastically accepted by the children, who turned in 26 bags of litter—more than 150 pounds. Most selected the Smokey Bear patches as their reward. Total cost of incentives was $3.00, with two man-hours required to implement the procedure. Collecting the same amount of litter using campground personnel would have taken about 16 to 20 hours and cost $50 to $60.

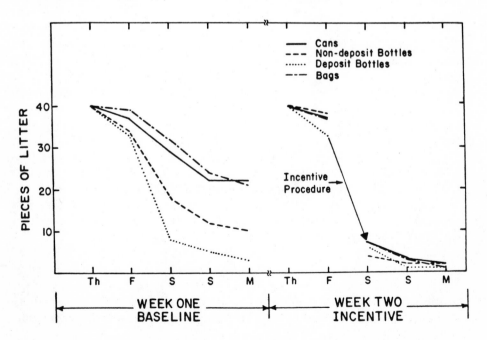

Abstract **106**

Fixed-Interval Work Habits of Congress

PAUL WEISBERG and PHILLIP WALDROP(University of Alabama), *Journal of Applied Behavior Analysis*, 1972, 5, 93-97.

Similarity between pigeons and politicians.

There is a large body of research that shows animals such as pigeons, rats, and monkeys behave differently under different schedules of reinforcement. Ratio schedules, for example, in which reinforcement is determined by the number of responses made, generally produce higher rates of responding than do interval schedules which require only one response at the end of a particular time period for reinforcement.

One common schedule, fixed interval, produces a familiar pattern of responding. A pigeon on a five-minute fixed interval (FI-5) schedule, for example, will stop responding immediately after reinforcement. As the minutes pass, the pigeon begins responding sporadically, then more frequently, until the five-minute point approaches. After precisely five minutes pass, a response is reinforced, and the pigeon again stops responding. This pattern, called Fixed Interval Scallops because of its characteristic shape on a cumulative recorder, is well known in basic operant research. In this study, members of the United States Congress seem to be guided by the same reinforcement delivery schedule as are pigeons.

Method

SUBJECTS AND SETTING: This was not an experimental study in the usual sense of the word. Instead, the behavior of the United States Congress was assessed, using data drawn from the *Congressional Digest*.

PROCEDURE: Congress processes legislation in time-limited sessions which require the bills to be passed before the session ends.

Result

The experimenters graphed the number of bills passed for Congressional Sessions 80 through 90, and as Figures 1 and 2 show, the rate of passing bills did indeed accelerate as the end of the session approached. It is argued that this pattern is not due to Fixed Interval escape behavior. Members of Congress are subjected to many forms of pressure from organized lobbies, special interest groups, and segments of their voting constituency. If bills of interest to these groups are not passed, the result will be the application of aversive consequences to the Congressperson after the session ends.

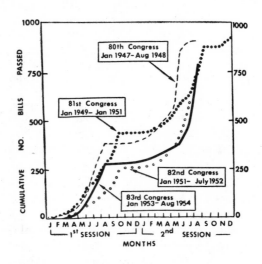

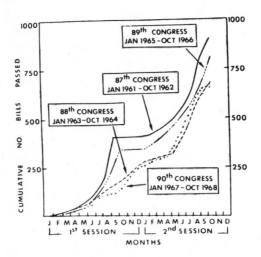

Abstract **107**

Effects of Bonuses for Punctuality
On the Tardiness of Industral Workers

JAIME HERMANN, ANA DE MONTES, BENJAMIN DOMINGUEZ, FRANCISCO MONTES, B. L. HOPKINS (University of Kansas), *Journal of Applied Behavior Analysis,* 1973, *6,* 563-572.

Behavior modification in a factory setting.

Although a number of behaviorists have suggested use of behavior modification in business, there has actually been very little experimental validation of such procedures in industrial settings. This study is an evaluation of a reinforcement procedure used to reduce the tardiness of industrial workers in a factory in Mexico City. The 131 workers at the plant had accumulated 750 tardies during the year preceding the study, in spite of annual bonuses for punctuality and a procedure that permitted supervisors to suspend a worker for one day on accumulation of three tardies.

Method

SUBJECTS: Twelve male workers with chronic tardiness problems were divided into an experimental and a control group. Most had little formal education, had worked for the company for an average of four years, and ranged in age from 19 to 40 years.

PROCEDURE: After the program was explained, each of the workers in the treatment group agreed to participate. Every day the worker arrived on time a slip was attached to his time card stating that he had been punctual. Each slip was worth about 2 pesos (16¢) which could be collected from the experimenter at the end of each working week. During the experimental period, the annual bonuses of a maximum 500 pesos ($40) and the suspension procedure were in effect. The slips were delivered to the men by a guard who was always present when the workers punched in for work. The control group was not told about the experiment.

Results

The Figure presents the results of the experiment. An average of about 10%

257

of the workers in the control group were tardy each day. The experimental group's tardiness was also high (15%) during the first Baseline, but dropped to a mean of 2.5% during the first treatment period.

The effects of treatment and Baseline on tardiness were replicated twice, indicating that the intervention was successful.

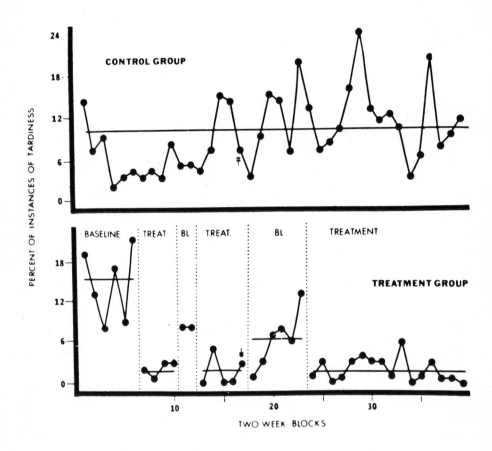

CHAPTER IX

Training Behavioral Engineers

Abstract 108

Instructions, Modeling and Rehearsal: Implications for Training

GERALD STONE and ADRIAN VANCE (University of Western Ontario), *Journal of Counseling Psychology, in press.*

Evaluating alternative methods for teaching counseling skills.

With increasing public demand on the services of the helping professions, there is a notable trend toward utilizing paraprofessionals as lay counselors and helpers. Training for these individuals has typically involved a combined package of instructions, modeling and rehearsal of human-relations skills. This study was conducted to examine the relative effectiveness of these three techniques in producing a paraprofessional skilled in empathic responses. An empathic response is one that communicates to a person experiencing an emotional difficulty that the listener understands.

Method

SUBJECTS AND SETTING: Forty-eight subjects from an introductory psychology course were randomly assigned to one of eight training groups with the restriction that there be four females and two males in each group.

The eight training groups were 1) instructions, 2) modeling, 3) rehearsal, 4) instructions and modeling, 5) instructions and rehearsal, 6) modeling and rehearsal, 7) instructions, modeling and rehearsal, and 8) control.

Training was conducted via prerecorded videotape in an experimental room with an experimenter present to operate the videotape player. All videotape presentations were identical except for the appropriate manipulation required by the particular condition.

PROCEDURE:

Instructions: Specific instructions on formulating an empathic response were given, including both positive and negative guidelines which would help in discriminating appropriate responses. No examples were given to minimize any confounding with modeling.

Modeling: Five examples of empathic communications were shown to the subjects in this condition. Each example included a low- and a high-level empathic response. Instructions about the desired response were excluded.

Rehearsal: General instructions concerning empathic responding were necessary here so that subjects would be aware of the direction in which they were to respond. Subjects were then presented with ten problems by male and female helpers to which they were to respond empathically. They were then given feedback ("Needs improvement"—red light; "Excellent"—green light). The criteria for these judgements were based on a scale of empathic communication.

Combined Conditions: These represented combinations of the above-noted conditions and were presented as follows: instructions, then models; instructions, then rehearsal; models, then rehearsal; instructions, then models, then rehearsal.

Control: Subjects were given no specific training, but were instructed on the general criterion behavior. Posttest followed one week after pretest for all conditions.

Dependent Variables: Two measures were used. Before and after training, subjects wrote replies to a standardized set of 16 stimulus statements. The ten-point Revised Carkhuff Empathy Scale was used to judge the statements.

Two weeks after training, all subjects were asked to assume a helping role in a six-minute critical incident interview. That is, subjects role-played a situation demanding empathic communication.

Results

Figures 1 and 2 present the results from the 16-statement standardized index for the pre- and posttest periods (Figure 1) and those for critical incident performance in the follow-up period (Figure 2). All groups except control improved significantly in empathic communication on the posttest measure. The follow-up data, from the critical incident interview, indicated that any combination of training methods was superior to any single method. Those groups trained in only one method functioned at their pretest level during the interview. The modeling component was shown through an analysis of variance to be critical. Although instructions and rehearsal appeared facilitative, they did not achieve significance statistically.

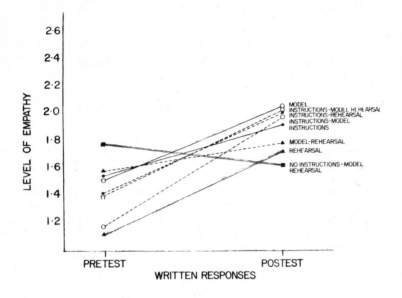

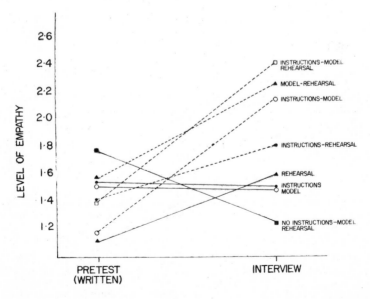

Abstract **109**

An Evaluation of Parent-Training Procedures Designed to Alter Inappropriate Aggressive Behavior of Boys

N. A. WILTZ (University of Oregon) and G. R. PATTERSON (Oregon Research Institute), *Behavior Therapy*, 1974, 5, 215-221.

A model parent-training program.

Although most children live with their parents from 16 to 18 years, it is an unfortunte reality that a position of this responsibility has rarely been the subject of systematic training. The study reported here investigated the effects of training parents to modify aggressive behavior in their sons and examined the effects of that training on the target behaviors.

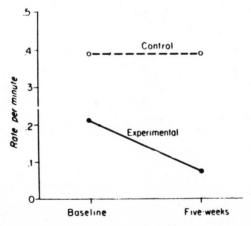

Mean rate of targeted deviant behavior for experimental and control groups.

Method

SUBJECTS: Six pairs of boys who had been referred for problems with aggression were selected. They were matched on the basis of age, socioeconomic status, and Baseline aggressive behavior. Parents of one of each pair were assigned to the parent-training condition, while the other parents were assigned to a control condition. Control-group parents were told that treatment was not to begin until five weeks after the initial home-observation period. During that five-week period, the experimental parents were trained. Boys in the experimetal group averaged 9.8 years of age. Control group boys averaged 9.3 years.

PROCEDURE:

Parent Training: Parents were required first to read *Living with Children: New Methods for Parents and Teachers* (G. R Patterson, and M. E. Gullion, Champaign, Illinois: Research Press, 1968) to learn the concepts, language, and data-collection skills necessary to plan and carry out contingency management programs. This is a programmed text based on social learning principles. Second, parents were seen individually and required to identify (target) an aggressive behavior that they wanted to alter. They were instructed in observing and behavior-measurement techniques. Third, parents were invited to join a parent-group in which progress was discussed, and modifications of treatment strategies suggested by other parents and by the therapists for 30 minutes. When their case had been discussed, parents could leave or stay.

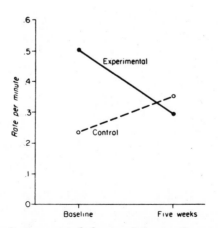

FIG. 2. Mean rate of non-targeted deviant behavior for experimental and control groups.

The therapists set three goals: 1) target behavior must be reduced to 30% of Baseline occurrence; 2) a second behavior was to be targeted and modified by the parents in a direction that they determined; 3) one set of parents helped another set through program suggestions during the group meetings.

Home Observation: A 29-category coding system for family social behavior, which included such classes as negative physcial contact, humiliation, noncompliance and disapproval, was used. Observations occurred when the entire family was home, continued for ten Baseline sessions, and included 100 minutes of observation data per family member. Five weeks after treatment began, both control and treatment group members were observed on two days. The target child was observed for 20 minutes and other family members for five.

Results

Data on the mean rate of targeted aggressive behavior for experimental and control groups is presented in Figure 1. The experimental group decrease was statistically significant. Figure 2 depicts the rate of nontargeted but deviant behavior recorded, using the 29-category coding system. Although the data are in the direction favoring the experimental group, the difference was not statistically significant.

Abstract 110

Relative Effectiveness of Behavioral and Reflective Group Counseling with Parents of Mentally Retarded Children

JOSEPH TAVORMINA (University of Virginia), *Journal of Consulting and Clinical Psychology*, 1975, *43*, 22-31.

Comparing two popular methods of training parents.

Training parents to deal effectively with their retarded children is an important function of many psychologists. The situational stress and the day-to-day child-management problems of rearing special children can have major ramifications on parent and child alike in terms of the personal development of both. This study compared two popular orientations toward dealing with these difficulties: behavioral counseling and reflective counseling.

Method

SUBJECTS AND SETTING: Fifty-one mothers, whose age averaged 37.4 years, participated. They had been in school for a mean of 12.8 years. Their children averaged 6.7 years. Although there were no reliable estimates for most children, it appeared that the majority would score below 50 on an IQ test.

PROCEDURE: Mothers were administered six outcome measures during Baseline 1. The measures were as follows: 1) Herford Parent Attitude Survey, which measures parental feelings of adequacy in their role, the responsibility they feel for their children's behavior, acceptance of the child, mutual trust, and understanding. 2) Missouri Behavior Problem Checklist, a children's behavior rating scale scored along dimensions of aggression, inhibition, activity level, sleep disturbance, somatization, and sociability. 3) Behavior observations which were taken during a 25-minute mother-child interaction in a playroom which could be observed through a one-way mirror. The behaviors were scored in terms of the following: antecedent conditions (mother or child could command, ignore, or attempt to affiliate), response (compliance, noncompliance, or ignoring), and consequence (initiator's response, positive reinforcement, punishment, or ignoring). These in turn were coded as appropriate or inappropriate. The mother was instructed prior to the observation session to allow unstructured free play during part of the observation sessions and to provide structured command play (e.g., "Please have your child pick up the toys and put them away") during the other part. 4) Ratings of target behavior. Mothers listed the three most troublesome problems and rated them on a nine-point scale from "No disruption" to "Significant Disruption." The mother also rated her emotional reaction from "none" to "considerable." 5) Frequency count of target behavior. Mothers recorded the frequency of the behaviors for a one-week period during Baseline 2 and post-treatment periods. 6) Multiple-choice questionnaire of the worth of the group, which was administered after treatment.

Baseline 1 measurements were taken two months before the first training began. At Baseline 2, which occurred just prior to the beginning of the groups, the first five measures listed above were readministered and mothers were assigned to treatment groups or to control groups on the basis of their stated time preference. Those who preferred training in February and March were placed in treatment groups; those who preferred April and May were controls. The 38 mothers in treatment conditions were assigned to one of two groups using behavioral methods (Ns = 11 & 8) or to one of two groups using reflective counseling (Ns = 10 & 6). There were no

265

significant pretreatment differences between the groups.

All treatment groups received eight weekly 14-hour counseling sessions, and both treatment and control subjects were retested on all measures. Mothers in the control group were later counseled using a combined behavioral and reflective approach.

Reflective Counseling. The book *Between Parent and Child* (Haim Ginott, New York: Avon, 1959) served as a reference text for dealing with the feelings of children and for guidelines to setting appropriate limits and providing alternative activities for children.

Group discussion in the reflective counseling groups focused on empathy, acceptance, and understanding, and their application to each mother's situation.

Behavior Counseling. The book *Parents Are Teachers: A Child Management Program* (Wesley C. Becker, Champaign, Illinois: Research Press, 1971) was used to teach the application of operant techniques to specific child-rearing difficulties. Group discussion centered around teaching the use of praise and positive consequences, rather than aversive techniques, to change behavior. Role-playing, modeling, and discussion were used to help mothers work out programs for their own children.

Results

Differences from Baseline 1 to Baseline 2 occurred only on the Missouri Behavior Problem Checklist, Aggression Scale. Mothers across all groups reported a decrease in the amount of aggressive behavior by their children. No other differences were found.

Analyses of variance indicated that both reflective and behavioral counseling were equally effective in decreasing the number of problems listed by mothers, and that there were no differences among the two treatment groups and the controls in terms of the frequency count of target behavior occurrence. On the remaining four measures, the Herford Attitude Survey, behavioral observations, the Missouri Behavior Problem Checklist (aggressive scale) and mothers' evaluation of the worth of the groups, the behavioral counseling group improved significantly more than both the reflective and the control group.

Abstract **111**

Training Parents of Behaviorally-Disordered Children in Groups: A Three Years' Program Evaluation

R. C. RINN, J. C. VERNON and M. J. WISE (Huntsville-Madison County Mental Health Center), *Behavior Therapy*, 1975, *6*, 378-387.

Long-term effects of child-management courses.

Positive Parent Training, the program developed by the authors and evaluated in this study, represents a meaningful alternative to individualized therapy. More than eleven hundred parents were involved in classes to help them deal with their "problem" children in a community mental health center. The program included a long-term, six-months-to-three-years evaluation of effectiveness.

Method

SUBJECTS: All parents referred to a mental health center, regardless of source, were placed on a waiting list and notified two weeks prior to the first class of a Positive Parent Training course. Both parents were required to attend if they lived together. The mean age of the children was 8.7, although anyone under 18 was considered a child for this study. The mean latency between referral data and first class was 45 days. Thirty-six percent of the referrals did not attend. In total, 1,128 parents of 639 children were instructed.

Positive Parent Training Program. Five two-hour sessions were held per course. Twenty-four courses were conducted ranging in class size from 16 to 90 parents with a median of 41. Parents were required to pay a $30 fee, with $10 refundable if parents were on time, attended all sessions, completed homework and produced positive change in target behaviors. Homework involved mastering five tasks: 1) specifying behavior; 2) measuring baserate behavior and setting a goal; 3) identifying rewards and punishments; 4) developing a program for changing the consequences of behavior; 5) measuring the consequated behavior. Measures of progress were attendance, project completion and goal attainment measured in the home by the parents, and behavior change reported in the last session and at follow-up.

267

PROCEDURE: A random sample of parents who had completed the course at least 6 months previously were interviewed by telephone for follow-up data. Of 240 calls made, 154 were completed, 46 parents from 1971, 44 parents from 1972, and 64 parents from 1973. The mean follow-up period was 17.3 months.

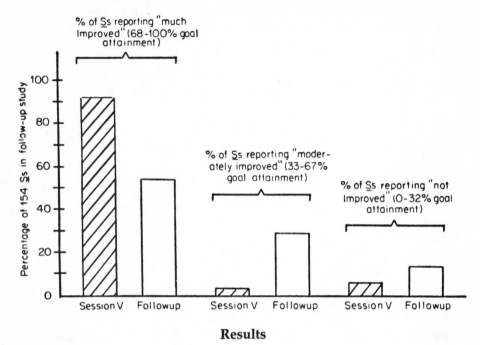

Results

The Figure shows the percentage of parents included in the follow-up study who were "much improved" (60-100% goal attainment), "moderately improved" (33-67% goal attainment) and "not improved" (0-32% goal attainment). The difference between those rated much improved at Session V and at follow-up was a significant decrement. Conversely, the greater number showing moderate improvement and no improvement from Session V to follow-up was also significant by a chi-square test. In total, for the parents of the follow-up sample 84% reported improvement when both "improved" categories were grouped.

Subjective measures of overall behavior of the problem child indicated that 88% of parents saw their children as improved. Sixteen percent of the follow-up sample sought further treatment.

Time required for treating the 639 families with Positive Parent Training was 654 hours as compared to 2,594 hours if all families were seen in outpatient therapy. The cost to parents for group training totaled $14,058. When the cost of additional therapy for those for whom training was unsuccessful is included, the overall cost for all parents is $26,479. Comparable costs if all families were treated as outpatients was $77,811.

Abstract **112**

Generalization to the Classroom of Principles
of Behavior Modification Taught to Teachers

Douglas McKeown, Jr., Henry Adams and Rex Forehand
(University of Georgia), *Behaviour Research and Therapy*,
1975, *13*, 85-92.

Effects of a behavior modification course on teachers' classroom behavior.

There have been a number of books written for teachers explaining learning
principles of behavior change. But do they actually affect teacher performance in the classroom? This study evaluates that question by comparing
teacher-training techniques.

Method

SUBJECTS: Twenty elementary school teachers were randomly assigned to
four groups (training group, training and text group, text group, and
control), matched on number of years teaching, number of children in
classroom, and grades taught (either kindergarten to grade three or grade
four to grade seven).

PROCEDURE: Two measures of training effectiveness were used. The first
was a 20-item multiple choice test on behavior modification principles,
administered before and after training. The second was a 60-minute
classroom observation of disruptive behavior, also taken before and after
training.

The training-only group (Tr group) met with the training and text group
(TT group) and the experimenter for six weeks, 1½ hours a week. Both
groups covered the same material, practising behavioral skills such as
reinforcement and the use of token economies. The difference was that the
TT group was given assignments and instructed that the material covered in
the text would be beneficial to them. The text was *A Teacher's Manual on
Behavior Modification in the Classroom* (Douglas McKeown, Jr., Georgia
Mental Health Institute, Atlanta, 1971). The text group (Te group) was
instructed to read one lesson a week, and were told that in eight weeks they
could participate in a training group. Two teachers actually chose to
participate. The control group (C group) was given no information on
behavior modification, but they were told they could participate in a

training group after postexperiment measures were taken. All five chose to participate.

Results

An analysis of variance indicated that participation in a training group (either Tr group or TT group) significantly influenced knowledge of behavior modification. In addition, for teachers who participated in a training group, there was a significant decrease in classroom disruptive behavior as compared to the classes of teachers in either the Te or Control group.

Abstract **113**

The Relative Effectiveness of Lecturing, Modeling and Role Playing in Training Paraprofessional Reading Tutors

JOERG GUELDENPFENNING (University of Guelph), unpublished Master's thesis.

Talking, show and tell, and practice: three methods of teaching tutoring.

The need for effective tutoring programs is apparent in most schools today. Yet there seems to be very little empirical validation of training programs for tutors. In this study, three common methods of training were compared to determine their relative effectiveness in training tutors to teach.

Method

SUBJECTS AND SETTING: Eleven university students, ten female and one male, enrolled in an undergraduate behavior modification course, served as tutor trainees. Training was conducted in a 30' by 15' room in an experimental school located on the university campus.

PROCEDURE:

Training Program. Seven essential tutoring skills were derived from a review of the teaching and tutoring literature. These included: 1) *specifying*—informing the tutee of material to be covered, tasks and consequences of task completion; 2) *signaling*—asking questions, giving direction, and prompting at relevant points; 3) *recognition*—signaling rather than criticizing errors; 4) *reinforcing*—praising correct responses; 5) *correcting*—signaling an error and helping the tutee correct it; 6) *data-collection*—gathering data on tutee; 7) *enthusiasm*—varying loudness, rhythm, pacing and pauses in voice when interacting with tutees. Each skill comprised one unit and was presented during one half-hour training session. Total training required eight half-hour sessions. The first session introduced the program and the tutors were divided into three experimental groups. The remaining seven sessions involved teaching one skill per session. Evaluation consisted of eight five-minute videotaped tutoring tests, one at the conclusion of each session. Each tutor role-played tutoring a student in oral reading.

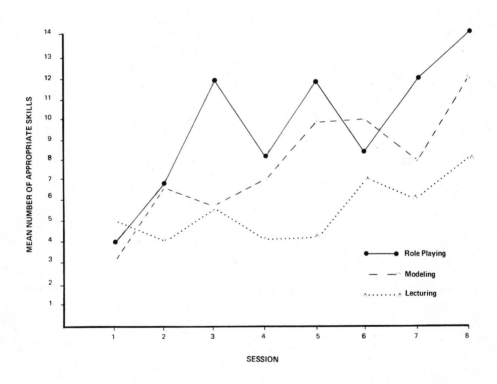

271

Experimental Groups. Three tutors were assigned to a lecture condition, four to the modeling condition, and four to the role-playing condition. The lecture group received a 20-minute lecture on the skill to be taught, and was allowed a 10-minute discussion period. In the modeling group, the experimenter modeled each skill with a subject. Each subject acted as tutee and observed for part of the session. As tutee, the subject played the role of a child reading and was to question when parts of the skill were unclear; as observer, the subject was to discriminate relevant features of the demonstrated skill. The experimenter gave subjects feedback on the correctness of their discriminations. A 10-minute discussion period followed. In the role-playing condition, each subject acted as tutor, tutee, and observer. As tutor, the subject performed the skills; as tutee, the subject role-played a child with reading difficulties; as observer, the subject gave feedback to the tutor on the accuracy of the skill. A 10-minute discussion period followed.

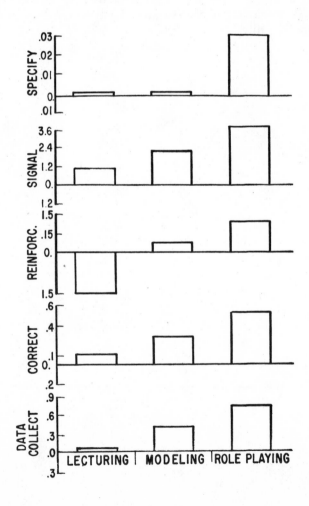

Results

Figure 1 shows the mean number of appropriate tutoring skills presented by each group. All improved over session one, the Baseline period. The lecture group increased appropriate skills 33% over the initial presentation. Modeling improved group performance 238% and role playing improved performance 250%.

Figure 2 shows gain scores between pretraining and posttraining for each skill. Role playing was a consistently superior technique for training the five skills shown, with modeling second in terms of effectiveness except for the specifying skill, which was the same for both lecturing and modeling. One skill, enthusiasm, was not considered, because no reliable means of measuring it were developed.

Abstract 114

A Reinforcement Program for Psychiatric Attendants

MELVYN HOLLANDER (Bronx State Hospital and New York University) and ROBERT PLUTCHIK (Albert Einstein College of Medicine), *Journal of Behavior Therapy and Experimental Psychiatry*, 1972, *3*, 297-300.

Contingent rewards for appropriate behavior in a psychiatric hospital.

The typical perspective of behavior modification programs designed to alter the behavior of institutional attendants revolves around initiating operant procedures. The attendant is reinforced for beginning the change process. In this study, the focus is switched to reinforcement of the completed task assignment.

Method

SUBJECTS: Three male and ten female attendants with considerable hospital experience served as subjects.

PROCEDURE: Attendants were given a six-week course on behavior modification principles and were then assigned to specific tasks which were clearly posted. Included were such tasks as observing and recording bedmaking behaviors, grooming behaviors, and work behaviors, as well as distributing and collecting work supplies. They could also voluntarily complete tasks not specifically assigned.

Baseline: The rate of assigned tasks completed was computed during this phase.

Stamp Contingency: During this condition, trading stamps redeemable in local stores were made contingent upon task completion. Each task completed resulted in about $4.00 worth of stamps. Bonus stamps were also available for nonscheduled tasks. Trading stamps were delivered at the end of each week. Trading stamps were chosen because union regulations prohibited extra cash or vacation days, two commonly used reinforcers.

Extinction: This phase constituted a replication of Baseline.

Results

Trading stamp contingency effectiveness was clearly demonstrated as shown in the Figure. During Baseline the mean number of tasks completed was 61%. When stamps were contingent, it jumped to 94%. Behavior was clearly controlled by reinforcement, because extinction, that is, no stamp reinforcement, resulted in an almost immediate decrease to a mean rate of 50% task completion.

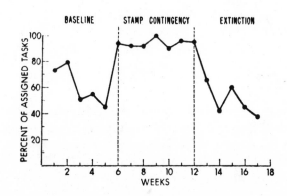

Abstract **115**

Modifying the Dispensing of Reinforcers:
Some Implications for Behavior Modification
with Hospitalized Patients

ROGER KATZ, CLAUDIA JOHNSON and SIDNEY GELFAND (University of Utah), *Behavior Therapy*, 1972, 3, 579-588.

Changing staff behavior.

In any behavioral intervention, a central principle is that behavior is primarily a function of the reinforcement it produces. In spite of this emphasis, little attention has been given to providing consequences for those responsible for behavioral change in the patient. Since behavior, too, should be a function of reinforcers received, this study compared the effectiveness of instructions, verbal prompts, and monetary reinforcement in modifying the behavior of psychiatric aides involved in a token economy.

Method

SUBJECTS AND SETTING: Three male psychiatric patients evidencing withdrawn and unsociable behaviors, and four psychiatric aides trained in behavioral principles, and with at least one year of experience on a token-economy ward, were selected as subjects. Observations were conducted for one hour regularly in the hospital occupational therapy workshop.

PROCEDURE: The Table summarizes patient and aide behaviors observed. A frequency count was kept for each subject using a time-sampling technique which resulted in 40 15-second observations for each behavior. Aide behaviors were recorded simultaneously with patient behaviors.

Baseline. Rate of the behaviors was recorded for eight sessions with no attempt at intervention.

Instructions: Prior to session nine, aides were instructed that two patients were doing poorly and the third, although doing better, was not being reinforced. Aides were then told that appropriate behavior could be strengthened if rewards such as praise or cigarettes were dispensed. In addition, inappropriate behavior could be decreased by reinforcing incompatible behaviors. No consequences were delineated.

Table 1
Behaviors Selected for Observation

Patient behaviors	Aide behaviors

1. *Task-oriented behavior* (T-O): occurrence scored if patient had hands on work materials at any time during the observation interval, or if patient was receiving assistance on a project from a staff member.
2. *Inappropriate behavior:*
   a. squatting: knees fully bent and patient stationary for the duration of the interval.
   b. sleeping: patient seated or lying on the floor with eyes closed for duration of the interval.
   c. hand chewing: hand in mouth with accompanying movement of the jaws occurring at any time during the interval.
   d. pacing: nongoal-directed walking characterized by two or more ambulatory circuits between any two points in the OT area. Occurrence scored if observed during the entire interval.
	1. *Positive interaction:* occurrence scored when patient either praised, congratulated, or reinforced with tokens, cigarettes, or candy for his performance.
	2. *Negative interaction:* patient scolded, reprimanded, threatened, given a command to "stop it," or fined by a loss of tokens for his behavior.
	3. *Neutral interaction:* indicated for interactions not characterized by either (1) or (2) above; e.g., aide questions the patient, attends to patient's verbalization, etc.

Verbal Prompts: Aides were informed that instructions had not been sufficient and that they would be reminded to reinforce behavior whenever appropriate by an undergraduate (who was also recording behavior). Aides would also be encouraged to prompt patients into task-oriented activities.

Monetary Reinforcement: Prompts were discontinued, and aides were told that if they reinforced patients at least 50% of the time during which patients were recorded as behaving appropriately for at least two days, they would receive a $15 bonus. Aides were also told that they could receive daily feedback on reinforcement rates, should they so choose.

Follow-up: This replicated Baseline as a check on maintenance of behavior change. The $15 reward was discontinued.

Results

The Figure illustrates the effects of each phase on both aide and patient behavior. Throughout Baseline, instruction and prompting conditions, aide reinforcement was minimal. The monetary reinforcement condition resulted in a notable increase in aide reinforcement, and a concomitant increase in patient task-oriented behavior for subjects one and two. Subject three had a fluctuating but generally high rate of task-oriented behavior during all conditions. In the follow-up period, aide reinforcement behavior decreased to some extent, although it was maintained above Baseline levels. Task-oriented behavior for subjects one and two varied considerably but was also maintained at a higher rate than during Baseline.

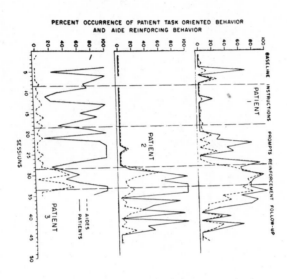

PERCENT OCCURRENCE OF PATIENT TASK ORIENTED BEHAVIOR
AND AIDE REINFORCING BEHAVIOR

Abstract **116**

Feedback to Attendants as a Reinforcer
for Applying Operant Techniques

MARION PANYAN, HOWARD BOOZER, and NANCY MORRIS
(State Home and Training School, Wheatbridge, Colorado),
Journal of Applied Behavior Analysis, 1970, 3, 14.

Training a hospital staff to use behavior modification.

An important difficulty in maintaining any program for behavior change lies in the reinforcers available for the person or institution implementing

277

the program. Immediate improvement in a target behavior can be very rewarding in itself, but what of behaviors which are slow to change? This study investigated the effects of one form of reinforcement, feedback, on maintaining the behavior of nonprofessional staff in an institution for mentally retarded children.

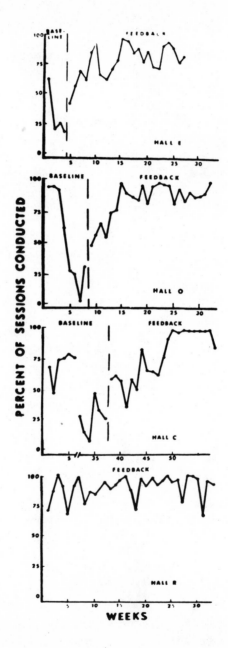

Method

SUBJECTS: Thirty-four staff attendants on four wards (E,O,C, and R) served as subjects. All staff members had been trained to modify self-management skills such as handwashing, dressing, toileting, and self-feeding, and they were to teach these skills to residents on their wards.

PROCEDURE: Staff were instructed to keep daily performance records for each child trained. They were each assigned residents to train. During Baseline, all performance records were collected and a percentage of assigned self-help skill-training sessions carried out was calculated by a research assistant and the psychologist who had requested them. Staff were not informed of the results of these calculations. Baseline lasted four weeks for Hall E, eight weeks for Hall O, 38 weeks for Hall C and was not conducted for Hall R. In the feedback condition, which was instituted after Baseline, the calculated percentages were written on a feedback sheet and given to the staff member. The percentage of training sessions was rank-ordered, so that each hall would be informed of its position relative to other halls.

Results

As can be seen in the Figure, immediately after the staff was trained the percentage of training sessions conducted was fairly high. As Baseline continued, however, (in Halls E, O, and C), the number of sessions decreased dramatically. When feedback was instituted, whether from the beginning as on Hall R or after as many as 38 weeks as on Hall C, there was a sharp increase in the percent of self-help, skill-training sessions.

Alternative Topical Outline

Note: Some professors prefer to structure their course around the basic principles that are assumed to underly practice. Several recent texts are organized along these lines, and the table of contents given below should be helpful to those who use these texts and wish to coordinate readings, chapter assignments, and lectures. Some abstracts are listed more than once.

All numbers refer to Abstract numbers.

Subject Index

Note: All numbers refer to Abstract numbers.

Target Behavior Index

Note: All numbers refer to Abstract numbers.

Target Behavior Index

Information-seeking behavior 47
Institutionalization, number of people 99
Interruptions, number of 91
Interview behavior, modification of therapist 51
I.Q. 68
Job level 104
Language development 16
Lever pressing 85
Litter, amount of 105
Math 75
Medication, amount taken 81
Misconduct reports 51
Motor behavior 67
Movements 73
Negotiation 97
Occupational skills 78
Participation
  in discussion 94
  in government 95
Penile circumference 76, 77
Phobia 61, 62, 63
Placement follow-up 100
Playing 14
Politeness 96
Posture 73
Prosocial behavior 17, 19, 50, 72, 78, 110
Public speaking 54
Punctuality 89
Questionnaire, money-saving 93
Questions
  number of 35
  type of 35
Racial attitudes 20
Reading 15, 75
  achievement 34
  time spent 32
Recidivism 89, 91
Reinforcement 66, 73, 115
Salary, starting 104
Self-control 44

Self-help training sessions for patients 116
Self-mutilation 83, 84
Sexual
  fantasies 77
  urges 77
Silence, amount of 91
Smiling 67
Smoking 63
Social interaction 35
Social skills 80, 88
Speech problems 4
Stammering 4
Study behavior 18, 38, 40, 74
  lack of 38
  time spent 44
Stuttering 4
Symptom substitution 54
Tantrums 10, 65, 66
Talking 67
Tardiness 107
Task completion 88, 102, 114
  quality 86
  quantity 86
Task-oriented behavior 115
Tests
  behavior 68
  score changes 110
  scores 25
  scores, final examination 25
  Wide Range Achievement Test scores 36
Thoughts 70
Tutoring skills 113
Typing errors 3
Verbal behavior 8
  inappropriate 52
Verbalization 79
Vocabulary 36
Volunteering a response in classroom 48
Weight 69, 70

Treatment and Research Design Index

Note: All numbers refer to Abstract numbers.

Treatment and Research Design Index